CW01467041

YOUTH JUSTICE

Towards a Contextualised Understanding of Policy Making

Stephen Case

First published in Great Britain in 2024 by

Policy Press, an imprint of
Bristol University Press
University of Bristol
1–9 Old Park Hill
Bristol
BS2 8BB
UK
t: +44 (0)117 374 6645
e: bup-info@bristol.ac.uk

Details of international sales and distribution partners are available at policy.bristoluniversitypress.co.uk

British Library Cataloguing in Publication Data
A catalogue record for this book is available from the British Library

ISBN 978-1-4473-6966-0 hardcover
ISBN 978-1-4473-6968-4 ePub
ISBN 978-1-4473-6969-1 ePdf

Cover design: Lyn Davies Design
Front cover image: alamy/YAY Media AS
Bristol University Press and Policy Press use environmentally responsible print partners.
Printed and bound in Great Britain by CPI Group (UK) Ltd, Croydon, CR0 4YY

Contents

List of abbreviations

ASB	antisocial behaviour
ASBO	Antisocial Behaviour Order
AWYOS	All Wales youth offending strategy
AYJ	Alliance for Youth Justice
AYM	Association of YOT Managers
CDA	Crime and Disorder Act
DCSF	Department for Children, Schools and Families
DfE	Department for Education
HMIP	Her/His Majesty's Inspectorate of Probation
KEEPs	Key Elements of Effective Practice
KPI	Key Performance Indicators
MoJ	Ministry of Justice
NDPB	non-departmental public body
NPCC	National Police Chiefs Council
OCC	Office of the Children's Commissioner
QDA	qualitative documentary analysis
RFPP	Risk Factor Prevention Paradigm
RQ	research question
RTA	reflexive thematic analyis
SPAD	senior policy adviser
WYJAP	Wales Youth Justice Advisory Panel
YCAP	Youth Crime Action Plan
YCS	Youth Custody Service
YIP	Youth Inclusion Programme
YISP	Youth Inclusion and Support Panel
YJB	Youth Justice Board for England and Wales
YJB Cymru	Youth Justice Board Cymru/Wales
YJS	Youth Justice System of England and Wales
YMC	YOT Managers Cymru
YOT	Youth Offending Team

Acknowledgements

Three expert and inspirational colleagues have been crucial to this project. I would like to sincerely thank Dr Anna Souhami, Professor John Drew and Professor Neal Hazel for generously giving up their time to offer expert feedback on and support for this project. But their contribution is more than this.

Without Anna's ground-breaking, brave and thoroughly captivating ethnographic research with the Youth Justice Board (YJB) and the exceptional publications that accompany it, I would not have had the motivation to conduct this research. Her work is the reason this book has been written.

Without John's remarkable, ceaseless commitment to principled youth justice policy making and to nurturing critical friendships with academics, I would not have had the confidence or belief that I could have an impact on policy. His support has given me faith that this book and its author can make a difference.

Without Neal's tireless and insightful advocacy of the 'Child First' principle through his scholarship, his research, our collaborations and particularly his dedicated work with the YJB, I would not believe so strongly that a principled policy trajectory for youth justice is possible. His efforts give me faith that Child First will continue to change the Youth Justice System for the better.

Introduction: a contextualised understanding of youth justice policy making

> [A] wider view is required of what constitutes [youth justice] policy and where and by whom it is 'made' in order that youth justice policy-making can be better understood as 'a complex arena of social practice, incorporating a diverse range of actors, practices, relationships and networks.'
>
> (Souhami, 2015a: 152, 164)

Despite the significant influence of policy on the socio-historical construction of youth justice (Case, 2018/21), there has been little critical investigation of its complex nature. This is illustrated by the consistent conflation of policy with static 'products' or 'measures' such as legislation and ministerial speeches, and by reductionist and decontextualised assumptions that politicians dominate the 'making' of policy (see Souhami, 2015a). Neglect of complexity has come at the expense of understanding policy as constructed (made) through dynamic, situated and contextualised processes and interactions. In order to address this shortfall in the knowledge and evidence bases regarding youth justice policy making, this book pursues a contextualised analysis of how policy is made in the Youth Justice System (YJS) of England and Wales. The central aim of the book is to interrogate youth justice policy making as a dynamic, contested and contingent social construction (Case, 2018/21) that is created and shaped by a range of policy 'actors' working and interacting within and across different professional contexts. Accordingly, there will be detailed examination of the inherent complexity, non-linearity and chaos of youth justice policy making with the goal of identifying elements of coherence, consistency and instrumentalism that can enhance understandings and guide and improve policy making and its realisation in practice in the youth justice sector.

The evidence-based, expert-led, context-sensitive understandings of youth justice policy processes generated through the analyses underpinning this book should be of significant value to a broad range of professional stakeholders or 'policy actors' from different contexts (for example, policy, strategy, practice, third sector, academia) working in governmental and non-governmental systems and organisations that provide support services for children within and outside the YJS. Professional stakeholders supporting children operate in contexts of sustained socio-economic and socio-political insecurity, instability and uncertainty. They experience significant pressure to effectively respond to long-term social problems through restricted and diminishing resources: economic, practical, evidential and intellectual. Consequently, innovative, contextualised knowledge and evidence bases for understanding and actualising youth justice policy through policy making should be of immense benefit when seeking improved effectiveness, efficiency, economy and sustainability in the 'making' of policy to address social problems, notably 'youth offending'. Deeper historical analyses of the youth justice policy-making landscape since 1996 (moving beyond Goldson's [2020] macro-level 'excavation' of youth justice reform) will pursue an enhanced knowledge base to address the 'floundering and incoherent nature of policy formation' and offer insights that can 'guide future youth justice reform' (Goldson, 2020: 330) in contexts of uncertainty and instability (see also Lawrence, 2012). Analyses will extend and challenge hegemonic constructions of youth justice policy making as politically dominated, wherein the influence of non-governmental actors (such as practitioners) can be marginalised, restricted and even ignored, especially outside of policy implementation processes.

In my professional opinion,[1] the book's originality lies in the application of a new, contextualised lens to analyses of youth justice policy making, enabling investigation of the extent and nature to which youth justice policy making is constructed, experienced and enacted within and between a wide range of key stakeholder policy actors and policy-making contexts. These new, innovative lenses are:

- Conceptual/focal: conceptualising policy making as a *constructed reality* (see Case, 2018/21) – a real, objective, tangible phenomenon that is 'made' (constructed, created) and 'remade' (reconstructed) as part of contextualised, dynamic identities, relationships and interactions that are re/experienced and re/interpreted subjectively by stakeholders. In other words, the realities of policy making for stakeholders are experienced, interpreted and re/constructed within and between the relational contexts they inhabit. Analyses explore youth justice policy *making* as shaped by inter/intra-personal *relationships* between a wide range of professional stakeholders and organisations operating within and between *professional contexts*, including philosophy/rationale development, political policy making, strategic direction/governance, policy implementation, oversight and policy implementation in practice. These contextualised relationships are seen to operate within and across *multiple levels of the social system*: macro (for example, socio-historical, socio-political, economic, cultural, national), meso (organisational cultures and relationships, for example) and micro (for example individual/professional expertise, training, skills, attitudes).
- Contextual: investigating the 'constructive influence' of *context* as the relational (interacting) and dynamic (changing) features or 'forces'

that shape the *mechanisms* through which policy is constructed and experienced – policy-making mechanisms (potentially) shaped and influenced at multiple levels (contexts) of the social system by dynamic themes including power, evidence, expertise, professional identities, national cultures and socio-political change. The book's empirical research adopts a social constructionist-realist perspective of context as operating in dynamic, emergent ways over time across multiple contexts (Coldwell, 2019) rather than existing as merely static, observable features (space, place, people, things), general circumstances and background information that trigger/block access to policy-making processes at specific moments in time (see Greenhalgh and Manzano, 2021). As such, context is understood as 'comprised of individuals, interpersonal relationships, institutional settings and infrastructure' (Greenhalgh and Manzano, 2021: 587), not conceptualised in terms of what it is, but in terms of what it *does*.

- Methodological: examining policy making from a *social constructionist, contextualised perspective* through qualitative analysis of policy documents and reflexive thematic analysis (RTA) of semi-structured interview data. This triangulated approach facilitates deeper, more holistic examination of the inherent dynamism, contradiction, non-linearity and contentiousness of youth justice policy making. Instead of imposing academic conceptual frameworks on definitions and understandings of policy making (a typical bias in this field), the study is largely *ethnomethodological* (that is, it examines how social order is produced through processes of interaction), interrogating how professionals develop *situated knowledge* and *make sense/meaning* of policy making in the real world and how professional perspectives drive and shape contributions to policy formation, development and implementation nationally and locally. Analyses will consistently acknowledge and explore the influence of author and stakeholder subjectivity and *positionality*.

Critical commentary: professional reflection on my 'skin in the game'

My academic research career in youth justice has been shaped by close collaboration with a range of professional stakeholders, including children, youth justice staff, third sector professionals, local and national politicians, strategists and academics. Every ounce of my experience tells me that the 'making' of policy is far more complex than traditional government-led, linear explanations suggest, indicating that a broader range of stakeholders 'make' policy in different ways at different stages in different contexts. Consequently, this project is part evidence based and part experience based. I am seeking to look behind the curtain of the often hidden processes/mechanisms of and influences upon youth justice policy making in order to uncover the realities of these dynamics from the perspectives of those involved, namely policy actors. An overriding question I have at this stage is whether clear and coherent understandings of youth justice policy making can be discerned in an ostensibly chaotic and complex arena.

It is important at this early stage to be as transparent and explicit as possible about my 'positionality' in this endeavour – the professional identity, experiences, perspectives and acquired subjectivity and partialities (preferences, biases) that influence my understandings and arguments (see also the discussion of methodology in Chapter 2). Throughout my professional career as a youth justice academic and researcher, I have adopted a critical criminological lens when analysing the origins, trajectories and animation of youth justice policies in practice arenas and how these policies are experienced by children in the YJS. I have reached the scholarly and – in my view and experience – evidence-based conclusion that 'youth justice' is a socio-historical construction with multiple influences and influencers, but that the role of policy and politicians/government in the making of this policy dominates the social construction of youth justice (Case, 2018/21). Concurrently, I have been highly critical of the nature and development of youth justice policy making, particularly the partial (biased and incomplete), self-fulfilling and adult-centric risk management approach that has dominated 21st-century youth justice policy and prescriptions for its implementation in practice (see Case and Haines, 2009; Case, 2022). This so-called 'evidence-based' model of youth justice appears to prioritise the political agenda and political expedience over the broad-minded generation of a range of evidence, most notably evidence provided by the practitioners and children whose relationship is central to the ultimate success or otherwise of youth justice policy in practice.

My professional scepticism of hegemonic youth justice policy and related practice has been motivated by a long-term body of research with children and practitioners that has produced a significant evidence base that now underpins the 'Child First' guiding principle for youth justice in England and Wales (Case and Browning, 2021a). Consequently, I have a deep and longstanding professional and principled vested interest ('skin in the game') in better understanding why, how and by whom youth justice policy is made in order that the Child First principle is realised effectively across England and Wales. In particular, it is vital to me that Child First is further evidenced, validated and insulated from the socio-political and socio-economic uncertainties, insecurities and rapid changes that could undermine its success.

The structure of this book

Following this Introduction, Chapter 1 analyses the 'Contextualised construction of youth justice policy', exploring the extent and nature to which youth justice policy can be understood as 'made' through complex processes of social construction within and between different policy-making actors and contexts. The chapter addresses *what* makes youth justice by outlining the complex, constructed and contextualised nature of youth justice policy making across its socio-historical trajectories, leading into detailed discussion of the consistent, recurring dichotomisation (representation as polar opposites) and bifurcation (splitting into two different directions at once) of policy principles. Such consistency and recurrence implicate a degree of coherence, order and even predictability across ostensibly random and chaotic youth justice policy trajectories. This is followed by a discussion of the centrality of policy as the key 'constructive influence' on what is understood as 'youth justice', augmented by critical discussion of *what* is understood by youth justice 'policy'. The chapter then asks *who* are the 'makers' of youth justice policy in terms of the key stakeholder groups or 'policy actors' operating at governmental and non-governmental levels in England and Wales. There follows an exploration of *how* youth justice policy is made, evaluating the hegemonic Policy Cycle Model through a lens of 'necessary complexity' and focusing on the competing and conflicting discourses and rationales shaping the socio-historical trajectories of youth justice policy making. The summative discussion coheres around the role of power as a constructive influence on policy-making relationships within and between youth justice contexts and stakeholder groups, with particular focus on the exercising of power to govern and the power of experts/expertise and the generation of evidence to guide youth justice policy making.

The 'Methodology' (Chapter 2) sets out the aims that structure the analyses reported across this book:

- to identify, trace and critically examine the key constructive influences on the trajectory of youth justice policy making in England and Wales within and between different contexts;
- to enhance stakeholder and sector understandings of in/effective youth justice policy making, in order to fill the vacuum of political, policy, strategic, practice and academic understandings of the dynamic trajectories of youth justice policy development;
- to establish key recommendations for enhancing youth justice policy making (such as the faithful translation of policy into practice), collaborative partnership working and knowledge sharing cross/nationally and locally.

The chapter then establishes the five research questions (RQs) that guide the analyses across the book:

1. What is youth justice 'policy'?
2. Who are the 'makers' of youth justice policy?

3. How is youth justice policy making understood, re/constructed, experienced and made meaningful by policy makers working in different contexts?
4. What are the barriers, challenges, enablers and opportunities for youth justice policy making?
5. How can youth justice policy making be improved?

The chapter goes on to outline and substantiate the qualitative, ethnomethodological approach adopted to explore the RQs, which consists of qualitative documentary analysis of youth justice policy documents followed by semi-structured interviews with expert stakeholders. There is discussion of why and how the interview data will be interrogated using RTA (Braun and Clarke, 2022) to develop, analyse and interpret patterns across the qualitative datasets. There is an accompanying critical reflection on the positionality, subjectivity and role of both the researcher and stakeholder in the construction of knowledge. Discussions of the RTA and researcher positionality populate the rationale for the contextualised and social constructionist epistemology adopted, which examines how youth justice policy is created/constructed (made) through processes of social interaction that are situated in and animated by relationships within and between stakeholder organisations.

This is followed by two contextualising chapters founded in the critically analyse works of youth justice policy since 1996. The first of these chapters is entitled 'Expansionist "new youth justice" policy' (Chapter 3). It traces the socio-historical trajectory of youth justice from the mid-1990s onwards, prioritising the influence of policy and policy making on the reconstructions of youth justice (which are most notably philosophical, socio-political, strategic and practical) that coalesced to form the new *prevention* policy focus across the United Kingdom. The chapter discusses the origins of evidence-based prevention as a youth justice policy priority in the 1996 'Misspent youth' review of the YJS, formalised in government in policy 'products' (for example, the 'No more excuses' 1997 White Paper and the revolutionary Crime and Disorder Act 1998) and consolidated by policy implementation structures, notably the creation of the Youth Justice Board (YJB) for England and Wales. The reported context-specific influences on the construction of these policy products will be identified and explored, establishing a series of critical themes for interrogation in subsequent stakeholder interviews. These themes include the intra-system, cross-national differences emerging from the 'dragonised' youth justice agenda in Wales, first animated in the 'All Wales youth offending strategy' (2004). The chapter ends with a critical review of youth justice developments in policy and related policy making during the dying days of the Labour government (2008–10). These key developments include the abolition of the 'offences brought to justice' police arrest targets for children and the continued affirmation and consolidation of 'new youth justice' strategies through the Youth Crime Action Plan 2008 and the 'Scaled Approach' risk-led assessment and intervention framework.

Chapter 4, 'Austerity youth justice as tentative policy progress', explores the socio-historical trajectory of youth justice from 2010 onwards, analysing how its re/constructions have been shaped by policy and policy making during a period of widespread economic austerity and political instability. The first half of the chapter explores the policy-led trajectory of youth justice over the first half of the decade under the coalition Conservative–Liberal Democrat government, which is characterised as a consolidation of prevention policy mobilised by 'new youth justice' strategies. In 2010, for example, both the 'Breaking the cycle' Green Paper and the Independent Commission on Youth Crime and Antisocial Behaviour advocated for more emphasis on effective prevention in the YJS. It is then explained how these preventative recommendations were mobilised by the new Early Intervention Grant in 2011, the introduction of 'interventionist diversion' as a reconstructed and reframed form of prevention policy in the Legal Aid, Sentencing and Punishment of Offenders Act 2012 and the reconstruction of prevention-focused assessment and intervention practice through the introduction of the AssetPlus framework in 2014. The second half of the chapter examines the policy-led, austerity-based trajectory of youth justice since 2015 (when the Conservative government took power), which was characterised by the retrenchment of children's services, sweeping economic efficiencies and a relative policy inertia in the youth justice field. There is also discussion of progressive, strategic moves away from neo-liberal prevention policy and towards the more holistic 'Child First' approach recommended by the Taylor Review in 2016. It will be outlined that this period evidenced more strategic influence from non-governmental actors, including from the YJB of England and Wales and more discretionary practitioner influence over how prevention policy is 'made' locally.

Across both contextualising, policy analysis chapters, a number of 'key features' are integrated to facilitate constant critical reflection by the reader on the documents being analysed and the nature of the policy contained within them:

- Policy points: concise summative statements reflecting critically on the nature of a policy development and the key influences implicated in its construction (for example, political, conceptual, thematic, empirical, academic).
- Policy questions: targeted questions, both rhetorical and analytical, focused on key elements of policy making (stages in the cycle, constructive influences and important policy actors, for example). These questions are provided to encourage the reader to critically analyse what can be

discerned from key policy documentation and to critically reflect upon the sources and validity of their own views regarding policy making.
- Critical commentaries: reflexive evaluations of key policy documents that are aligned with the researcher's disciplinary background and consequent 'positionality' (see this chapter) as a sociologically orientated criminologist, critical youth justice scholar, strident critic of 'new youth justice' strategies and zealous proponent of child-centric and 'Child First' modes of youth justice.

Chapters 5 to 7 present a detailed analysis of the data obtained through a series of semi-structured interviews with expert key stakeholders in the youth justice sector, conducted to explore the five central RQs guiding this project.

Chapter 5, entitled 'Exploring youth justice policy-making contexts and mechanisms', begins by asking 'What is youth justice policy-making?' The chapter explores expert stakeholder views of the complexity and lack of consensus surrounding policy and policy making. It presents stakeholder perceptions of the multi-layered, multi-systemic and fragmented nature of policy-making structures and processes that foster conflict and role ambiguity, but also their views that these complexities can also be cohered through multi-agency collaboration promoting universal policy, shared objectives and seeking alignment of agendas. The following section asks 'Who makes policy?', focusing on the roles of governmental policy actors (three politicians/ministers, senior policy advisers and civil servants, as well as right-wing newspapers) and non-governmental actors (for example, the YJB, Office of the Children's Commissioner [OCC], youth justice practitioners, third sector coalitions). There is a focused discussion of the YJB's contested and ambiguous identity, role and status in policy-making contexts, alongside discussion of the unique influence of the OCC. These discussions cohere by identifying the *soft power* of non-governmental organisations in youth justice policy-making contexts. The final section asks 'How does youth justice policy making happen?', framing its analysis in terms of trajectories of *stability* and *change* as indicative of the messy complexities and conflict and ambivalence of youth justice policy. The stability of youth justice policy trajectories is illustrated by their *cyclical* nature and contexts of *gradual development* encouraged by mechanisms of consensus, clarity and consistency of approach. Contexts of policy change in different directions and at differing speeds are understood as influenced by commonly identified mechanisms such as *churn* (later known as 'churnover') of key staff and in the policy agenda (for example, cyclical, sudden) and *chaotic, sudden* policy making resulting from structural changes, critical events, opaque and incoherent policy influences, *political* and *financial short-termism* and *opportunistic, instrumental* policy making, all with varying levels of (un)predictability. The chapter concludes with a general overview of the 'implementational mode' of policy making (Fergusson, 2007) and the role of managers and practitioners in policy-making contexts, including their perceived responsibility and culpability (relative to governmental actors) for policy implementation failure (discussed in more detail in subsequent chapters).

Chapter 6 explores 'Professional identities, expertise and evidence'. The chapter examines how relational contexts influence the *identities* of policy-making organisations and professionals, including the *expert* identities often prioritised when generating evidence and implementing evidence-based policy and practice in the YJS. It begins with a discussion of *policy discourses* as representing the identity of governments, including analyses of the sustained populist punitiveness discourse, contrasted with the hybrid and conflicted prevention–support–diversion discourse emerging from the 'new youth justice' and the distinct 'dragonised' identity associated with youth justice policy in Wales. This is followed by discussion of stakeholder perceptions of governmental open-mindedness and receptiveness to civil servant and YJB influence, which challenges discourses of governmental prescriptiveness and agenda as dominating policy-making processes. There follows a detailed exploration of the policy-making identity, role, status and influence of the YJB, exploring its role as a policy influencer and as a strategic influencer, with particular focus on the evolution of the YJB policy-making identity from *managerialist prescription* to *engaging with and empowering practitioner experts*. There follows an investigation of the policy-making role of *practitioners as experts by experience* and as 'street-level bureaucrats' engaged in bottom-up policy making through the localised mediation and moderation of government policy. Finally, there is an exposition of the broader role of *experts, expertise* and *experience* in youth justice policy making, including discussion of the central role of evidence in shaping policy.

Chapter 7, 'The centrality of relationships in youth justice policy making', extrapolates previous findings by scrutinising the constructive influence of *relationships* in shaping dynamic policy-making identities in different contexts. It begins with discussion of the *power dynamics* shaped by the identities and agendas of orgaanisations and individuals as influencing the nature of relational policy making, thereafter focusing on the *relational contexts occupied by the YJB* in their policy-making relationships with governmental actors (UK and Welsh Governments, ministers, civil servants) and non-governmental actors (His Majesty's Inspectorate of Probation, Welsh professionals, practitioners). What follows is a detailed exploration of the relational – relationship-based – contexts and mechanisms that are seen to shape *collaborative policy making*, particularly through:

- *power dynamics* within and between governmental and non-governmental policy-making organisations in the YJS;
- *seeking common ground* within collaborative policy-making relationships;

- *utilising communication* to build collaborative relationships; and
- *relational reciprocity* promoting equitable, supportive policy-making relationships.

The final chapter, 'Discussion: towards a contextualised understanding of youth justice policy making', coalesces the project findings into a central argument for improved understandings of policy making that move beyond reductionist, linear frameworks by examining youth justice 'policy' and its 'makers' and 'making' through a lens of *necessary complexity*. This leads into a discussion of youth justice policy making as a series of dynamic constructive influences/mechanisms, trajectories, processes, relationships and interactions that are constantly re/constructed by a range of governmental and non-governmental policy actors in relational contexts. The chapter concludes that while these contacts present as ostensibly chaotic, random and unpredictable, and that it is impossible to discern a degree of 'coherence from chaos', consistency and predictability or 'patterns in the noise' can explain and enhance the effectiveness of policy making in terms of sustainability, coherence, validity, evidence and the faithfulness of its transfer into practice. The chapter then outlines and explores a tentative selection of lessons learned and recommendations for enhanced policy making, which cohere around rejecting reductionism/embracing complexity, rejecting fear-embracing challenges and power-embracing expertise experience and evidence in the YJS.

The chapter and book conclude that there are multiple ways of viewing and constructing reality and knowledge in the YJS. Therefore, holistic and ecologically valid understandings (by both policy actors and researchers) of youth justice policy making necessitate the management of power dynamics, empathy to the needs, challenges, constraints and realities of others, sensitivity to context and the representation and legitimisation of diverse voices. Furthermore, in order to successfully execute such a challenging and complex project, it is essential to critically reflect upon the positionality, assumptions and biases that shape the perceptions, experiences, instructions, decisions and practices of policy actors and of the researchers seeking to understand their world.

1

The contextualised construction of youth justice policy

Following from the contextualising rationale set out in the Introduction, this opening chapter explores the extent and nature to which youth justice policy can be understood as 'made' through complex processes of social construction within and between different policy-making contexts. The chapter begins by asking *what* makes youth justice, outlining the complex, constructed and contextualised nature of youth justice policy making across its socio-historical trajectories. This analysis leads into detailed discussion of the often dichotomised and bifurcated nature of policy *principles*, which implicates a degree of coherence and order across ostensibly random and chaotic youth justice policy trajectories. There is then discussion of the centrality of policy as the key 'constructive influence' on what is understood as youth justice, augmented by critical discussion of *what* is understood by youth justice 'policy'. The analysis then turns to *who* are the 'makers' of youth justice policy in terms of the key stakeholder groups or 'policy actors' operating in governmental and non-governmental contexts in England and Wales. There follows an exploration of *how* youth justice policy is made, evaluating the hegemonic 'Policy Cycle Model' through a lens of necessary complexity and a focus on the competing and conflicting discourses and rationales that have shaped socio-historical trajectories of youth justice policy making. The chapter concludes with a discussion of the role of *power* as an influence on policy-making relationships within and between youth justice contexts and stakeholder groups, with particular focus on the exercising of power to govern (that is, exercising *governance*), the power of *experts* and the generation of *evidence* as guides of youth justice policy making.

What 'makes' youth justice policy? Complex constructions, conflicts and coherence

Before exploring the nature of the complex influences on policy making in the youth justice field, it is instructive to operationalise what we understand by 'youth justice', the context within which this policy analysis is situated. The concept of youth justice can be understood as a social construction – a creation or product that is made by institutions and people in specific societies in specific historical periods – that is, it is a socio-historical construction – through the definitions, labels and measures given to specific behaviours, groups and individuals (Case, 2018/21). The same can be said of the behaviour labelled 'youth offending' to which youth justice responds. For the purposes of clear, consistent and accessible argument going forwards, 'youth justice' is operationalised as the socially constructed label given to formal systemic responses to offending behaviour by children[1] and young people. In other words, youth justice is conceptualised as a multi-faceted social construct consisting of relationships within and between the philosophies/principles, theories, laws, systems, structures, statistics, legislation, policies, strategies, practices and organisations[2] that coalesce to shape official responses to youth offending (Case, 2022). Due to its socially constructed nature, the trajectories of youth justice and related policy development/changes/reforms are inherently:

- dynamic – varying widely and rapidly in extent and nature over time and place;
- contingent – dependent on (dynamic) historical, cultural, social, economic, political contexts; and
- contested – subject to disagreement or a lack of consensus, debate and contextual differences (contingencies) across history and between and within countries, contexts, organisations, professions and individuals.

(After Case, 2018/21)

The socially constructed nature of youth justice is contextualised and illustrated in the following section in a concise summary of the socio-historical trajectories of youth justice in the United Kingdom (see Case, 2018/21; see also Bateman, 2017; Goldson, 2020). The main influences on these socio-historical constructions of youth justice (hereafter 'constructive influences') are discussed as variously systemic, legal, legislative, structural, political strategic and principled. As will be demonstrated, these trajectories have led into and away from the systemic devolution of youth justice in the UK and the creation of the Youth Justice System (YJS) of England and Wales through the Crime and Disorder Act 1998 (CDA 1998), which constitutes the stepping off point for the analyses populating this book.

The complex and constructed socio-historical trajectories of youth justice in the UK

Social construction of the contemporary YJS can arguably be traced back to early to mid-19th century, between 1820 and 1850, when the development of the first detailed, categorised prison statistics highlighted the lack of segregation by age in custodial institutions and the potential for a toxic mix between innocent children and hardened adult offenders. In 1838, Parkhurst

Prison was opened in 1838 as a bespoke youth justice structure to respond to the need for segregation and special treatment in custody for children who had offended. The Youthful Offenders Act 1854 followed as the first significant piece of government legislation to contribute to the construction of a distinct 'youth justice' policy in the UK. Most notably, it allowed for bespoke youth justice responses to children who offend to be differentiated from criminal justice responses to adult offenders through the creation of a new structure – the Reformatory School. Children in these schools received correctional, rehabilitative and reformative training to compensate for the criminogenic influence of defective parenting and damaging neighbourhood experiences. This new structure evinced a policy change/shift in youth justice in terms of its guiding *principle*, from punishment (that is, punitive treatment) to reform and rehabilitation for children who offended. The Act also foregrounded a bespoke *structure* for responding to neglected, needy, victimised, 'pre-criminal' children in the form of the Industrial School (legislated into existence by the Industrial Schools Act 1857), underpinned by a principle of vocational employment training, rather than punishment.

In the early 20th century, the Children Act 1908 was introduced as government legislation animating a shift in youth justice *policy* and associated principle away from punishment and towards education and reform through the formal introduction of the Borstal. This new *structure* housed education-focused custodial institutions/wings for 16- to 21-year-olds who offended, with the dual purpose to instruct/socialise and to reform/treat rather than primarily to punish. This was followed 25 years later by the Children and Young Persons Act 1933, which cemented the view (construction) of children as vulnerable and innocent victims of social disadvantage through a change in law, raising the minimum age of criminal responsibility ('MACR') from seven to eight years old. The Act also reconstructed understandings of children who offend through a youth justice *principle* of non-criminalisation, stating that 'there is little or no difference in character and needs between the delinquent and neglected child' (cited in Hendrick, 2015: 182). The legislation further cemented the growing hegemony of the child welfare *principle* through the creation of new *structures* (such as probation, approved schools, boarding schools) favouring welfare over punishment- and justice-based responses to children who offended. Soon afterwards, the Children and Young Persons Act 1948 created and established welfare-based, social work provisions for children in the form of new *structures* (organisations), which included the first professional social workers exclusively for children. The Act also introduced new *structures* (remand centres, attendance centres, probation hostels) to pursue a policy *principle* of restricting the use of custody (as a sentence) and thus punishment (as a principle) for children who offended. However, the requirement persisted to punish adolescents who offended through newly created detention centres to provide 'short, unpleasant sentences' (reaffirmed in the subsequent Criminal Justice Act 1982), illustrating socio-historical conflict and ambivalence in youth justice responses to the children when they offend.

In the 1960s, the Children and Young Persons Act 1963 focused on responding to offending through social work-based therapeutic relationship building and a proposed change in law to extend the MACR from eight to ten years old. The 1969 version of the same Act proposed a further *law* change, the extension of the MACR from ten to 14 years old, along with changes in *structures* through abolishing Borstals and detention centres. However, neither change (reconstruction) proposed in the 1969 Act was implemented due to a change in government in 1970. The next substantive pieces of legislation affecting youth justice were the Criminal Justice Acts of 1988 and 1991, which restricted use of custody for children and provided specified activities as statutory alternatives to custody, thus espousing changes to youth justice philosophy and processes. Youth custody centres and detention centres combined to form a new structure, the Young Offender Institution (in 1988 – still in existence). The Juvenile Court was renamed the Youth Court in 1991 (still in existence), and the age that it could impose custody was raised from 14 to 15 years old.

The complex socio-historically constructed trajectories of youth justice culminated in the 20th century with the CDA 1998, which radically re-orientated and reconfigured youth justice by establishing a new, formalised *system*, the YJS of England and Wales.[3] The Act also introduced a new strategic approach dubbed the 'new youth justice' (see Goldson, 2000), which was less concerned with welfare and justice policy *principles* and more focused on managerialist, interventionist, responsibilising and risk-based prevention and early intervention *strategies* (see Chapter 3). In legal terms, the Act reconstructed youth justice by abolishing 'doli incapax', the legal presumption of innocence for children aged ten to 14 years old that previously had to be rebutted in court in order to secure a conviction.

The conflict and ambivalence of youth justice policy principles

The preceding broad-brush overview of the trajectory of youth justice in the UK up to 1998 indicates a complexity and dynamism to youth justice developments that has been shaped by and has resulted in a persistent *conflict and ambivalence* in its socio-historical re/construction, which has been consistently illustrated by tensions, hybridity and unreconciled rationales (Goldson, 2020). It has been animated further through a multiplicity of – often contradictory – influences and priorities such as laws defining 'offending' by children, theories explaining offending by children and principles, systems, strategies, mechanisms and processes for responding to offending by children (May, 1973; Magerey, 1978; Shore,

2011; Hendrick, 2015; Brett, 2018). Historians, criminologists and other critical commentators have distilled this socio-historical, socially constructed trajectory of youth justice (in the UK and, latterly, England and Wales) into a generalised series of *dichotomous* (oppositional) and *bifurcated* (twin-track) responses (see Case and Smith, 2023 for a detailed critical overview) while acknowledging that such reductionism (over-simplification, narrowing, over-generalising) risks diluting and caricaturing the essential *complexity* and dynamism of youth justice (policy) realities. Notwithstanding the dangers of reductionism, the hegemonic theoretical and evidential constructions of 'youth offending' have been consistently dichotomised, with children constructed as innocent-threatening, mad-bad, deprived-depraved, rational-irrational, responsible-irresponsible, in need or at risk and so on (Case, 2022). These dichotomised constructions have shaped bifurcated youth justice responses prioritising reform or punishment, welfare or justice, care or control, needs or deeds, Child First or offender first principles and so on (Case and Smith, 2023). The prevailing dichotomy in analyses of the socio-historical construction of youth justice has been the 'welfare vs justice debate' (Smith, 2006), wherein the nature of youth justice at any given point in time is characterised as dominated by one of two competing priorities, either *welfare-based*, child-focused responses to the child's needs, or *justice-based*, offence- and offending-focused responses to the child's deeds/offending behaviour (discussed further subsequently). Crucially, the notion of consistently and discernibly dichotomised forms of youth justice suggests a degree of *coherence* and revolution/repetition in an otherwise complex, conflicting and chaotic (unpredictable, random) context. This resonates with assertions that youth justice policy trajectories of reform/change are *cyclical* in the sense of constantly returning to these welfare–justice policy positions (Bernard and Kurlycheck, 2010). This cycle of reform allegedly begins when policy makers and the public identify youth crime as increasingly problematic and youth justice responses as increasingly ineffective, which engenders support for more punitive (justice-based) approaches, before eventually reverting to support for a more lenient (welfare-based) treatment when policy makers believe that harsh punishment is ineffective and criminal (Bernard and Kurlycheck, 2010).

The reality of how youth justice is socially constructed and how its constructive influences interact is, of course, less reductionist/generalised and more necessarily complex than suggested by traditionally dichotomised and bifurcated explanations and discourses (see Case and Smith, 2023). The socio-historical nature of youth justice, frequently manifested in policy, has been messy, contradictory and often *polyfurcated* (that is, travelling in multiple directions at once), characterised by multiple, often competing discourses (see Fergusson, 2007). These discourses have themselves been characterised by broad trends and themes that overlap and conflict within and between countries to create complex, hybrid trajectories for youth justice internationally (Dunkel, 2014; McAra, 2023), reflecting Goldson and Muncie's (2009: vii) depiction of youth justice internationally as operating within multi-faceted, hybrid contexts wherein '[d]iscourses of child protection, restoration, punishment, public protection, responsibility, justice, rehabilitation, welfare, retribution, diversion, human rights, and so on, intersect and circulate in a perpetually uneasy and contradictory motion'.

The centrality of *policy* contexts in the construction of youth justice

Notwithstanding the espoused multiplicity of constructive influences on the 'making' of youth justice, however, it is widely asserted that the constructive (political) influence and context of policy is paramount (see Brett, 2018; see also Souhami, 2015a; Case, 2018/21). This accords with understandings of policy reform as

> very much a *political* process. It is governed not by any criminological logic but instead by ... political actors and the exigencies, political calculations and short-term interests that provide their motivations. In its detailed configuration, with all its incoherence and contradictions, [it] is thus a product of the decidedly aleatory history of political manoeuvres and calculations. (Garland, 2001: 191, original emphasis)

Youth justice policies often reflect dominant political constructions of the issue/problem of 'youth offending'. As such, policy making is arguably *the* most influential process in shaping and constructing what is understood as 'youth justice'. Policy shapes the very nature of youth justice and the outcomes expected from it (Bateman, 2017), while youth justice strategies and models are manifested in policy (Yates, 2012). Nevertheless, there are significant challenges to studying and understanding youth justice policy *making*.

The evolving trajectory of youth justice and its related socio-historical constructions and reconstructions can be understood as the 'product' or manifestation of relationships and interactions between a range of different constructive influences. These influences operate in different contexts situated within and between different levels of the social system ('Ecological Systems Theory' – Bronfenbrenner, 1995): the *macro* (national, socio-structural, socio-economic, cultural and political contexts), the *meso* (interactions and relationships within and between systems) and the *micro* (the individual and immediate environment level).[4] These contextualised, constructive influences have been identified in critical youth justice and historical-criminological literature (for example, Magerey, 1978; Muncie, 2014) as predominantly

- socio-economic – for example, macro-level changes due to industrialisation and urbanisation, the emerging influence of middle-class values and behaviours, the creation of juvenile-specific institutions, the economically driven representations of children by the media, economic austerity (chronosystemic);
- political – for example, macro-, meso- and micro-level law making, evolving government legislation and policy regarding the behaviours and treatment of children and young people, rhetoric from politicians, (mis) representations of mass media (exosystemic);
- statistical – for example, the creation of new sources of statistical information to categorise groups and behaviours in order to measure the extent and nature of (youth) crime and justice-based responses to it;
- professional – for example, micro-level investigations, experiences and practices of key stakeholder professionals working directly with children in youth justice systems, including lawyers, magistrates, police, social workers and others working with these stakeholders (such as strategists, non-departmental public bodies [NDPBs], inspectorates, politicians, civil servants, mass media), along with the meso-level interactions and relationships between them and the macro-level organisational practices and occupational cultures that shape their work;
- intellectual – for example, changing perceptions of children promoted by key thinkers such as philanthropists, moral entrepreneurs and social reformers, combined with scholarly, academic explanations of youth offending/justice (the effectiveness of different sentences and interventions, for example), including those generated through empirical research.

The identification of these constructive influences and influencers (such as policy makers) implicates youth justice as constructed and shaped within and between multiple sites or *contexts* of influence, including the cultural, historical, economic, national, cultural, political, legal, academic/intellectual, conceptual, empirical, statistical, professional, media and public (see also Goldson's 2020 macro-level 'excavation' of youth justice reform). The socio-constructionist lens adopted throughout this book enables context to be operationalised as the *relational and dynamic features* shaping the *mechanisms* through which policy can be in/effective and conceives of context operating in dynamic, emergent ways over time at multiple different levels of the social system (Greenhalgh and Manzano, 2021). Accordingly, youth justice policy making can be analysed by eliciting the dynamic constructions, perspectives, experiences and meaning making within and between key stakeholder organisations and individuals.

What is youth justice 'policy'?

A thorough examination of the 'making' of youth justice policy for children should be underpinned by a clear working definition and understanding of 'policy'. Levin (1997) has argued that although recognising policy can be difficult, policy makers,[5] such as politicians, their officials (civil servants, for example) and academics, typically conceptualise policy as the 'principles applied to a situation' through a proposal or set of proposals committing to further action. These policies are often framed in deliberately broad, generalised ways (such as 'prevention') to allow more options for the translation of this commitment into policy 'action' (for example, policy mobilised by strategy and animated in practice). Accordingly, Levin distinguishes between different constructions of the goals, roles, statuses and manifestations of policy as a *stated intention* (by governments in manifestoes and White Papers, for example), as a *current or past action*, as the *formal or claimed status of a past, present or proposed course of action* (for example, 'government policy' – assuming the dominance of governmental actors as primary policy makers) and as an *organisational practice* (such as rules, regulations, responses, attitudes).[7]

In addition to distinguishing these different yet potentially reciprocal interrelated constructions of 'policy', it is possible to further distinguish policy *measures* as the things done to implement the policy. These measures typically manifest as policy *products* (see Souhami, 2015a) or *instruments* such as government *legislation* (Acts of Parliament, for example), 'Green Papers' (discussion and consultation documents outlining proposed policies), 'White Papers' (documents setting out proposals for future legislation), policy briefings and ministerial speeches, public expenditure (spending plans, for example), organisational structuring (creating, abolishing, modifying structures) and management activities (for example, appointments to positions, setting performance targets, prescribing practices, supervising activities of organisations). Therefore, policy making is traditionally and essentially understood as a stance which, once articulated, contributes to the context/s within which a succession of future decisions will be made. With that said, according to Souhami (in Case, 2018/21): 'Of course, these [products] are vitally important and powerful instruments in the policy process. However, … policy is something much wider than this.'

Clearly, therefore, there are attendant challenges to developing knowledge and related evidence of youth justice policy making. For instance, youth justice 'policy' is a social construction in itself, situated within the broader social construction of 'youth justice', so it is extremely difficult to conceptualise as a specific, concrete phenomenon. Indeed, 'policy' is not a self-evident term but rather a web of decisions or actions, each potentially subject to the different interpretations and reconstructions of stakeholders based on their respective agendas, perspectives and experiences. However, this narrow explanatory lens has encouraged a reductionist analytical focus on policy measures and products rather than a more dynamic, relational focus on 'making' policy through processes, relationships and interactions between a broader cadre of policy actors (as within this book). For example, government ministers and their civil servants, who tend to dominate narratives of policy construction (see Croci et al, 2022), are not necessarily primarily responsible for enacting or delivering those policies in the real world. Rather, these tasks of implementation and the associated mediation, moderation and re/construction of centralised policy prescriptions are typically those of stakeholders and organisations operating in non-governmental, localised and relational contexts (see Goldson and Briggs, 2021).

How is youth justice policy made? Processes of cyclical complexity

The processes of making youth justice policy have been most commonly conceptualised in the academic literature as sequential, with policy development moving in a linear manner through a series of parts or stages, often labelled the 'Policy Cycle Model' (Howlett, 2018; Klammer et al, 2021). According to the model, as policy makers work through its stages, they decide on the best course of action based on specialist advice (expertise) such as expert reports, consultations and cost–benefit analyses. In this model, the sequential, staged, linear policy-making process is typically represented as:

1a. Problem emergence – issues emerge on the policy agenda (resulting from governmental agenda and/or media reporting, for example) as 'the list of subjects or problems to which governmental officials, and people outside of government closely associated with those officials, are paying some serious attention at any given time' (Kingdon, 2011: 3).
1b. Agenda setting – a social problem is initially sensed by policy actors and a variety of solutions are put forward.
2a. Policy formulation (also known as policy 'formation') – the development of specific policy options within government when the range of possible choices is narrowed by excluding infeasible ones and efforts are made by various actors to have their favoured solution ranked highly among the remaining few.
2b. Decision making – formal actors in government (central, local) adopt a particular course of action to address the problem and realise the policy.
3a. Policy implementation – governments put decisions into effect using some combination of tools of public administration in

order to alter the distribution of goods and services in society in a way that is broadly compatible with the sentiments and values of affected parties.

3b. Policy evaluation – policies are monitored by both state and societal actors, often leading to the reconceptualisation of policy problems and solutions in the light of experiences encountered with the policy in question and the start of a new iteration of the cycle.

(After Howlett, 2018)

The Policy Cycle Model is considered to be an effective basic framework for understanding the complex field of policy studies and policy making (Capano and Pritoni, 2020) and as the basis for further research in this field (Perl, 2020). Additionally, the model can help identify which policy actors are relevant in which stages of the cycle, as well as providing a helpful and practical way to describe and understand the process of policy making (Jann and Wegrich, 2007). However, the model has significant limitations as an empirical description of policy-making realities and risks oversimplifying, narrowing and restricting (or dumbing down) our understandings of highly complex, dynamic, contingent, contested and non-linear policy processes (Croci et al, 2022). In particular, the model supports constructions of policy *contexts* as static, linear and deterministic, thus overlooking the *dynamic* and *relational* aspects of multi-faceted policy contexts, for example the role of relationships and interactions between policy 'makers' (see Introduction; see also Greenhalgh and Manzano, 2021). In practice, policy issues are likely to be interconnected, and policy operates in contexts of uncertainty and internal/external constraints and political and practical realities. The realities of policy 'making' are not necessarily systematic and linear, as the Policy Cycle Model might suggest, with stages often compressed, skipped, overlapping or changing their order entirely, such as policy formulation proceeding agenda setting as 'solutions seek problems' to which they can be applied (Howlett, 2018). In particular, the reductionist and decontextualised nature of the policy-making narratives emerging from the model may render them unable to adequately answer key questions regarding what influences the actual substance of policy, such as the potentially significant role of policy implementation, the numbers and types of relevant policy actors involved in policy-making processes and the exact manner in which actual policy development processes occur (Savard and Banville, 2012; Klammer et al, 2021). Furthermore, the cycle does not consider the interaction between different policies and their parallel implementation (Croci et al, 2022). Therefore, the Policy Cycle Model is, at best, a baseline for the analysis of the potentially more complex, messy, opportunistic and chaotic reality of policy making in the YJS.

Policy point: youth justice policy making from inside the melting pot

Youth justice policy making has been subject to a limited, yet steadily increasing, degree of empirical study and critical scrutiny. These studies have explicitly challenged the reductionist focus, methods and conclusions of the broader social policy-making studies that conflate policy formulation with policy making and privilege the role of governments, politicians and administrators/civil servants as the primary makers of policy (Souhami in Case, 2018/21). In stark contrast, this nascent, evolving body of studies has deliberately examined a broader range of policy-making processes (beyond policy 'products', for example), stages (such as addressing the vacuum of policy implementation research) and contexts (beyond the role of government and related officials, for example). A key example of such research is Souhami's (2011, 2015a) in-depth ethnographic study of the complex policy-making role, identity and experiences of the Youth Justice Board (YJB), the NDPB responsible for advising government on the development of youth justice *policy*, devising youth justice *strategy* to facilitate policy implementation and managing and guiding the implementation of policy on the ground in *practice* (such as work with children). This ground-breaking study (a significant inspiration for the current book) has been complemented by empirical research by Case and colleagues exploring policy-making relationships between politicians/government (traditionally understood as 'policy makers'), strategists (for example, YJB, YJB Cymru) and practitioners (such as youth offending team staff), focusing on the policy barriers, challenges, enablers and opportunities presented by the dynamic nature of context-specific relationships within and between stakeholder groups (Case, 2014; Case and Hampson, 2019; Case et al, 2020). Findings from relevant empirical studies of youth justice policy making will be integrated into the critical analyses that populate this book.

Who is making youth justice policy, and *whose* policy is it?

It has been argued that there is a growing necessity to understand the 'makers' of youth justice policy through the application of a much broader lens (Souhami in Case, 2018/21). This necessity emerges, at least in part, because academic definitions and empirical analyses of policy-making processes can fail to capture the most salient features of youth justice policy and tend to impose their own conceptual frameworks on the analysis rather than those of a full range of participant actors in policy-making processes (Vergari, 2015). Consequently, in order to understand policy and policy making in the most valid and comprehensive ways, it is important to acknowledge and accommodate a broader range of policy actors/makers of policy, such as distinguishing between those located inside and outside of government and between those who are considered to be in/visible to varying degrees (Vergari, 2015).

Governmental policy actors

Youth justice policies and policy making can be understood, at least in part, as reflections of the power structures within and between formal, permanent institutions typically located within and driven by the machinery of government and the wider political system. Indeed, according to Croci et al (2022: 5), '[t]he primary agent of public policy making is the government'. Actors working in governmental contexts include politicians/government ministers such as the Home Secretary and the Minister of Justice[6] and their elected and appointed officials (such as senior policy advisers/'SPADs' – senior civil servants working closely with ministers and government officials to develop and implement policy) and other civil servants working for governments, rather than for specific political parties. These 'visible' actors often fulfil prominent roles in placing social problems on the policy agenda and are thus privileged in analyses of how policy is made. However, privileging the policy influence of visible actors can engender reductionist understandings of policy-making processes that are characterised by partiality (incompleteness, bias towards particular stakeholder groups and analysis of earlier stages of the policy process) and *decontextualisation* (insufficient appreciation of contextual influences). The enduring assumption in academic and policy debates has been that government bureaucracy is unconnected to the formation of policy, which is viewed as the sole domain of ministers and a relatively narrow group of SPADs who advise them, while the role of supporting bureaucracy (for example civil servants) is largely confined to policy implementation (Page and Jenkins, 2005). The privileging of the policy-making role of ministers and SPADs reflects a 'normative institutional understanding' (Gains, 1999: 716) of a clear split between responsibility for policy formation and for its administration, seeing the primary purpose of government bureaucracy as supporting ministers but without political authority to define its own objectives (Page and Jenkins, 2005): '[I]f politicians knew how they wanted the problem solved sufficiently to give their administrative support and strict instructions, they would not need policy bureaucracies' (Page and Jenkins, 2005: vi).

In reality, division of policy-making responsibility is less clear. Government officials can be intrinsically involved in policy-making processes (see Souhami, 2015b), with civil servants often elaborating on ministerial decisions in order to put them into action, being routinely involved in formulating policy and having discretion in relation to small questions of implementation that define and change the shape of policy (Page and Jenkins, 2005). In addition, civil service bureaucracy can be a site from which policy ideas emerge and are promoted or resisted. As well as providing formal advice, government officials at all levels are engaged in informal processes of influence and negotiation. Rather than always functioning as neutral arbiters of technical information, civil servant officials can instead create particular constructions of problems and solutions – 'good stories' which can be presented to ministers (Stevens, 2011). Therefore, central government officials are not only routinely involved at the decision-making stage of policy making but can also shape how problems are constructed and thus what is considered possible (albeit potentially mediated by governmental agenda). Thus, the institutional context of government administration is of central importance to any meaningful analysis of youth justice policy making (see Souhami, 2015a).

Policy point: the YJB as a constructed policy-making context

The contextualised complexity of government bureaucracy and non-governmental influence in the making of youth justice policy is illustrated by the special case of the YJB for England and Wales. In April 2000, created in accordance with the CDA 1998, the YJB was introduced as a new youth justice structure that took the form of an NDPB, also known as a 'quango' (quasi-autonomous non-governmental organisation). The YJB's dual remit was to advise government on youth justice policy (notably agenda setting and policy formulation) and to support youth justice professionals and organisations in their implementation of policy in practice. Its NDPB status and broad remit gave the YJB a hitherto unprecedented and significant influence in shaping the direction and realisation of youth justice policy in England and Wales and a broad, flexible arena in which to act; as well as the capacity to act according to values and objectives potentially and connected to ministerial outcomes. As such, the YJB was and continues to be a unique youth justice construction and occupied a new policy-making context for youth justice. The YJB's scope for discretion was considerable, at least initially, as exemplified by the ambiguous parameters of its statutory functions, such as the duty to 'advise the Secretary of State' (Home Secretary), which was open to multiple interpretations (Souhami, 2011). Furthermore, working in a politically charged arena such as youth justice, the strategic and practical implementation decisions formally delegated to the YJB as an NDPB could themselves be seen to constitute policy (Gains, 2003). The unique policy-making context and identity of the YJB, therefore, situates the organisation in an ambiguous space, both between and within the categories of governmental and non-governmental policy actors.

Non-governmental policy actors

Academic analyses have traditionally considered non-governmental policy actors to be less visible and less influential as policy makers than governmental actors. According to Souhami (in Case, 2018/21), "youth justice policy isn't made just by senior civil servants and ministers, but by all kinds of people working in government and in partnership elsewhere [so] ... if we want to understand youth justice policy making, we need to look at what youth justice policy makers do". However, the policy-making involvement of 'hidden' expert actors such as other political parties (for example, the Shadow Justice Minister), interest groups, mass media, strategists, academics and practitioners[7] can be neglected, as can (by extension) analyses of the latter stages of policy-making processes, such as developing policy solutions for problems (see Kingdon, 2011). Indeed, policy *implementation* as policy making is much neglected in analyses of the policy-making processes, which often privilege the problem emergence/agenda-setting (political) context of policy making, typically led by politicians and government officials (Braithwaite et al, 2018; Hudson et al, 2019). Relatedly, the constructive influence of the non-governmental actors typically responsibilised for policy implementation continues to be marginalised (but see Case and Browning, 2021b; Day, 2022). As Souhami reflected in an interview for my *Youth Justice: A Critical Introduction* textbook (Case, 2018/21): 'What becomes of the practice expertise which is so important in how youth justice services work? Does this play a part in how policies are made in central Government, and if so, how?' This long-term failure to acknowledge the full complexity of policy making in policy analyses has limited understandings of why policy is not always successfully translated into practice, otherwise known as 'policy implementation failure' or the 'policy implementation gap' (Gunn, 1978; see also Day, 2022). Instead of detailed, contextualised explanations, there has been a political tendency to assign responsibility for policy 'failure' to ineffective implementation by practitioners, rather than to poor agenda setting and policy formulation/decision making by government actors (see Davies et al, 2008). This has led critical scholars to assert that meaningful consultation with practice should be prioritised in order to better understand how youth justice is 'made' in local contexts by practitioners mediating and moderating national policy and strategy through their relations, discretion, decisions and adaptations (see Goldson and Briggs, 2021). Such an approach appears sensible because frontline practitioners functioning as 'street-level bureaucrats' (Lipsky, 1980) are typically closer to, and have a better understanding of, the realities of implementing policy in the real world[8] compared to centralised governmental and governance organisations (Hudson et al, 2019). This argument strongly recommends consultation with a range of policy-making stakeholders at multiple levels of social and organisational systems to explore the 'messy engagement of multiple players with diverse sources of knowledge' (Davies et al, 2008: 188).

A contextualised understanding of youth justice policy making

> [Youth justice is] a complex arena of social practice, incorporating a diverse range of actors, practices, relationships and networks.
>
> (Souhami, 2015a: 164)

Policy making in the youth justice field is a complex undertaking that has been conceptualised as involving a series of processes: establishing strategic direction, agenda setting, making decisions/formulating policy and defining/identifying workable solutions to youth crime (Huckel-Schneider and Blyth, 2017). However, this representation of policy making appears somewhat over-simplified and linear (akin to the Policy Cycle Model) in a contemporary, complex context of youth justice policy making that appears confused and contradictory (Muncie, 2008; Hopkins-Burke, 2016; Goldson, 2017), excessively politicised (Smith, 2006; Smith and Gray, 2019) and bereft of consolidating principles (Goldson and Muncie, 2006; Case, 2022). Phoenix (2016: 124) succinctly articulated this complexity by observing a fundamental rupture in the relationship between '*how* we deal with youth crime (i.e. the processes, procedures and provisions) and *why* we do it (i.e. any higher philosophical or ethical goals)'.

Observations and conceptual, philosophical and methodological critiques of contemporary youth justice policy making strongly implicate the importance and urgency of examining how youth justice policy is constructed/made. Such an examination could promote more ecologically valid understandings of the inherent complexities of youth justice policy making to enable a greater appreciation of its possible future trajectory (Lawrence, 2019). However, the challenge of explaining youth justice policy making illuminates a central paradox for the YJS – the political, policy and practice imperative to evidence simplicity, certainty, security and stability in a context (of policy making) that is fluid, unpredictable, unstable and evidentially limited (see Case and Hampson, 2019). This paradox was encapsulated by Dr Anna Souhami when reflecting on her detailed ethnographic research of the YJB's policy-making role:

> If responses to troubling behaviour are necessarily individual, fluid and uncertain, how do Government officials make broad policies? If there is no clear criteria or mechanism for success, how do governments show themselves to be successful? How do they cope with uncertainty in a political climate in which it is not tolerated? (Souhami in Case, 2018/21)

Critical commentary: youth justice as a melting pot of multiple policy discourses

In his seminal critical analysis of the youth justice policy-making context, Fergusson (2007) discerned a 'melting pot' of 'multiple discourses' in youth justice policy, reflective of the political tensions that have produced inconsistencies within and between policy positions and historical periods and the perennial conflict and ambivalence in the construction of youth justice (Case, 2018/21) and disjunctures or 'ruptures' between policy and practice (see Phoenix, 2016). This explication of a 'melting pot' of multiple discourses resonates with Goldson's notion of historically competing 'rationales' for youth justice policies, identified through his excavation of the 'complex and seemingly incoherent nature of youth justice reform' (2020: 318). Goldson asserts that such complexity 'derives from attempts to reconcile and balance competing rationales and fractious relations with an overriding context of shifting social, economic, and political conditions' (2020: 318).

Relatedly, Fergusson notes that (often contradictory and competing) youth justice policy discourses are closely related to political-philosophical traditions. For example, the welfare principle links with traditions of paternalism and children's rights, while justice links to neo-authoritarianism and neo-liberal responsibilisation strategies (see also Muncie et al, 2002). However, Fergusson (2007) also cautions against classifying and representing youth justice policies as falling within a single discursive framework, instead emphasising the importance of teasing apart the constituent elements of what policies are and how they are presented, applied and enacted (or 'made'), so not taking any aspect of policy at face value (Fergusson, 2007). Indeed, it is recognised that the 'architects of reform' (politicians, civil servants) are entirely capable of presenting policies in one way (bureaucratic framing), applying them in another and evaluating them in a third.

Fergusson's critical analyses of youth justice discourses cohere around the distinction between how governments present policy rhetorically, how they codify it and how those policies played out in practice, not least because they are under the direct influence of different people with differing priorities. He distinguishes between different *modes* of policy:

- rhetorical – where the power of professional politicians brings to the fore the punitive discourses founded in conservative-authoritarian values;
- codificational – where civil servants steer government towards statutes that maintain continuities with the welfare traditions of the preceding era and secure the customary discretion for professional practitioners;
- implementational – where discretion is exercised collectively, such as within rehabilitative and welfarist approaches.

Ostensibly, these modes appear to map on to the broad categories of *policy* (rhetorical), *strategy* used to guide policy transfer in practice (codificational) and the *practice* employed to make policy a reality (implementational), but such potentially reductionist assumptions will be subject to scrutiny as analyses progress.

Power as a constructive influence on youth justice policy making

Policies and their related 'measures', 'products' and policy-making processes have been understood as manifestations of power such as uneven power relations and power structures between policy actors in different contexts. Indeed, the very notion of 'power structure' reminds us that institutions and positions carry with them a certain degree of 'power' that their constituent actors are able to exercise, while linkages between institutions, positions, inhabitants bind them to a recognisable 'structure' (see Vergari, 2015). Power in the making of social policy can be exercised and manifested in a number of different guises (Vergari, 2015), such as the power *to do* and to take action (the Prime Minister appointing cabinet members, for example), power *over* (as when one stakeholder or organisation has power over another) or the power *to achieve* (for example, to realise an agenda, to determine the characteristics of a policy or measure). The identification of power as a significant influence on policy making strongly indicates that the relationships and interactions within/between stakeholders with different agendas require more detailed attention if policy making is to be better understood and ultimately enhanced. However, it remains immensely challenging for any analysis of youth justice policies to characterise, theorise and demonstrate the influence of the dynamic power relations between different policy-making groups and actors (for example governments/politicians, civil servants, strategists, managers, practitioners). Hill and Hupe (2015: 197) cite paradigmatic and conceptual shifts in political theory, away from vertically conceptualised *government* towards horizontally conceptualised *governance* – the decisions and actions of those in power to control and manage less powerful populations (Phoenix, 2016). Whether this governance paradigm leads to a picture of horizontally organised, multi-levelled policy making or fudged policy determinations with messy outcomes, it has been argued, depends on how power is understood to operate within it (Rose, 1996).

The policy-making power of expertise and evidence

Enhanced understanding of youth justice policy making can be facilitated by interrogating the processes by which organisations and professional stakeholders become privileged as 'experts' with specialist knowledge of youth justice and its evidence base (for example government ministers, developmental criminologists), while other stakeholder groups are compelled to avoid the development of expertise, such as generalist civil servants avoiding political attachment and fostering a range of experience (Souhami in Case, 2018/21), or may have their contextualised expertise marginalised or rejected (for example practitioners, critical academics). Analyses will consider the role of expertise and the generation and use of evidence in shaping policy-making relationships and how expertise interacts with and is mediated by power to construct policy.

Although the systematic generation of evidence by experts and its utilisation in policy-making processes is typically expected to produce more accurate policy advice (such as the 'evidence-based' policy and practice of post-1996 youth justice – see Chapter 3), these scientific aspirations will always be constrained by the realities of democratic political debates, stakeholder lobbying and popular opinion (Head and Alford, 2015). This situation has prompted repeated criticisms of the use of evidence in policy making. For example, critics highlight the 'oversaturation' of expertise and evidence sources in policy debates (Stevens, 2011),[9] while others assert that its role and utilisation is poorly understood and its linear impact on policy overstated and misrepresented (Belfiore, 2021). In his noteworthy study of civil servant policy making, Stevens (2011) explores how evidence is used for '[t]elling policy stories' persuasively to support policy making around particular political agendas. The ostensibly selective use of evidence can be seen as ideological and supportive of systemically asymmetrical power relations in policy-making contexts, for example by creating 'problems' to be solved. Accordingly, the complex, contentious nature of the policy–evidence relationship introduces questions about whether the youth justice sector is shaped by 'evidence-based policy' (as is often claimed by government) or by 'policy-based evidence' (Sanderson, 2011; Brown, 2013). Therefore, subsequent analyses throughout this book will explore the role and influence of evidence (or lack of it) in youth justice policy making in England and Wales and the role that ideas and values have in shaping policy (see also Oliver and Boaz, 2019; Belfiore, 2021).

Conclusion: the contextualised construction of youth justice policy

Nascent critical scholarship and empirical research evidence bases have sought to improve upon explanatory reductionism across socio-historical analyses of youth justice policy making. Consequently, it is essential that contemporary empirical studies continue to pursue more necessarily complex, non-linear, multi-faceted and contextualised understandings of how youth justice policy is constructed/made. This can be achieved through an original, broadened focus on the potential complexity and dynamism of policy-making processes and contexts and the context-specific influence of contextualised relationships between governmental and non-governmental actors in the 'making' of youth justice policy. Furthermore, there should be more detailed analysis of the extent and nature to which these relationships are influenced by power dynamics and the degree to which they enable/hamper the generation and utilisation of expertise and evidence. It is crucial that the knowledge and evidence bases associated with understanding youth justice policy making be consolidated and expanded so that the youth justice sector (politically, legally, professionally, intellectually) can break away from reductionist, partial and decontextualised explanations. Consequently, broadened understandings of youth justice policy making must encompass how and why policy is decided, understood, informed, experienced, enacted, developed, changed (that is, reconstructed) and evaluated, focusing on the relationships between key stakeholders engaged in policy-making processes across a range of professional contexts.

So … how should such a challenging project be undertaken?

2

Methodology: exploring contextualised constructions of youth justice policy

The opening chapters have established the rationale for a research project that pursues socially constructed, contextualised and necessarily complex understandings of youth justice policy making. Therefore, the analyses underpinning this project have a number of overarching research aims:

- to identify, trace and critically examine the key constructive influences on the trajectory of youth justice policy making in England and Wales within and between different contexts;
- to enhance stakeholder and sector understandings of in/effective youth justice policy making, in order to fill the vacuum of political, policy, strategic, practice and academic understandings of the dynamic trajectories of youth justice policy development;
- to offer recommendations for enhancing youth justice policy making (such as the faithful translation of policy into practice), collaborative partnership working and knowledge sharing nationally and locally.

Research questions

These overarching aims will be unpacked and pursued through a series of objectives, framed as targeted research questions (RQs):

1. What is youth justice 'policy'?
2. Who are the 'makers' of youth justice policy?
3. How is youth justice policy making understood, re/constructed, experienced and made meaningful by policy makers working in different contexts?
4. What are the barriers, challenges, enablers and opportunities for policy making?
5. How can youth justice policy making be improved?

The research methodology and analyses adopted are necessarily qualitative, contextualised and ethnomethodological to enable examination of how policy is produced through processes of social interaction. The chosen research ontology[1] is *social constructionism* (see also 'Researcher positionality' statement later in this chapter), which represents realities as created through processes of social interaction and contingent on human perception and experience, thus viewing all knowledge as constructed (Taylor, 2018).

Methodology: qualitative documentary analysis and semi-structured interviews

The chosen approach to exploring the project aims and RQs is an iterative, two-stage qualitative methodology consisting of qualitative documentary analysis (QDA) and semi-structured interviews. This methodological decision accords with the assertion that 'almost all likely sources of information, data, and ideas fall into two general types: documents and people' (Bardach and Patashnik, 2015). The central inclusion criterion guiding the sampling of both documents and stakeholders is relevance to the political/policy and legislative period from 1996 to the present. This period marked a significant stepping-off point for youth justice in the United Kingdom, evidencing repeated efforts to define and rationalise policy making (Institute for Government, 2011) and has experienced a revolution in youth justice policy making of an unprecedented nature. This included the construction of a distinct Youth Justice System (YJS) of England and Wales and the devolution of youth justice policy-making responsibilities to Scotland and Northern Ireland. Consequently, the socio-historical period from 1996 to to the time of writing (early 2024) provides the parameters for a focused, coherent and manageable analysis of youth justice policy making.

QDA of youth justice policy literature

A QDA of pre-existing youth justice and related policy literature (since 1996) was conducted to identify and examine policy-making patterns, themes, agendas and author meanings (latent and explicit) within those documents, for example, those illustrated by published/documented stated objectives, legal changes, introduction of new legislation, structures, strategies, practices and mechanisms (see also Merriam and Tisdall, 2016). The QDA of policy documents was supplemented by equivalent analyses of policy-focused scholarly literature over the same period.

QDA was employed as a systematic procedure for reviewing and evaluating youth justice policy documents as they evolve over time and differ across geographies. This methodology provided context, generated questions, supplemented other types of research data (for example from the interviews) and tracked the trajectories of policy (Dalgliesh et al, 2020). Like any research method, QDA is subject to concerns regarding validity, reliability, authenticity, motivated authorship (for example political agenda, researcher positionaility), lack of representativity and so on. These potential sources of bias were acknowledged, mitigated and moderated by using standard techniques to enhance qualitative rigour, including triangulation (within documents and across study methods), ensuring adequate sample size and 'engagement' with the documents, and peer validation[2] and.

For analysis purposes, policy literature is broadly defined in this project as:

- government legislation/policy, publications including Green and White Papers (for example, the Crime and Disorder Act 1998), published speeches, Ministry of Justice (MoJ) reports, Welsh Government strategies;
- grey and non-governmental literature, including Youth Justice Board (YJB) strategy documents, practice guidance and information papers, independent/commissioned reviews, think tank reports.

The body of policy literature identified and analysed was (largely) publicly available and was rendered more accessible through longstanding author networks and professional relationships. The findings of this QDA are presented in Chapters 3 and 4.

Analysing the policy documents: the READ approach

Youth justice policy documents were interrogated using a systematic documentary analysis technique popular in health policy research called the 'READ' method (Dalgliesh et al, 2020), an iterative approach consisting of four stages: (1) **R**eady your materials, (2) **E**xtract data, (3) **A**nalyse data, (4) **D**istil your findings.

1. Ready your materials: criteria were established around the topic (youth justice policies) and dates of inclusion (1996 to time of writing), then the researcher made notes on the type of information required from the documents (that is, what needed to be learned and how this helped to answer the RQs). As the initial criteria and data required evolved over the course of the research, it was considered useful to consult a mix of formal documents (for example official policies and strategies) and 'grey literature' (for example Green/White Papers, organisational reports, audits) that provided rich veins of insight into how youth justice policy actors were thinking through the issues under study.
2. Extract data (meaning making): the RQs focused largely on process, and documents were used to compile a timeline of events and to trace processes across time. Data extraction began with close, thorough reading of the selected documents, reading for overall meaning and the generation of ideas and working theories about what was being learned and observed in the data, akin to grounded theory methodology.

3. Analyse data: as in all types of qualitative research, data collection and analysis were iterative and characterised by emergent design, meaning that developing findings continually informed whether and how to obtain and interpret data (see Creswell, 2013). In practice, this meant that during the data extraction phase, the researcher was already analysing data and forming initial theories.
4. Distil your findings: once 'saturation' had been achieved (that is, the researcher felt that the phenomena were fully or sufficiently understood), findings were refined through presentation as a policy narrative. The final product of the distillation process enabled findings to be stated relative to the RQs and policy-relevant conclusions to be drawn, both of which were triangulated with and further interrogated by the findings from the semi-structured interviews.

(After Dalgliesh et al, 2020)

Semi-structured interviews with expert stakeholders

The QDA findings were complemented, triangulated[3] and extended by data generated from a series of semi-structured interviews with key stakeholders from the youth justice sector who are 'experts by experience' due to working in professional policy-making contexts during the analysis period.[4] Semi-structured interviews explored professional experiences, perspectives and constructions of youth justice policy 'making' and were framed by a series of broad stimulus questions that aligned with the research questions:

- What is your professional background in and experience of the youth justice sector? (Introductory/context-setting question)
- What do you understand as constituting youth justice 'policy' and policy 'making'? (RQs 1, 3)
- How do the key 'makers' of youth justice policy operate and relate to one another? (RQ 2)
- Are specific policy makers more influential at certain stages of the policy-making 'process'? (RQs 2, 3)
- What do you see as the enablers/facilitators of, barriers/challenges to, opportunities for effective policy making in the YJS? (RQs 3, 4, 5)

Semi-structured interviews: sampling expert stakeholders

The identification of suitable expert stakeholders to interview was undertaken through a staged sampling strategy of purposive sampling evolving into snowball sampling. Mirroring the sampling of documents in the QDA component, the sampling and accessing of expert stakeholders was guided and facilitated by the professional experiences, networks and relationships the researcher has developed over an applied research career in the sector beginning in 2000. These connections enhanced access to interviewees in many cases, such as when seeking representatives from governance and practitioner organisations. However, access was inevitably limited by the availability and willingness of particular individuals to participate. Consequently, certain stakeholder/policy actor groups are somewhat over-represented in the sample (for example, the YJB, Association of Youth Offending Team [YOT] Managers [AYM]), while others are under-represented, largely through unavailability of either suitable or selected participants, rather than unwillingness to participate. Under-represented expert stakeholder groups include government ministers, civil servants at the MoJ and officials from the Youth Custody Service, while police and court perspectives are not represented at all.

Interviewees were accessed in a range of professional youth justice contexts (for example national, local, organisational, community, custody) across the trajectory of youth justice policy development. An inclusion/purposive sampling strategy was developed for the interviews whereby the researcher attempted to access all former government justice secretaries since 1996 (largely unsuccessful), all chairs and chief executives of the YJB, all chairs of AYM and YOT Managers Cymru (largely successful), key staff from His Majesty's Inspectorate of Probation (HMIP) (again, largely successful) and key strategic and operational staff from these and other important policy-making organisations (for example, MoJ and Welsh Government civil servants, academics, YJB board members).

Interviews were conducted over a six-month period (September 2022 to February 2023) with 41 stakeholders[5] working in a range of national, local and organisational/occupational policy-making contexts (see Appendix 1 for a detailed list of interviewees and their occupational contexts). The decision was taken to anonymise interviewee quotes and to instead attribute quotes to occupational role (see Table 2.1), with the caveat that they reflect the views and experiences of individual professionals rather than their organisations. However, all interviewees consented to having their details shared and for directly attributable quotes to be used where anonymisation is insufficient (as for example in the case of the government minister interviewed).

Analysing the interview data: Reflexive Thematic Analysis

The semi-structured interviews were interrogated using *thematic analysis*, a common form of analysis within qualitative research which emphasises the identification, analysis and interpretation of patterns of meaning (or 'themes') within qualitative data (Braun and Clarke, 2006). Thematic analysis is often understood as a method or technique, in contrast to several other qualitative analytic approaches (for example grounded theory, discourse

Table 2.1: Interviewees and their occupational contexts[7]

Stakeholder group	Organisation	Role	n
Politicians	Government	Minister of Justice	1
Civil servants (governmental)	MoJ	Youth Justice Division	1
	MoJ	SPAD	1
	Welsh Government	Crime and Justice Unit	3
Civil servants (non-governmental)	HMIP	Managerial	3
	YJB	Chief Executive	4
	YJB	Chair	6
	YJB	Policy/Strategy lead	3
	YJB	Board member	5
	YYJB/YJB Cymru	Chair	1
	OCC	Commissioner	2
	OCC	Policy adviser	2
Practitioner representative	AYM	Chair	4
	AYM	Deputy Chair	1
	YMC	Chair	3
Practitioners	YOTs	Manager	9
Academics	Universities: Bedfordshire, Bristol, Derby, South Wales (2)	Expert scholar	5
Third sector	Alliance for Youth Justice	Chair	1

analysis, narrative analysis) which are better described as methodologies or theoretically informed frameworks for research. The thematic analysis adopted was *narrative* in form, revolving around the question of what the (policy-making) story is about and wherein the story content is central to the analysis, particularly to the meanings and codes derived from the data (see Sandberg, 2021). In this way, it remained essential to the researcher that the themes identified were not considered unique to one story or individual but instead represented something greater. Accordingly, the central themes of stories in the datasets generated were employed as a starting point for identifying broader findings and seeding discussions about policy making.

The overarching form of (narrative) thematic analysis employed to examine the interview data was reflexive thematic analysis (RTA), an advanced data analysis technique for data coding, identifying themes and developing, analysing and interpreting patterns across qualitative datasets (see Braun and Clarke, 2022). RTA was chosen to enable understandings of the situated meanings and interrogation of the meaning-making practices of research participants in order to generate *contextualised* and *situated knowledge* of policy making. Therefore, the analytical approach prioritised *process* and *meaning* over cause and effect, thus facilitating critical reflection on the dominant assumptions embedded in the cultural and occupational contexts (of youth justice policy making) under investigation. Indeed, employing RTA privileges understandings that are necessarily nuanced, complex, uncertain and often contradictory, as opposed to neat and unequivocal explanations, thus accepting that 'knowledge comes in a position' rather than lying in the infeasible pursuit of 'a singular universal truth' (Braun and Clarke, 2022).

The qualitative data generated from the semi-structured interviews were analysed using the six-stage RTA process outlined by Braun and Clarke (2022) in their text *Thematic Analysis*:

1. Dataset familiarisation: becoming deeply and intimately familiar with the content of the dataset through processes of immersion, re/reading the data, listening to recordings, taking brief notes about analytic ideas and insights.
2. Coding: working systematically through the dataset to identify segments of data that are potentially interesting, relevant or meaningful, to which the researcher attaches analytically meaningful descriptions ('code labels') that capture their 'analytic take' in terms of single meanings or concepts, from explicit or surface meaning (semantic) to more conceptual implicit meaning (latent).
3. Generating initial themes: identifying shared patterns/meanings in the dataset and compiling clusters of codes to illustrate a core idea or concept that could address the research question/s. At this stage, 'codes' typically capture specific or particular meaning, while 'themes' describe broader shared meanings.
4. Developing and reviewing themes: checking that themes make sense in relation to coded extracts and the full dataset by asking whether, collectively and individually, the themes tell a convincing, compelling story about important patterns and shared meanings across the dataset. For example, the researcher reflected upon whether certain 'candidate' (potential) themes should be collapsed together, split into new themes, retained or discarded. What is the 'character' of each individual theme – its core focus idea or central organising concept? What is the relationship between the themes in existing knowledge and/or practice in the wider research context?
5. Refining, defining and naming themes: fine tuning analyses to ensure that each theme is clearly demarcated and built around a strong core concept that tells a story and can be given a clear synopsis and concise, punchy and informative name.
6. Writing up: weaving together the analytic narrative and compelling, vivid data extracts to tell the reader a coherent and persuasive story about the dataset that addresses the research question/s.

Embracing researcher positionality, subjectivity and reflexivity

In his seminal analysis of policy making, *Making Social Policy*,[6] Levin (1997) asserted that academics studying policy tend to neglect or at least fail to accurately capture the policy-making world of politics and government. He characterised academic analyses of policy making as somewhat egocentric, shaped by the imposition of the academic's own concepts and preferences at the expense of the perspectives and experiences of other key stakeholders, particularly politicians and their officials (such as senior policy advisers [SPADs], civil servants). Levin's central conclusion, therefore, was that the role of the academic social scientist should be to *reveal* order rather than to *impose* it. The academic should solicit a wide range of expert stakeholder observations that fit together and may (ultimately) form a unified whole, for example a convincing story or set of arguments that help others to understand the complexity of social policy making. Therefore, it is important to stress that the perspectives and experiences explored and the themes identified in this book are, and must remain, those of the youth justice expert stakeholders (for example document authors, interviewees), *not* those of myself as the academic researcher. The researcher believes it to be crucial that these caveats and recommendations remain at the forefront of the analyses of the policy documents and semi-structured interview data in the current project.

The *reflexive* nature of the RTA process encourages (even demands) consistent critical reflection on the constructive role and influence of the researcher on the research process, including through my professional practices, disciplinary perspective, preferred epistemology, preferred methodology and professional subjectivity. The influential (constructive) elements of researcher reflexivity are neatly summarised by Braun and Clarke (2022) as:

- disciplinary – how the researcher's academic discipline and background influences knowledge production (for example due to their preferred paradigms, ideals and so on);
- functional – how the chosen research methods and other aspects of design impact the nature of the knowledge produced;
- personal – how the researcher's values shape the research and the knowledge it produces.

Embracing researcher reflexivity and its central constructive influence of subjectivity is key to conducting successful RTA (Braun and Clarke, 2022). These elements are especially pertinent to the current project, which rests on a fundamental assumption that knowledge and evidence generation occur in a socially constructed context of youth justice as part of inherently subjective policy-making processes shaped by key actors and constructive influences.

Consequently, it follows that the same assumptions should be applied to my role as researcher. For example, the experiences, identities, values, disciplinary perspectives preferences/biases that the researcher brings to and visits upon the research and the participants within this process will inevitably shape their (my) decision-making regarding chosen methods, research design, sampling (such as the purposive sampling discussed earlier), analytical techniques and, perhaps most importantly, the interpretation of data generated and the conclusions and recommendations that flow from that. Consequently, for this qualitative research project to be defensible, transparent and robust, it is crucial that the generative role of (my) researcher reflexivity/subjectivity is consistently and thoroughly acknowledged and interrogated. A useful starting point is to set out my researcher *positionality* – how my professional contexts and identity influence, shape and bias my perspectives, beliefs and understandings of the focal area of youth justice (see Reed and Rudman, 2023; see also Chapter 1).

Critical commentary: researcher *positionality* statement

In *disciplinary* terms, my professional trajectory, experience and perspective is that of a lapsed psychologist reborn as a sociological/critical criminologist (under the mentorship of Professor Kevin Haines) employing a social constructionist lens. As such, I view 'youth offending' and 'youth justice' as socially constructed concepts (see Chapter 1) rather than as objective 'facts' or 'realities' that exist and can be measured externally to individual perception and experience, akin to critical realist philosophy (Taylor, 2018). For explanatory purposes, I have always sought to understand youth offending as (largely) the product of *processes of criminalisation* within society more broadly and the YJS and its agencies (that is, a critical criminological perspective). I have explicitly eschewed assumptions that complex social behaviour can be understood through the reductionist, decontextualised, deterministic, quasi-experimentalist, yet hegemonic, approaches of positivism in its pursuit of universal laws and linear 'cause and effect' relationships. My research experience compels me to acknowledge the inherent complexity and non-linear nature of youth offending and youth justice by viewing both as socially constructed through personal perceptions, experiences and social interactions situated in different contexts (see Case and Haines, 2014). Therefore, my positionality is that once constructed, different elements of 'youth justice' (for example laws, systems, structures, strategies) can be discerned in critical realist terms as objective realities, albeit dynamic, contingent and contested realities subject to constant reconstruction, and therefore 'constructed realities' (Case, 2018/21, 2022).

Methodologically, as a critical criminologist examining social issues through a social constructionist lens, I have privileged qualitative, ethnomethodological approaches that explore meaning making, although I have always attempted to maintain a semblance of epistemological balance by critically reflecting on the use and utility of quantitative methodologies for knowledge and evidence generation. In policy/strategy terms, my disciplinary, functional and personal preferences, considered alongside my academic background working in the distinct Welsh social policy context (see Chapters 3 and 4), have stimulated robust, passionate (evidence-based) criticisms of the artefactual 'Risk Factor Prevention Paradigm' that has exerted significant influence within the 'new youth justice' (see Chapter 3). My professional preferences have stimulated similarly robust, passionate, evidence-based support for/proselytisation of child-centric, 'Child First' forms of youth justice that have emerged to counter the negative excesses of the 'new youth justice' (such as criminalisation through adulterisation, responsibilisation, interventionism, net-widening, labelling). These biases will be reflected upon throughout my critical analyses and interpretation of identified policy documents and the semi-structured interview data generated with key stakeholders.

Throughout the research and data analyses that populate this book, I will be critically reflexive, thoughtful, self-questioning and committed to interrogating the positions, values, choices and practices adopted within the research process in terms of their influence on knowledge generation (see also Luttrell, 2019). At all times, my intention is to privilege the perspectives of expert stakeholders over my own as researcher. My concern to demonstrate appropriate awareness of the necessary complexity of the research process and subject matter under examination will be acknowledged throughout by representing the positions informing the research as inevitably multiple, complex and evolving. In this way, I openly subscribe to the insightful and balanced observation that 'any reflexive analysis can only ever be a partial, tentative and provisional account' (Finlay, 2002: 542–3) of the subject under examination, in this case the 'making' of youth justice policy.

3

Expansionist 'new youth justice' policy

The following two chapters present the findings from the qualitative data analysis of youth justice policy documents, adopting a chronological approach that separates the analyses into two socio-political periods:

- New Labour policy influence (1996) and government (1997–2010);
- Coalition (Conservative–Liberal Democrat) government (2010–15) and Conservative government (2015 to the time of writing).

This chapter explores the extent and nature of the revolutionary youth justice policy reforms and the factors that influenced them under the Labour goverment (1997–2010). This socio-historical period was underpinned by an *expansionist* approach to youth justice, with large amounts of money, resources and time invested into sweeping policy reform, mobilised by the construction of a plethora of youth justice systems, structures, laws, sentences, strategies and practices. The chapter begins by tracing the emergence of a new brand of Labour Party ('New Labour') in the first half of the 1990s, one espousing radically new youth justice policies, strategies and practices. It then outlines the recommendations from the influential Audit Commission 'Misspent youth' review of youth justice in the United Kingdom (1996) and the subsequent 'No more excuses' government White Paper (1997), which formalised the requirement for a set of strategies that coalesced to form the 'new youth justice'. There follows a detailed discussion of the radical reconstruction of youth justice in England and Wales through the new principles, structures, systems, laws, strategies and practices introduced in the Crime and Disorder Act 1998 (CDA 1998), most notably the creation of the Youth Justice System (YJS) of England and Wales, with its central aim/policy of *prevention*. The chapter concludes with an investigation of youth justice developments following the first decade of the 'new youth justice' and immediately preceding New Labour's fall from power (2008–10), evaluating the extent to which these developments evidenced an extension of and progression from 'new youth justice'.

The emergence of a 'new youth justice'

In 1993, Shadow Home Secretary Tony Blair catalysed the Labour Party's bid to seize the mantle of the 'party of law and order' from the incumbent

Conservative government by proclaiming that the new incarnation of Labour would be "tough on crime and tough on the causes of crime". This move towards the political centre/right from a traditionally more socialist, welfare-focused political agenda constituted a major rebranding exercise for the 'New Labour' Party (Hopkins-Burke, 2016), pursuing the dual goals of modernising their dated policy agendas and making Labour more attractive to voters (Solomon and Garside, 2008). In 1994, Blair became Labour Party leader and was replaced as Shadow Home Secretary by Jack Straw, who worked closely with the Shadow Home Affairs Minister Alun Michael and Norman Warner (Straw's senior policy adviser or 'SPAD'). Straw and Michael had professional experience of the relationship between socio-economic disadvantage and high youth crime rates in their local constituencies (Blackburn and Cardiff South respectively), which also offered them first-hand experience of widespread, albeit localised, public perceptions of a 'youth crime problem' (see Michael in Case, 2018/21).

In their policy proposal documents 'Safer communities, safer Britain' (Labour Party, 1995) and 'Tackling the causes of crime' (Straw and Michael, 1996), Labour distanced themselves from more principled and historically embedded welfare-based approaches to youth justice policy development (see Chapter 1) by proclaiming that 'the welfare needs of the young offender cannot outweigh the needs of the community ... individuals must be held responsible for their own behaviour, and must be brought to justice and punished when they commit an offence' (Straw and Michael, 1996: 6). The politically attractive focus on holding young people more responsible for their offending was theoretically underpinned by realist academic/intellectual explanations that understood crime as a real problem with real impacts on real people. Realists from the political right identified the main causes of (youth) offending as rational choice and immorality among the working classes (for example Murray, 1994), while left realists fused rational choice explanations with consideration of the socio-economic contexts in which offending takes place (for example Lea and Young, 1984). The realist emphasis upon rational choice as a central explanation for 'youth offending' explicitly influenced the New Labour strategy of neo-liberal responsibilisation (Dunkel, 2014), which de-emphasised the social contexts of behaviour[1] and focused more on individual, family and community responsibility and accountability, while in return, the child would receive community and government support to reintegrate back into society (Muncie, 2014). A further responsibilising strategy was introduced, *communitarianism*, an ideology emphasising the responsibility of the individual to their community and the social importance of the family unit (Etzioni, 1995). Therefore, Labour wished to balance the rights afforded to the individual with their responsibilities to their community and to the state (for example their responsibility not to commit crime or to harm others) when formulating their youth justice policies.

Policy point: expedience, experience, evidence

The rebranded 'New Labour' Party began the 1990s by developing policy responses to 'youth offending' based on strategies of responsibilisation and communitarianism, both born of what Professor Roger Smith (2014) conceptualised as political *expedience* (the need to be popular with the voting public), the personal and professional *experience* of key constructors/influencers of the new approach to youth justice (for example Straw, Michael, Warner) and selective research *evidence* (particularly realist explanations). There was arguably a fourth 'E' at play during this time, *economy*, in the guise of large amounts of money available to the new government to invest in policy reform.

'Misspent youth': managerialist pragmatism over principle in policy development

In 1996, the Audit Commission published a review of youth justice policy, strategy and practice in England and Wales. The review was entitled 'Misspent youth', a double entendre suggesting – in my professional opinion – that huge amounts of money were being wasted on ineffective and inefficient responses to youth offending and that large numbers of children were wasting their adolescent years committing crime and damaging communities. The review concluded that '[t]he present arrangements are failing children – who are not being guided away from offending to constructive activities … Resources need to be shifted from processing young offenders to dealing with their behaviour … efforts to prevent offending behaviour by children need to be coordinated between the different agencies involved' (Audit Commission, 1996: 6).

Following a secondary data analysis of system outcomes and a consultation exercise with key stakeholders (for example, policy makers, practitioners, academics), the review authors found that the current system of implementing youth justice was

- ineffective due to rising levels of youth offending, accompanied by the observation that annual decreases in youth offending rates were more 'apparent' than real – the artefact of demographic changes, reclassification of offences and the increased use of cautioning;
- inefficient because multiple agencies were very poor at working together to address youth offending in practical terms, resulting in the very slow systemic processing of children;

- uneconomical because it allegedly spent around £1 billion per year responding to youth offending.

(Audit Commission, 1996; see also Renshaw and Perfect, 1997)

'Misspent youth' made a series of practical recommendations to make youth justice more *effective*, *efficient* and *economical*, recommendations that would shape New Labour youth justice policy over the next ten years (Muncie, 2014). The review recommended that the government implement a strategy of *managerialism* – a set of techniques and practices to transform (that is, reconstruct) the existing structures and processes of youth justice through close, intensive management and control (Muncie, 2008). There was a related recommendation that coordinated *multi-agency partnerships* be constructed to pursue shared objectives enabling children who offend to be processed and dealt with more quickly, efficiently and economically. Furthermore, these multi-agency partnerships and the organisations within them should be subject to rigorous and consistent *performance management* to ensure that they were working effectively and efficiently. The second radical recommendation for youth justice reform was that partnership should focus on one central policy aim, the *prevention* of youth offending. As formal youth justice responses (for example out-of-court cautioning, court sentences, custody) were allegedly ineffective, inefficient and expensive, it was considered preferable to prevent offending from occurring in the first place, and when offending occurred, to divert children from formal youth justice systems, structures and processes in order to prevent further criminalisation and expense. Notably, 'Misspent youth' advocated that the managerialist pursuit of prevention should be *evidence based* – demonstrably, measurably, transparently, accountably and justifiably 'effective' in preventing and reducing youth offending. However, the identified evidence base cited for 'effective' youth justice policy and practice was characterised by some critics as *partial* (biased and incomplete), privileging as it did evidence from the hegemonic Risk Factor Prevention Paradigm (RFPP) (see detailed critique by Case and Haines, 2009) and strategies of *risk management* (discussed later in this chapter), neo-correctionalist approaches seeking to correct the 'deficits' in individuals that allegedly lead to offending.

Policy point: practicality over principle

'Misspent youth' provided a blueprint for a radically revised approach to youth justice policy and practice, replacing the historically dominant philosophies/principles of welfare and justice (see Chapter 1) with recommendations for an overarching pragmatic strategy of managerialism and an underpinning policy aim of prevention to be pursued through a strategy of risk management.

Critical commentary: examining the *partiality* of 'Misspent youth'

Critical commentators have raised important questions about the independence, comprehensiveness and appropriateness of the review's findings and recommendations. In particular, critics have accused the report of partiality, in the dual sense of being biased and limited in scope, presentation and interpretation of evidence. The claims from 'Misspent youth' were subjected to significant scrutiny by Denis Jones (2001) in his polemical article 'Misjudged youth', in which he criticised the Audit Commission's focus on performance management as a move away from its main area of expertise, that of reviewing financial efficiency. This expansion beyond its original remit was seen as evidence of the Audit Commission 'adapting new roles from bases of limited knowledge, or indeed ignorance' (see also McSweeney, 1988). Jones also criticised the selective interpretation and use of evidence across the report, citing the authors' 'use of their own surveys instead of more detailed research, when it seems to suit', combined with 'numerical sleight of hand' (Jones, 2001: 3). In particular, Jones criticised the report's claim that 'a quarter of known offenders are under 18' (Renshaw and Perfect, 1997), citing this as based on very questionable assumptions and generalisations from adult offending figures, with no evidence that these extrapolations were valid. Similarly, the claim that 'public services spend around £1 billion a year processing and dealing with offending by young people' (Audit Commission, 1996: 7) was viewed as lacking criticality because two thirds of this expenditure was by the police, and there was a lack of evidence of how this had been calculated, which gave 'serious cause for concern' (Jones, 2001: 5). Finally, the argument that recent decreases in youth offending rates were more 'apparent' than real was criticised for overlooking any tangible 'success revolution' in offence-focused youth justice practice in the 1980s and early 1990s (see also Jones, 1993).

Others have criticised the final recommendations as the product of significant political influence and the cherry picking of evidence and experts to support preformed policy priorities (Pitts, 2003), despite the claim that the review authors had consulted with a range of academics, practitioners and other key stakeholder professionals, According to both Professor Haines (whose evidence was ignored in the report, despite being consulted) and Michael, political influence was exerted by politicians from New Labour (who were on the brink of winning the 1997 General Election) in order to shape and bias the report findings and recommendations (both interviewed for Case, 2018/21). Arguably, this accusation was born out by the subsequent appointment of report author Mark Perfect to the role of Chief Executive of the first incarnation of the Youth Justice Board (YJB). Like all potential new governments, New Labour were keen to dismiss previous policies as ineffective and even keener to offer new and progressive alternatives (see McAra, 2023). Consequently, the imminent Blair government was seeking a 'third way' to move youth justice beyond the 'distractions' of welfare and justice (Michael in Case, 2018/21). Welfare in any form was not considered a politically viable option for a party looking to distance itself from universal provision. Similarly, justice was a non-starter for a political party that had committed to the view that previous approaches to tackling youth offending had done little to address the 'problem'. Consequently, the recommended (partial) risk management approach of 'psychologically oriented criminologists' (Case and Haines, 2009) can be seen as affording the incoming New Labour government their desired model of youth justice: evidence based, managerialist and practical (Case, 2018/21).

'No more excuses': responsibilisation and punitiveness over principled policy

In 1997, the New Labour Party took control of the UK government, with Blair as Prime Minister and Straw as Home Secretary, the government minister responsible for internal affairs and criminal justice matters in England and Wales. Straw collaborated with close colleagues Michael (now Home Affairs Minister/Deputy Home Secretary) and Warner (SPAD) to further develop the new government's youth justice policy. Indicative of the continued policy significance of youth justice, one of the new government's first acts was to produce a White Paper building on the 'Misspent youth' recommendations by proposing a 'root and branch' reform of what constituted youth justice in England and Wales. The resulting report, 'No more excuses: a new approach to tackling youth crime' (Home Office, 1997), officially announced a new youth justice policy stance that would comprehensively 'draw a line under the past' (Straw in Home Office, 1997) by heavily promoting a new policy priority of prevention and a strategic emphasis on responsibilisation and risk management. These neo-liberal, neo-correctionalist emphases were reflected in the document title (just as they were in 'Misspent youth') and consolidated in the Home Secretary's preface: '[The YJS] too often excuses the young offenders before it, implying that they cannot help their behaviour because of their social circumstances. Rarely are they confronted with their behaviour and helped to take more personal responsibility for their actions.'

Critical commentators have portrayed the White Paper as reflecting Labour's ideological commitment to responsibilising forms of punishment (Goldson, 2020), with others perceiving an 'alarming' absence of a philosophical/principled basis in the context of this new, explicitly strategic and technical approach (Case and Haines, 2009). Taken together, 'Misspent youth' and 'No more excuses' formalised and mobilised a new, responsibilising, risk-focused, preventative model of constructing and responsibilising children who offend that contrasted with the traditional dominance of welfare and/or justice principles for youth justice. In addition, this modernised, strategic model of youth justice was to be very closely managed in order to ensure efficiency and economy, distancing youth justice responses from the existing system that 'excuses itself for its inefficiency' (Home Office, 1997: 3).

Policy point: 'new youth justice' conflict and ambivalence

'No more excuses' as a legislative influence on the reconstruction of youth justice (policy) illustrates the perennial conflict and ambivalence in how to respond to children who offend. The White Paper embodied a dual, bifurcated strategy of responsibilisation, apparently blaming and punishing children for their offending alongside offering recommendations to support children to stop offending, to appease public anxieties about reoffending. The responsibilising nature of these early policy proposals was strongly indicated in the document title, which itself built on the equally responsibilising 'Misspent youth' label of its predecessor review.

The CDA 1998: realising a 'new youth justice'

> It shall be the principal aim of the youth justice system to prevent offending by children and young persons.
>
> (CDA, 1998: section 37.1)

The systemic recommendations of 'Misspent youth' and the policy proposals of 'No more excuses' were 'legislated into existence' (Muncie, 2014) by the CDA 1998, the first substantive piece of policy legislation from the incumbent Labour government. The CDA 1998 introduced radical, wholesale reforms of existing youth justice policies, philosophies/principles, systems, structures, strategies, processes and practices in the UK. While this appetite for policy reform typified a new government seeking to stamp its political identity on key policy areas by being seen to effect change, either real or rhetorical (McAra, 2023), the extent and nature of youth justice policy reform/change was unprecedented. Primarily, 'youth justice' responses would now be located within a formal YJS, a fully formed, comprehensive, modernised *system*, as opposed to the previous collection of piecemeal responses to offending by children largely subsumed within the adult-focused Criminal Justice System. Although the new government had jurisdiction over the whole of the UK, the new YJS would have authority over England and Wales only, with youth justice policy-making responsibilities elsewhere ceded to the recently (partially) devolved governments of Scotland (see Whyte, 2009) and Northern Ireland (see Chapman and O'Mahony, 2007).[2]

Rather than pursuing a central *philosophy/principle*, typically the welfare or justice focus of previous youth justice legislation (see Chapter 1), the CDA 1998 cohered around a central policy aim. The prevention of offending was to be the focal point for an effective, efficient and economical YJS. Six associated youth justice 'objectives' were identified to facilitate the prevention aim: swift administration of justice; confronting young offenders with the consequences of their offending; intervention tackling the factors – personal, family, social, educational or health – that put young people at risk of offending; proportionate punishment; encouraging reparation to victims; and reinforcing parental responsibility. The prevention policy aim would be facilitated by a series of youth justice *strategies* that would shape practice, notably the managerialism, responsibilisation and risk-based early intervention(ism) pre-empted in 'Misspent youth' and 'No more excuses'. The largely strategic, pragmatic, technical and modernising[3] changes introduced in the CDA 1998 coalesced to form a 'new youth justice' (Goldson, 2000). Accordingly, the youth justice policy approach of the New Labour government was deliberately *expansionist*, expanding the remit, scope and size of the YJS in relation to the populations and behaviours addressed (net-widening), the extent of available responses to these behaviours (interventionism) and the practical or financial resources available to the sector (that is, economic expansion).

A key area of expansionism in CDA 1998 was the extrapolation of New Labour's commitment to the *responsibilisation* of children (also their families and communities) for their offending behaviour and for the success/failure of youth justice responses to it. This neo-liberal strategy for pursuing the prevention policy priority enabled the government to abandon the diversion/minimal intervention trajectory of the 1980s and early 1990s (for example, the Criminal Justice Act 1991) in favour of more punitive, retributive system objectives for achieving their prevention aim (Joyce, 2017). The responsibilisation policy agenda was born of political imperative and the professional experience of key policy actors (Smith, 2014):

> 'There was a political imperative to be seen to be doing the things that will make a difference to what the public is concerned about, but there's also the need to do it in a sensible way. That's why we had the slogan "tough on crime and tough on the causes of crime".' (Michael in Case, 2018/21)

Labour's responsibilisation agenda was further expanded by the abolition of *doli incapax*, the historical, legal and rebuttable presumption that children aged ten to 13 years old cannot distinguish between right or wrong to the extent that they should be held responsible for their criminal actions, unless this presumption could be refuted in court. As such, this abolition constituted a reconstruction of youth justice laws. For many years, the principle of *doli incapax* had functioned as a safeguard to effectively maintain the minimum age for a 'youth offender' at 14 years old, but its abolition in 1998 removed this safeguard and made all children from the age of ten 'unequivocally responsible and accountable for choices made and harm caused' (Bandalli, 2000: 86–7).

Policy point: the 'new youth justice'

The construction of the 'new youth justice' as a third way alternative youth justice policy approach superseded traditional 'welfare versus justice' principles (see Smith, 2006) through modernising and neo-liberal strategies of managerialism, responsibilisation and interventionist risk management. The 'new youth justice' embodied the government's overt indifference to the philosophical grounding of their policies and related youth justice mechanisms and processes, which were instead predominantly driven by technical, pragmatic, 'evidence-led' and 'what works' approaches (D. Smith, 2006) as a means of rationalising policy making through political discourse that works 'beyond ideology' (Fergusson, 2007).

The birth of the YJB: independent expert policy adviser

The CDA 1998 established the YJB for England and Wales as a new youth justice structure. The YJB was to function as a non-departmental public body (NDPB) or 'quango' (quasi-autonomous non-governmental organisation), sponsored and overseen by the Home Office, a civil service, ministerial department of the UK government with responsibility for criminal justice at that time (now the responsibility of the Ministry of Justice [MoJ]). The YJB's identity was to be shaped by a series of central objectives:

- monitoring the operation of the YJS;
- advising the Home Secretary on the operation of the YJS and on how the aim of preventing offending by children and young people can most effectively be pursued;
- identifying, disseminating and funding effective practice across youth justice services;
- commissioning a distinct Secure Estate for children and placing children in custody.

At its core, therefore, the YJB was to be a strategic body with a dual purpose: to advise/guide government on youth justice policy development and to advise/guide (also monitor) local youth justice teams on the 'effective' implementation of policy in practice. The status of the YJB as an NDPB was indicative of the 'hiving off' of executive functions of government to arm's-length organisations more broadly (see also Pliatzky, 1992). This enabled the YJB (at least in principle) to bypass civil service bureaucracy and to bring about change quickly. This, in turn, enabled the detailed management of the implementation of Labour's youth justice policy reforms that a vast, multi-function, conservative, cautious and bureaucratic civil service could not and would not do (Driscoll and Morris, 2001). Furthermore, the introduction of the YJB was intended to facilitate hitherto infeasible speed and innovation in the implementation of youth justice policy reforms, not least because the organisation would be removed from the 'closed and monolithic' (see also Kemp, 1990: 187) conservative, compliant and risk-averse civil service culture (Driscoll and Morris, 2001), which afforded the organisation clearer lines of accountability and greater transparency (Home Office, 1997). As a single-purpose, dedicated body, the YJB would provide operational oversight of Labour's youth justice reforms, providing a specific focus for youth justice both in operational management and in central policy making (Souhami, 2015b).

YJB as primary sector expert

Crucially, the newly created YJB would have the capacity to express ideas counter to ministerial agendas. Souhami characterises civil servants as "Whitehall Westminster captives. ... They don't have lasting, long-term, relationships of trust with the interests they need to work in" (Souhami in Case, 2018/21). Beyond its unique independent status, YJB also held expert status upon its inception, strongly differentiating it from Home Office civil servants. The YJB's expert status as an expert body was reinforced by its composition – as an NDPB, it could recruit outside the civil service, such that most of its board members were appointed from Youth Offending Teams (YOTs), local government or related fields. Furthermore, work in an NDPB requires a sustained period of office in a single area of executive activity, allowing for specialisation and continuity of knowledge, thus uniquely providing the structural opportunity for the expert administration of youth justice (Souhami, 2011). Therefore, the YJB was viewed by the sector as expert in comparison with civil servants or ministers who rarely had substantive knowledge, to the extent of being constructed as the organisation in which youth justice expertise was solely located (Souhami, 2015a). Therefore, locating the YJB outside departmental structures further recognised the limitations of the civil service in producing youth justice policy and the need for external, expert input (Souhami, 2015a, 2015b). The formal incorporation of *expertise* (a key constructive influence on policy as we progress) through YJB as expert independent adviser (as opposed to non-expert, generalist civil servants[4]) within central policy-making processes was explicitly designed so that 'new youth justice' strategies could be 'properly grounded in the experience of practitioners and other experts' (Souhami 2015a: 56; see also Chapter 1).

Policy point: YJB expertise as a constructive influence on youth justice policy making

The creation of the YJB as a specialised, independent, expert non-departmental governmental body was intended to influence youth justice policy making across multiple contexts. As such, it is a highly significant development in the socio-historical trajectory of youth justice policy making in England and Wales. The unique identity, role and constructive influence of the YJB as 'independent' and 'expert' policy maker will be interrogated in great detail from this point. The construction of the YJB as an expert body advising governmental policy makers disrupted the traditional organising logics and bureaucratic rationality of civil servant policy advisers, who work on behalf of elected government and supporting ministers, rather than pursuing personal or organisational goals (Page and Jenkins, 2005). Conversely, the YJB appointed staff based on their expertise (technical and practical), which encouraged decision making based on expert knowledge rather than ministerial agendas. Allied to this, the independent nature of the YJB's role and identity enabled it to *challenge* government by structuring decision making according to principles potentially unconnected to ministerial outcomes, for example the best interests of the child. This element of challenge was to render the YJB a highly risky and insecure organisation going forwards, as will be discussed.

YOTs: performance management of practice as prescription or support?

The YJB was required to use its unique role, identity and expertise to monitor and performance manage the practice of new organisational structures called YOTs. From April 2000, YOTs became a statutory requirement in all local authority areas in England and Wales, constituting a new structure to work with children who offended in order to pursue the statutory aim of the YJS to prevent offending. YOTs were required to be multi-agency, consisting of representatives from the five statutory agencies: police, local authority social services departments, local authority education departments, probation and health, while including voluntary, charitable and other third sector partners where appropriate and available locally. Although the basic structure of YOTs was statutory and prescribed by government, the number of representatives from each statutory agency was not, and neither were the type of staff member from each agency or the nature of any other stakeholder groups represented.[5] This indicated an element of 'flexible managerialism' from the centre/government through assigning discretion to empower local areas in how they executed their statutory responsibilities. Souhami (2007: 25) encapsulated this climate of cultural change in youth justice as: '[A] marked departure from the accustomed ethos of youth justice work. … The formation of YOTs demanded the development of new, multi-agency practice, new routines and ways of working.'

Policy point: introducing the policy-making influence of YOTs as experts

The introduction of YOTs as a new structure shaping the implementation of youth justice policy in practice also introduced YOT managers and practitioners as experts exerting a potentially important constructive influence on policy making. However, the expert identity and empowerment of YOTs was to be consistently tempered by the managerialist prescription of practice by government and the YJB over the next decade (see next section).

Although the composition of YOTs had a degree of flexibility, the practice of these YOTs was to become subject to increasing levels of managerialist prescription. A managerialist turn in youth justice policy and practice was encapsulated by the introduction of centrally prescribed performance management measures at the organisational (YOT) and individual (YOT practitioner) levels as methods to standardise practice and to increase organisational and practitioner accountability, transparency and demonstrable 'effectiveness' (YJB, 2003; Stephenson et al, 2007). These performance management measures were constructed as 'Key Performance Indicators' (KPIs), which were standardised performance statistics gathered from YOTs on a quarterly and annual basis by the YJB. The main KPIs required reductions in *first-time entrants* (FTEs) into the YJS, *reoffending rates* among identified offenders and the proportion of *custodial sentences* administered.[6] The new raft of performance management measures were subsequently complemented at the organisational level by 'Case management guidance' to assist and support YOT staff in working through the key stages of a child's case, from arrest to court to planning and managing post-sentence interventions (YJB, 2009). From April 2009, Her (now His) Majesty's Inspectorate of Probation (HMIP) commenced 'Core Case Inspections' of all YOTs within a rolling three-year programme, wherein YOT practice was assessed through case studies and interviews with staff, children and victims. Consequently, the HMIP governance organisation emerged as a potentially significant influence on youth justice policy making (see also Chapters 5 to 7), for example through their inspection criteria, their provision of guidance to practice (such as 'Academic insights' publications regarding key youth justice processes) and their relationships with the YJB and practitioner groups (for example Association of YOT Managers [AYM], YOTs).

At the individual/practitioner level, bespoke performance measures and guidelines were constructed. A new 'National standards' framework was produced by the Secretary of State for Justice (Justice Minister) and the Secretary of State for Children, Schools and Families following advice from the YJB. These standards for youth justice services were intended to establish 'the minimum expectations of staff and managers in the youth justice system' (YJB, 2003: 19) and were to be used in conjunction with the 'Case management guidance' and new 'Key Elements of Effective Practice' (KEEPs) guidance. The KEEPs[7] were constructed by the YJB as the 'essential elements of practice with all children at all stages of the YJS' (YJB, 2003: 6) – accompanied by bespoke guidance manuals commissioned from experts (typically academics) and drawing heavily on an international evidence base for 'effectiveness' in responding to youth offending through preventative interventions (Case et al, 2022).

YJB deprofessionalisation of practitioners through managerialist prescription

A common academic and practice critique of early YJB managerialism has been that its high levels of prescription, privileging instruction and restriction over guidance and empowerment, deprived practitioners of opportunities to exercise their expert judgement and discretion. In his notorious 2001 polemic entitled 'Korrectional karaoke: New Labour and the zombification of youth justice', Professor John Pitts asserted that youth justice practice had being thoroughly 'deprofessionalised', 'routinised' and 'technicised' by excessive performance management, prescription and an obsession with statistical outcomes. Pitts observed that practitioners were being compelled to adopt heavily prescribed, off-the-shelf practices focused on targeting a restricted group of psychosocial risk factors through the partial methods dictated by the YJB. A common counterpoint to such criticisms of managerialist prescription, however, is that of local mediation and moderation, with YOTs and their practitioners having the capacity to exercise a degree of expert discretion and experience/expertise when interpreting, reconstructing and implementing centralised guidance, such as risk assessment processes (Kemshall, 2008; Briggs, 2013). The respective constructive influence of prescription and local mediation/moderation will be explored further as analyses progress.

Policy point: managerialist prescription and responsibilisation

A plethora of new youth justice structures and performance management measures were introduced in the CDA 1998 to guide and shape youth justice practice through centralised, standardised, prescriptive mechanisms. This managerialist approach complemented the growing strategic responsibilisation of local communities/authorities/YOTs (itself complementing the individualising responsibilisation of children and families) to address offending behaviour through the 'effective' employment of centralised, prescribed mechanisms and processes – with 'effectiveness' measured against organisational KPIs. A cynic – such as myself – may argue, therefore, that this form of 'managerialist responsibilisation' constituted a strategy of simultaneous centralisation–decentralisation, whereby government was able to claim credit for successful youth justice outcomes (indicative of effective prescription), while assigning blame to non-governmental actors for youth justice failures (indicative of policy implementation failure).

Policy question: prescribing practice

Do critiques of the prescriptive and deprofessionalising nature of 'new youth justice' policy (for example those of Pitts) and related practice guidance offer a valid portrayal of the complex influences upon the realities of youth justice policy making (such as implementation in practice)? Similarly, do arguments for the local mediation of centralised policy prescriptions accurately reflect practice realities?

Evidence-based policy in youth justice: political power through prescription

The 'new youth justice' and its constituent strategies of modernisation, managerialism, neo-liberal responsibilisation and neo-correctionalist risk management were heavily influenced by the macro-level socio-economic, political, geographical and technological transformations catalysed by a period of globalisation that swept across the Western world from the late 1990s. The resultant public insecurities, uncertainties and anxieties coalesced into perceptions of these rapid and sweeping transformations as risks and threats needing to be predicted, controlled and managed (see Beck's 1992 'risk society' thesis). A concomitant 'punitive turn' emerged in both criminal justice[8] and youth justice, animated by prescriptions for managing the risks presented to the public by allegedly dangerous, threatening children (Case, 2018/21) through the expanded use of strategies of punishment, control, surveillance and restriction (Muncie, 2014): '[P]olicy decisions should be based on evidence. Good quality policy making depends on high quality information, derived from a variety of sources – expert knowledge; existing domestic and international research; existing statistics; stakeholder consultation; evaluation of previous policies' ('Modernising government' White Paper, Cabinet Office, 1999: 31).

A key vehicle for rationalising and mobilising expansionist and punitive youth justice strategies was the government commitment to evidence, particularly to their particular understanding of 'evidence-based policy' as a modernising and managerialist, 'scientific' criminal justice approach to ensuring that practice was accountable, transparent and defensible (Stephenson and Allen, 2013). The corollary of evidence-based policy, evidence-based practice (EBP), was to function as a managerialist tool for exercising centralised government *power* (a key policy-making influence going forwards), governance and prescriptive control over the implementation of youth justice policy in practice. EBP was prescribed through performance management measures such as auditing KPIs, guidelines, checklists and national standards (Kemshall, 2008; Turnbull and Spence, 2011) and used as a guide for resource allocation. As such, EBP signified a move away/culture shift from the purportedly overly discretionary, less consistent, uncoordinated and expensive systemic responses of the past (Wilcox, 2003; YJB, 2013) and represented 'the conscientious, explicit and judicious use of current best evidence in making decisions regarding the prevention of offending by individual children based on skills which allow the evaluation of both personal experience and external evidence in a systematic and objective manner' (Stephenson et al, 2011: 7).

The self-fulfilling partiality of EBP

The promotion of EBP served a higher evidential purpose than simply to facilitate the modernisation and managerialism of youth justice practice: it encouraged youth justice professionals to make more use of empirical, expert research evidence to guide their decision making, typically during policy implementation activities (Oliver, 2019). To this end, the YJB was charged by the government with 'commissioning research' to inform the development of 'effective practice' and 'developing and expanding [academic] research … to provide evidence that can constructively influence central policy decisions [and] enhance the existent knowledge base' (YJB, 2009: 1–2; see also MoJ, 2012). The YJB's espoused intention was that academic research/expertise take precedence in populating the youth justice evidence base over 'less robust' practitioner-generated evidence grounded in knowledge from training, prejudice and opinion, practice experience, anecdote, fads/fashions and advice from senior colleagues (Stephenson et al, 2011; see also Jones, 2001: 15). However, it soon became clear that 'the incoming government already knew what it wanted to do about youth justice' (Smith, 2016: 83). The YJB appeared to follow suit by commissioning and disseminating research from a select group of academic 'experts' in order to provide evidence to support their preformed neo-liberal policy position on youth justice (see McAra, 2023). This selectivity and partiality was indicative of a self-fulfilling strategy of generating 'policy-based evidence' to support preformed policy positions (see Goldson and Hughes, 2010), contrary to the espoused commitment to EBP, where policy is informed by evidence. For example, the government/YJB neo-liberal preference for quasi-scientific, risk-based and 'what works' evidence to populate the KEEP documents encouraged engagement with a limited, albeit hegemonic group of developmental psycho-criminologists (see Case, 2022) and rendered 'certain research questions … "unaskable" because they cannot be addressed using experimental methods' (Prior and Mason, 2010[9]: 219). Such 'political utilisation of research evidence' negated (possibly deliberately) the potential for the production of 'inconvenient evidence' (Goldson and Muncie, 2015), concurrently depersonalising and deprofessionalising the recommended practice of youth justice staff through a prescribed adherence to the risk lens (Turnbull and Spence, 2011). The corollary of this skewing of the explanatory evidence base was the reduction of complexity and explanations and responsive interventions by marginalising the impact of a broader range of contextual criminogenic factors – structural, political, economic, cultural, historical, interactional and situational influences (Myers et al, 2020; Ward, 2021). Accordingly, strategies of reductionism began to shape the application of EBP in England and Wales (Case, 2022), particularly in the form of the over-simplified explanations and responses to youth offending that provided 'an ostensibly neat and coherent approach to the messy and ill-defined complexities of practice' (Stephenson et al, 2011: 3). This reductionism is perhaps best illustrated by the privileging of neo-correctionalist risk management.

Risk management and risk-based early intervention as preventative EBP

Labour's strategic commitment to managerialist, prescriptive EBP as a central vehicle for pursuing their prevention policy aim was to be realised, at least in part, through the neo-correctionalist strategy of risk-based early intervention, which was operationalised in the YJS as risk management. In accordance with their 'tough on crime and tough on the causes of crime' mantra when in opposition, Labour resolved to address both the individual (micro-level) and socio-structural (macro-level) 'causes' of youth offending through risk-led prevention and early intervention approaches, marking an interventionist shift away from the diversionary 'new orthodoxy' of the 1980s (Bateman, 2016). Addressing individual, psychosocial causes of offending – that is, *individualising* the causes of youth offending – took precedence over identifying broader socio-structural and relational influences when shaping policy formation and practice guidance (Smith, 2014), aligning with neo-liberal responsibilising political and strategic goals. Subsequent YJB strategies and practice guidance focused exponentially on identifying children as 'at risk' of re/offending and targeting these children through 'individualised crime prevention' methods. Additionally, specific social groups and neighbourhoods were to be identified as 'high risk' of experiencing youth offending and then supported through 'targeted crime prevention' methods. The government and YJB increasingly employed both the lens and the language of 'risk' to emphasise the apparent danger and threat posed by children to others and the urgent need for the state to intervene in children's lives (thus justifying an *interventionist* agenda) in order to protect the public. In summary, 'New Labour would be tough on risk and tough on the causes of risk' (Porteus in Thom et al, 2007: 260).

> The evidence base employed to rationalise risk management in the YJS emanated from the growing international movement of Risk Factor Research (RFR), which utilised 'quantitative scientific methods that can identify potential offenders and reduce recidivism by predicting future behavior' (Kehl et al, 2017: 7–8). The explanatory theories of youth offending preferred by this hegemonic, quantitative, 'artefactual' form of RFR (Kemshall, 2008) were overwhelmingly developmental, deterministic and neo-positivist – identifying 'risk factors' in early life (childhood, for example) that are statistically predictive (not necessarily causal) of later offending (Case and Haines, 2009). The RFR evidence base dominating subsequent prescriptions for 'effective' and 'evidence-based' practice for preventing youth offending was to be animated by youth justice professionals through the RFPP (Hawkins and Catalano, 1992), which is founded on an evidence-based, preventative premise: 'Identify the key risk factors for offending and implement prevention methods designed to counteract them. There is often a related attempt to identify key protective factors against offending and to implement prevention methods designed to enhance them.' (Farrington in Maguire et al, 2007: 606)

Taken together, RFR and the RFPP provided the YJB with an evidence-based 'foundational scientific body of knowledge' (Day, 2020: 1) for managing, prescribing and governing practice, introducing a neo-liberal strategy of governance (see Chapter 1; see also Kuhn, 1996). The RFPP provided an attractive, timely and policy-expedient methodology for policy makers, particularly government, civil servants and YJB strategists, enabling them to rationalise and dictate prevention-focused practice through 'clear, unambiguous guidance on how to solve a problem as complex as offending by children' (Smith, 2016: 86). The RFPP had particular appeal to governmental policy makers working in a risk-averse political climate of increasing managerialism, audit-focus, accountability, transparency, defensible practice and cost-effectiveness, as it provided an ostensibly modernising, evidence-based and defensible paradigm to drive policy and practice (Stephenson et al, 2007). The espoused pragmatic benefits of the RFPP were encapsulated in the claim by Farrington (2000: 7) that 'the paradigm is easy to understand and to communicate, and it is readily accepted by policy makers, practitioners, and the general public'.

The central vehicle to mobilise the RFPP was to be the 'Asset' risk assessment instrument, commissioned by the YJB from the University of Oxford's Centre for Criminology, which was 'designed to identify the risk factors associated with offending behaviour and to inform effective intervention programmes' (YJB, 2003: 27). Asset[10] was intended to cohere youth justice practice approaches in pursuing the prevention policy aim and would underpin the 'National standards', 'Case management guidance' and the delivery of KEEPs, all adjudged 'effective' by utilising the 'what works'[11] evaluation framework (see also Sutton et al, 2021). Asset promoted the standardisation of practice through 'a common approach to the process of assessment that can assist practitioners in planning their work, gathering appropriate and relevant information and analysing that information … [as] the basis for arriving at judgements and making decisions' (YJB, 2003: 5).

Critical commentary: researcher positionality regarding risk management

In the spirit of reflexivity (see Chapter 2), I have a longstanding professional history of empirical research and scholarship evaluating and vociferously critiquing risk management as the dominant paradigm for delivering youth justice. This partiality inevitably shapes my interpretation of the policies, strategies, practices and research reported across this and subsequent chapters. In addition to critical articles published in a range of international journals and edited texts (for example Case, 2006, 2007, 2022; Case and Haines, 2015, 2021), I have also co-authored an entire book dedicated to a thorough critical dissection of the RFPP and its underpinning research and evidence base (Case and Haines, 2009). Arguably, I have been one of the staunchest critics of the use of risk management in the YJS over the past 15 years, so the reader is urged to account for this bias when evaluating my perspectives of the risk-based policy and practice highlighted through the qualitative analysis of policy documents. To summarise my main empirical, methodological and ethical criticisms of the RFPP (after Case, 2022: 175–6):

Factorisation: the RFPP oversimplifies the complexity of risk by converting it to quantifiable 'factors'. This 'factorisation' process reduces potentially dynamic, multi-faceted and interacting experiences, characteristics, individual meanings (constructions), circumstances and behaviours into crude, meaningless statistics that wash away their quality and (ecological) validity of the outcomes measured. So, in this respect, the RFPP is reductionist.

Developmental, psychosocial bias: the theoretical basis for the RFPP lies in developmental risk factor theories, which encourage the assessment of psychosocial (personal and immediate social) risk factors in the family, school, neighbourhood and personal life of a child, on the basis that these predict future offending. These developmental and psychosocial biases neglect the potentially criminogenic influence of broader socio-structural or contextual factors such as 'socio-economic status, local area ... cultural, political or historical context' (Case, 2007: 93). So, in this respect, the RFPP is reductionist.

Determinism: the RFPP evidence base is over-confident in concluding that risk factors exert a quasi-positivist, deterministic influence on future offending that should be targeted by preventative intervention. There remains much academic debate over whether risk factors function as determinants, causes, predictors or indicators of offending, with some suggestions that they may even be symptoms of offending or simply correlates with offending and therefore not risk factors in any predictive sense. So, in this respect, the RFPP is potentially invalid.

Adult-centrism: risk management processes (for example risk assessment) and the decisions relating to risk-led intervention planning are typically adult-led. Consequently, children's constructions – perspectives, experiences, voices, meanings, lived realities – are often marginalised and neglected. This being the case, the key stakeholder in the youth justice process who may have the best understanding of the (risk factor) influences on offending behaviour – the child – is often ignored, and resultant interventions may be crucially limited in their validity and practicality. So, in this respect, the RFPP is overly prescriptive and invalid.

Expansionist early intervention as EBP

In accordance with Labour's expansionist agenda, their RFPP-based strategy of risk management was soon extrapolated through a streamlined, pre-offending version of the Asset risk assessment instrument 'Onset' (YJB, 2003). This tool was created to identify children 'at risk' of offending for the first time who could be targeted for control and support by two new neighbourhood-based early intervention programmes. The first of these to be introduced was the Youth Inclusion Programme (YIP), established by the YJB in 2000 as a risk-based early intervention/prevention programme for 8- to 17-year-olds in 114 neighbourhoods in England and Wales who were considered to be at 'high risk' of experiencing youth offending due to their high levels of social disadvantage and crime levels (YJB, 2006). Referral to the YIP was the primary responsibility of all agencies working with children, notably statutory agencies (police, local authority, probation, health), who were instructed to identify the top 50 children in each neighbourhood who were measurably 'at risk of future offending, social and educational exclusion' (Morgan Harris Burrows, 2003). The second programme was the Youth Inclusion and Support Panel (YISP), established in April 2003 in 13 pilot, 'high-risk' neighbourhoods in England and Wales. The central objectives of the YISP were to prevent offending and antisocial behaviour (ASB) by 8- to 13-year-olds (or 14- to 18-year-olds in the case of the YISP+ programme) who were identified by referring agencies as 'at risk' of offending and to ensure that these children and their families could access mainstream services at the earliest possible stage.

Expansionist early intervention: ASB management

A central driver of New Labour's responsibilisation agenda was the social construction of a new category of 'problematic' and 'pre-offending' behaviour entitled 'antisocial behaviour'. This new construction functioned as a catchall category to justify early intervention by identifying individuals, typically 'at risk' children or 'problem families', whose behaviour was considered borderline criminal or otherwise problematic (annoying, nuisance, threatening, causing harassment) to communities and/or persons not in their household. The construction fulfilled and expanded upon the neo-correctionalist, net-widening and interventionist goals of identifying and targeting a larger population of 'at risk' children in order to prevent future offending. Children whose behaviour was identified as troublesome and problematic but not necessarily criminal or in need of referral to the formal YJS (for example by police, neighbours, landlords), could now be subject to an escalating scale of ASB management measures, led by local police, YOTs or newly formed 'Antisocial Behaviour Units'. Measures included home visits, warning letters, Antisocial Behaviour Contracts and Antisocial Behaviour Orders (ASBOs). The responsibilising ethos of these new ASB management processes was explicit in the strategic planning of government:

> 'I take quite a lot of personal responsibility for the way we [the Labour government] approached antisocial behaviour. Where you have a lot of low-level activity going on, it can escalate to the point of offending and the child can go into the Youth Justice System. However, if you're able to deal with the behaviour early then you can prevent the child from getting to this stage. That's the whole point of early intervention.' (Michael in Case, 2018/21)

In 2003, the government White Paper 'Respect and responsibility: taking a stand against antisocial behaviour' (HM government, 2003) officially kickstarted the government's neo-liberal responsibilising and (re)moralising 'Respect' agenda. The recommendations from the White Paper were manifested in the Antisocial Behaviour Act 2003 (HM government, 2003), which gave local authorities and the police broader, more flexible powers to address nuisance crime and low-level incivility. The Act served to expand (net-widen) the use of ASBOs, enabling local authorities, registered social landlords and the British Transport Police to apply for them. Subsequently, 'Dispersal Orders' were introduced to allow police and police community support officers to disperse groups of two or more people from designated areas if the group's behaviour was 'perceived' as likely to cause harassment, alarm or distress to members of the public. Like ASBOs, the use of Dispersal Orders fell disproportionately on children as they were more likely to be on the streets in groups and behaving in 'visible' ways that may cause alarm and distress to the general public. The Antisocial Behaviour Act 2003 also broadened the availability of (responsibilising) Parenting Orders, making them applicable to parents of children who had truanted or been excluded from school, rather than being restricted to parents of children who had offended (HM government, 2003).

Policy point: expanding early interventionism through ASB management

The social construction of ASB and associated powers expanded the net-widening and interventionist influence of the YJS by drawing in children who had not officially offended and subjecting them to formal intervention. The rationale was that ASB is indicative of irresponsibility – necessitating responsibilisation – and is a demonstrable risk factor for offending so should be prevented through control and support (necessitating early interventionism).

Expansionist early intervention: responsibilising, risk-based social policy

The expansionism of Labour youth justice policy was further illustrated by their broader social policy agenda for children (in England) immediately after the passage of the CDA 1998. This followed an equivalent responsibilising and individualising trajectory to that of youth justice policy by prioritising the prevention/reduction of negative behaviours and outcomes at the individual level (for example ASB, substance use, teenage pregnancy) and at the broader social level (social exclusion, academic underachievement, unemployment, for example). In 2000, the UK government's Social Exclusion Unit published their 'Report of Policy Action Team 12: young people' (SEU, 2000), which characterised children as potentially 'at risk' of exposure to risk factors and consequent negative behaviours, expanding the focus of the CDA 1998 on risk reduction and prevention of offending into the lives of children outside of and beyond the YJS. The UK government Department for Education and Skills followed-up with the Green Paper 'Every child matters' (DfES, 2003), which introduced a greater emphasis on the prevention of negative behaviours and outcomes (ASB, substance use, offending, educational failure, ill-health, teenage pregnancy) through risk-focused early intervention. The policy promised coordinated, multi-agency and responsive services for children that would 'maximise opportunities and minimise risk' (DfES, 2003: 2). Consequently, 'Every child matters' perpetuated the neo-correctionalist, 'deficit'-focused strategy that privileged individualised, deterministic explanations for personal and social problems experienced by children while responsibilising children to take advantage of the 'opportunities' given to them and to adhere to social norms and rules or have these opportunities forcibly removed (Goldson, 2003). At the same time, social policy for children in Wales was beginning to take a form that was distinct from England, being more focused on collective responsibility (compared to individual responsibility), social inclusion (compared to preventing social exclusion) and universal rights/entitlements to services, guidance and opportunities (compared to rights being accessed by demonstrating responsibility). Herein, 'entitlements' differ from and extend 'rights' in their promotion of maximum outcomes for children rather than simply the pursuit of minimum standards or expectations (Haines and Case, 2011).

Thereafter, the responsibilisation of children (and their parents) experiencing social problems was inextricably bound together with children's rights discourses in England, exemplified by Blair's proclamation that children should have 'no rights without responsibilities', rendering children's rights 'conditional' on acceptable behaviour (see Kemshall, 2008). The Labour government followed 'Every child matters' with 'Youth matters' (DfES, 2005), a strategy for meeting needs, improving services, increasing opportunities and enhancing support for 13- to 19-year-olds in England while also determining to 'challenging' these children to 'appreciate and respect the opportunities available to them' in order to strike the 'right balance between rights and responsibilities' (DfES, 2005: 4). 'Youth matters' outlined a twin-track (bifurcated) approach committed to 'engage more children in positive activities and to empower them [while providing] ... personalised intensive support' for children with serious problems and/or those in trouble with the law (DfES, 2005: 5). The 'Youth matters' policy framework extended the multi-agency, responsive service provision ethos of 'Every child matters' but similarly retained a focus on risk-focused targeted early intervention to address negative behaviours and outcomes. It even added educational exclusion, unemployment and victimisation to the list of negative behaviours and outcomes targeted within 'Every child matters', along with responsibilising rhetoric couched in the language of meeting needs. Subsequent social policies for children and young people, such as the 'Children's plan' (DfES, 2006) and the 'Youth Task Force action plan' (DCSF, 2008), furthered the emphasis on risk reduction and preventing negative behaviours and outcomes (now also including underachievement and disaffection) through risk-focused intervention using the RFPP (see Turnbull and Spence, 2011).

Expansionist early intervention: social, universal problem prevention

As discussed, the 'new youth justice' as a strategic driver of youth justice policy was characterised by a largely micro-level, individualised approach, pursuing prevention policy through identifying and targeting psychosocial risk factors located within the child. As such, macro-level socio-structural influences on youth offending were de-emphasised in explanations of youth offending and in responsive youth justice interventions. Where macro influences were acknowledged, they were typically addressed through prevention and support programmes that were designed as 'universal' – that is, available to all children – thus tackling social exclusion and disadvantage as manifested within the individual through programmes located outside the YJS (Joyce, 2017). For example, Labour implemented a series of universal prevention initiatives located within broader strategies to address social exclusion and the psychosocial risk factors associated with it (many of which were also related to youth offending), which included truancy and school exclusion, teenage pregnancy, substance use, unemployment and being in care (Social Exclusion Unit, 2001). Universal prevention initiatives included family support, community development and education, training and employment schemes (see Smith, 2014). In addition, a £900 million 'Neighbourhood Renewal Fund' was created and linked to a 'National strategy for neighbourhood renewal' (Social Exclusion Unit, 2001) to prevent social problems such as youth crime, ASB and educational failure. Ultimately, however, even 'universal' prevention programmes prioritised the criminogenic influence of psychosocial risk factors and the 'effectiveness' of targeted youth crime prevention programmes, which (perhaps inadvertently) fuelled the Labour agenda of responsibilisation by individualising the causes of crime and other social problems (Muncie, 2014). The individualising and responsibilising nature of this universal crime prevention can be seen to have emerged from Labour's political preference for realist academic explanations of youth offending as the product of rational choice and irresponsibility (right realism) being exacerbated by social disadvantage (left realism) – thus focusing on the symptoms of socio-structural problems rather than their specific influence on offending children's lives more broadly (Pitts, 2003).

Critical commentary: governmentality through risk management

Risk management provided the 'makers' of youth justice and social policy with an expedient strategy/method for controlling and managing risk in an age of uncertainty and anxiety. As such, risk management perpetuated 'governmentality', a political strategy prioritising the governance, control, monitoring and management of 'at risk' and offending populations, along with the over-control and prescription of youth justice practice (Pitts, 2003) while marginalising alternative methods and concerns related to the receipt of welfare, justice or rehabilitation (Muncie, 2014).

Policy question: academic constructions of policy-making 'realities'

Are post-CDA 1998 representations by critical scholars (including myself) of governmental policy making as predominantly shaped by risk-led, managerialist prescriptions accurate and fair, or were the realities of policy-making contexts and relationships during that period much more nuanced and complex?

Welsh youth justice policy (1998–2010): introducing dragonisation

Following the CDA 1998, a tension emerged between the (arguably positive) Welsh social policy agenda and the (arguably negative) 'new youth justice' agenda prescribed by the UK-based government when dealing with children who offend. The partial devolution of Wales in 1999 created a particularly complex policy context, as youth justice remained non-devolved, while associated policy areas for children (for example education, health, social services) became devolved policy-making responsibilities for the Welsh Assembly government. It is claimed that a 'dragonised' model of youth justice (the dragon being Wales' national symbol) emerged in this Welsh policy context, underpinned by a 'children first, offenders second' (CFOS) philosophy/principle (Haines and Drakeford, 1998[12]) and by an evidence-based model of 'Positive Youth Justice' (Haines and Case, 2015). CFOS responsibilised adult professionals (rather than children) by asserting that they should take primary responsibility for enabling children's access to a series of universal 'entitlements' to support, guidance, information and services (National Assembly Policy Unit, 2002), for addressing children's social needs and for treating children in the YJS as 'children first and offenders second' (WAG and YJB, 2004: 3).

The Welsh Assembly government and the YJB produced a coordinated policy document in 2004, the 'All Wales youth offending strategy' (AWYOS) (WAG and YJB, 2004), which provided a 'national framework for preventing offending and reoffending among children and young people in Wales' (WAG and YJB, 2004: 1). The AWYOS echoed the prevention focus of the CDA 1998 by asserting that 'whenever we can prevent offending there is benefit for us all … the best way to stop offending is to prevent it from happening in the first place' (WAG and YJB, 2004). Most notable in the strategy, however, was the commitment to responding to young people who offend as 'children', in line with Welsh social policy principles by treating them as 'children first and offenders second' (WAG and YJB, 2004: 3), which directly challenged the offender-first, risk-focused, adulterising and responsibilising strategies of 'new youth justice' (see Haines and Case, 2015). Elsewhere in the strategy, however, there was a clear attempt to balance 'new youth justice' strategies of 'early intervention, restorative justice measures, appropriate punishment and supported rehabilitation' with Welsh social policy principles by 'promoting the welfare of children and young people' (WAG and YJB, 2004: 3).

Despite a degree of adherence to the preventative strategies of the 'new youth justice', the AWYOS officially marked a point of divergence in Wales from UK government/English youth justice policy. It introduced a set of principles more aligned with broader social policy principles in Wales, including collectivism, universal entitlement to services and children's rights (Drakeford, 2010) and associated legislation such as the 'Extending entitlement' youth inclusion strategy (NAPU, 2002; see also Case et al, 2005), which supplemented and enabled a national (Welsh) challenge to youth justice strategies prescribed by the UK government in Westminster. The Welsh principles of CFOS, rights/entitlements-focus, promoting social inclusion and promoting positive behaviours/outcomes contrasted with the ostensibly more punitive, responsibilising and risk-based strategies of the 'new youth justice' (see Muncie, 2008; Haines and Case, 2015). However, the extent to which these principles were understood and actualised in practice in Wales at that time or since (see Chapter 4) is debatable, as is the degree of divergence between youth justice *practice* in England and Wales, despite a clear divergence in policy expressed through strategic documents.

The death throes of the 'new youth justice'? Emerging polyfurcation

As the New Labour government entered its final years (2008–10) under a new prime minister in Gordon Brown, its official, documented youth justice policy became increasingly contradictory and confused (see Smith, 2014). Indeed, youth justice policy discourse and strategy seemingly moved beyond bifurcation (see Case and Smith, 2023) into the realms of hybridised *polyfurcation*, adopting multiple trajectories and directions contemporaneously. This ongoing conflict and ambivalence within youth justice policy was encapsulated in Labour's final significant legislative policy statement, the 'Youth crime action plan 2008' (YCAP 2008) (DCSF, MoJ and Home Office, 2008), which constituted a series of light-touch, rebranded reconstructions of 'new youth justice' strategies, presented alongside ostensibly more supportive, progressive policy intentions. YCAP 2008 outlined Labour's strategy for moving youth justice forwards and 'tackling youth crime' through a 'triple track' (polyfurcated) approach of 'enforcement and punishment where behaviour is unacceptable, non-negotiable support and challenge where it is most needed, and better and earlier prevention' (DCSF, MoJ and Home Office, 2008: 1). Specifically, the YCAP 2008 prioritised the polyfurcated strategic goals of:

- enforcement and punishment – setting clear boundaries for 'acceptable behaviour' and clear consequences for failing to meet them (reflecting 'new youth justice' punitiveness);
- prevention – tackling the 'root causes' of youth offending by improving universal services and committing to further early intervention to identify vulnerable children and families (reflecting 'new youth justice' risk-based prevention and early intervention);
- support – non-negotiable intervention with children and families 'at risk' of offending, including extra funding and re-emphasis of parental responsibility (reflecting 'new youth justice' responsibilisation and interventionism, alongside supportive intent).

An important (bifurcated) distinction was made between vulnerable children in need of support and those who were considered more threatening and irresponsible, illustrated by the assertion that 'for those who are struggling we will offer more support; and those who do not take their responsibility seriously we will challenge them to do so' (DCSF, MoJ and Home Office, 2008: 5). The more punitive, enforcement-led and 'non-negotiable' elements of youth justice were acknowledged as essential to the government's preventative aim, thus giving the Act a 'veneer of toughness' (Smith, 2014). There were also increased emphases upon public protection as a goal of youth crime prevention and upon the responsibilisation of individuals and communities (for example through a consolidated commitment to restorative justice).

Concurrently, the Criminal Justice and Immigration Act 2008 (HM government, 2008) further reconstructed youth justice by introducing the 'Youth Rehabilitation Order' to replace all existing community sentences/ orders. This new order prioritised the prevention of reoffending through individualised, risk-focused interventions and placed a statutory requirement upon YOTs to more explicitly link their intervention planning to assessed levels of risk. A new process and structure was created to enable this expanded neo-correctionalist objective, the 'Scaled Approach' assessment and intervention framework (YJB, 2009), which replaced the existing 'Assessment, planning interventions and supervision' KEEP guidance

(YJB, 2008). The origins of the Scaled Approach lay in the 'Youth justice 2004' report (Audit Commission, 2004: 142), the somewhat perfunctory follow-up to 'Misspent youth', which recommended that 'YOTs should make better use of the Asset risk assessment tool to determine the amount as well as the nature of interventions with individuals using a scaled approach'. Henceforth, YOT practitioners would be required to tailor/scale the frequency, duration and intensity of planned interventions to the level of risk assessed, with their Asset scores categorised into three indicators of future offending that were then linked to the frequency and intensity of intervention: low risk-standard, medium-enhanced and high-intensive (YJB, 2009). As such, the Scaled Approach constituted the 'zenith' of Labour's commitment to risk management through the RFPP (Haines and Case, 2012).[13] The pilot process evaluation of the Scaled Approach concluded that there was a 'broad and clearly defined consensus among the practitioners in the four pilot YOTs that the risk-based approach results in better outcomes for children' (YJB, 2010: 15). However, this definitive, policy-friendly and ostensibly evidence-based conclusion was at odds with detailed critical reviews of the original process evaluation and empirical testing of the framework, which raised concerns about the inconsistent application of, support for and effectiveness of the framework (Sutherland, 2009; Haines and Case, 2012).

Tentative policy progress 'in principle'

Over the same timeframe (approximately 2008–10), tentative policy development was occurring locally in the guise of a return to the youth justice principle of diversion from contact with the formal YJS (hence progress 'in principle'). In 2007/8, a major review of policing practice concluded that the 'Offences Brought to Justice' (OBTJ) target (also known as 'sanction detections') had served as a 'perverse incentive' that encouraged police to formally process excessive numbers of low-level offences and incivilities that would previously not have warranted arrest or conviction (Flanagan, 2008; see also Smith, 2014). These concerns consolidated the vociferous complaints of Professor Rod Morgan (YJB Chair) that OBTJ targets had led to unnecessary *criminalisation* by increasing the numbers of children 'ending up in the youth court when magistrates complained many cases do not warrant their attention' and because children were easier targets for police activity because they were 'low hanging fruit' (Morgan, 2009; see also Bateman, 2011 – both interviewed for this book). The government responded to the Flanagan Review by revising (reconstructing) its approach to processing offences and effectively abolishing the OBTJ target measure as of April 2008 (Solomon and Garside, 2008). The impact on KPIs of this reconstruction of youth justice processes was significant, with decreases from 2008 to 2010 in relation to FTEs (55 per cent), reoffending (29 per cent) and custody rates (30 per cent), along with the use of pre-court disposals falling 62 per cent from its 2006/7 peak (YJB/MoJ, 2012).

There was subsequent debate, however, over the extent to which these system performance 'successes' could be directly attributed to the centralised abolition of the OBTJ targets by politicians and civil servants, as opposed to being the result of ongoing, more effective systems management, decision-making processes and local mediation by a broader range of key stakeholders (for example police, magistrates, YOT staff); in other words, the results of local mediation and moderation of centralised policy prescriptions. Rob Allen (formerly of the YJB) has suggested that a range of dynamic structural and systemic factors should be considered as explanatory of the sharp change in direction in youth justice practice and outcomes since 2008. He observed the growing frustration of enforcement agencies (for example police, courts) in having to deal formally with minor offences committed by children. He argued that this frustration had motivated 'a greater engagement between the Youth Justice Board and Youth Offending Teams on the one hand and courts on the other, which may have developed a shared view that custody should be a last resort' (Allen, 2011: 4). Furthermore, structural relationships within government were changing around the time that the OBTJ ceased, with youth justice policy responsibility transferring from the Home Office to a new partnership (2007–10) between the MoJ (led by Straw as Justice Secretary) and the new Department for Children, Schools and Families (led by Ed Balls).[14] Allen viewed this transfer of responsibility as encouraging a more liberal perspective on youth justice, cohering with Bateman's (2012) view that professional attitudes were motivating changes in youth justice outcomes rather than any particular change in public mood or 'overt political enthusiasm' (Allen, 2011: 9). This begs the policy and practice development question as to what may have motivated changes in professional attitudes? Structural and systemic changes in the delivery of youth justice may well have been more strategic than principled on the part of youth justice agencies: instrumental changes in order to pursue the newly introduced KPIs from 2007 (evidence to House of Commons Justice Committee, 2012). Indeed, it was argued that YOTs were now 'taking a more systemic and targeted approach to the provision of alternatives to custody, while also working to improve their credibility with the courts' (Allen, 2011: 20). There are clear similarities here with the new orthodoxy thinking and systems management of the 1980s, where practitioner decision-making processes stimulated decreases in recorded youth offending and custodial sentencing (see Haines and Drakeford, 1998). To this end, Bateman (2012: 46) observed that punitiveness remained the dominant ethos for youth justice policy at that time, although it was mediated by various 'institutional frameworks, cultural constructions, national dynamics and local political or economic considerations'. Therefore, the possibility of local mediation and moderation emerges, as it was increasingly evident to critical commentators that local staff were mediating and moderating centralised youth justice policy and practice prescriptions to suit their own contexts and circumstances, either in collaboration with the YJB and/or conducted by innovative practitioners and progressive managers 'under the radar' of centralised monitoring processes (Morgan, 2009).

Policy point: prescription and locally mediated policy change

The final years of New Labour governance were characterised by conflict, ambiguity, ambivalence and polyfurcation surrounding the identity and direction of youth justice policy and practice. Contemporaneous to the centralised consolidation of 'new youth justice' strategies for pursuing the prevention policy agenda (for example, responsibilisation, neo-correctionalist risk management, managerialism), a locally driven, pragmatic moment of diversionary practice was evolving in the latter years of Labour, illustrated by the reframing and reconstruction of centralised policy prescriptions (with and without explicit political support), based on professional discretion, moderation and mediation.

Policy question: mediating policy prescription?

What was the extent and nature of constructive influence of local discretion/moderation/mediation on youth justice policy making (particularly implementation) over this period? Did this influence extend into other areas of policy making (such as policy formation)?

Conclusion: 'new youth justice' policy – expanding conflict and ambivalence

The expansionist 'new youth justice' strategies of the 'New Labour' government from 1997 to 2010 departed from traditional, principled welfare versus justice concerns. These strategies radically reformed the YJS of England and Wales through the systemic focus on *effectiveness*, *efficiency* and *economy* required by the CDA 1998, constructive influences reframed by Smith (2014) as political *expedience*, academic and other *evidence* and the professional/personal *experience* of key policy influencers. The 'new youth justice' drove the radical reconstruction of youth justice by introducing a new pragmatic policy priority for the YJS, the *prevention* of offending and reoffending. This prevention priority was mobilised by managerialism and the creation of a new *system*, new *structures* for delivering youth justice, new priority *strategies* of neo-liberal responsibilisation and neo-correctionalist risk management and reconstructed *processes* such as revised out-of-court and court sentencing frameworks.

An overarching goal of the 'new youth justice' was *modernisation* of the YJS, moving past traditional (philosophical) welfare–justice concerns and creating an 'evidence-based' and (cost-)effective set of practical responses that were transparent, accountable and defensible in the increasingly globalised world. However, the underlying policy context constructed was one of conflict and ambivalence, notably between multiple, polyfurcated discourses and objectives of support and control, which were seemingly contradictory and irreconcilable when pursued simultaneously within the same policy. Youth justice policy from 1997 to 2010, therefore, appears ambiguous – simultaneously supportive and punitive, diversionary and interventionist, preventative and criminalising, evidence based and evidence lacking.

What was equally new about the 'new youth justice' was what it lacked, namely discernible *principles*. The 'new youth justice' was simultaneously preventative and punitive, with youth justice policy principles abandoned in favour of the structures, strategies and practices that modernised the YJS into a tightly managed focus on mechanised processes and statistical outcomes, which were a world away from the dichotomised care–control and welfare–justice considerations of youth justice past (Case, 2018/21). Throughout Labour's 'unprecedented corpus of youth justice legislation', it remains difficult to discern any unifying jurisprudential basis or coherent philosophical principles (Goldson, 2010). Instead, what is more discernible is a hybrid and uneasy mix of impulses and rationales (Goldson, 2010), akin to the 'melting pot' of multiple discourses and intrinsic tensions and complexities (see Fergusson, 2007; see also Chapter 1). For instance, strategically, control- and risk-based early interventions were pursued alongside more welfare-based principles of support. Furthermore, alternatives to custody indicative of decarceration and decriminalisation principles have been pursued in a context of the escalating strategic/practical use of custody (Goldson, 2010). In practice, the managerialist control over and retraction of practitioner discretion flourished in an expansionist context of increasing, expanding court powers and practice prescription. Finally, perhaps the zenith of the 'new youth justice's' multiple, polyfurcated and competing discourses and rationales was the YCAP 2008 legislation, with its incongruous and arguably irreconcilable 'triple track' policy emphases.

The expansionist 'new youth justice' movement of 1997–2010 has continued to be criticised by youth justice scholars, who represent its policy influence as a mass of dynamic and contingent contradictions, constantly reconstructed in response to political priorities, selective interpretation of evidence and mass media misrepresentations (Goldson, 2010; Bateman,

2012; Case, 2018/21). Of course, the constant ambiguity, reconstruction and myriad of key stakeholder influences is not new to youth justice. Indeed, the 21st-century trajectory of youth justice is pitted with 'conflict, contradictions, ambiguity and compromise' (Muncie et al, 2002: 1) and the 'ambivalent and ambiguous character of New Labour's copious youth justice policies [are] … a melting-pot of contending, competing or directly contradictory measures' (Fergusson, 2007: 192). Consequently, analysing and understanding youth justice policy making is a complex and challenging enterprise.

Analysing expansionist youth justice (1996–2010)

So at this early stage, what are we able to conclude from the foregoing policy analysis in relation to the research questions (RQs) that frame this project?

What is youth justice 'policy'? (RQ1)

The identification and analyses of government documents and grey literature from 1996 to 2010 indicates that youth justice 'policy' was typically framed as a stated intention and a present or proposed course of action (see Levin, 1997) defined by an incumbent government (the New Labour government). In the period analysed, the dominant youth justice policy narrative was *prevention*, but other (related) youth justice policy agendas are discernible, including *punitiveness* (for example support for custody), interventionist *support* (for example ASB management, tackling social exclusion) and a dragonised, CFOS approach emerging in the Welsh policy context. The overarching policy of prevention was reflective of a trajectory of *expansionism* in the construction of youth justice animated by a 'new youth justice' cohered by strategies of responsibilisation, risk management and managerialism.

Who are the 'makers' of youth justice policy? (RQ2)

Analyses implicate governmental actors, notably government ministers working closely with their SPADs and other civil servants, as the primary 'makers' of youth justice policy from 1997 to 2010, particularly in terms of agenda setting and policy formulation. However, during this period, a new policy-making structure/organisation was created, the YJB, as an independent, expert policy adviser to government and practice adviser to the sector. The unique role, identity and status of the YJB introduced unique policy-making relationships with government and practice, such that the organisation inhabited a policy-making grey area situated somewhere between governmental and non-governmental policy actors. In turn, this unique policy-making context introduced a new level of complexity into the making of youth justice policy. Finally, the policies and scholarly critiques analysed suggest a slowly emerging role for practitioners in policy-making processes, not limited to the policy implementation phase, through their developing relationships with government (typically civil servants), their relationships with the YJB and the construction of new representative/advocacy organisations such as the AYM.

Elsewhere across the analyses, there are some latent, yet discernible, indicators of how youth justice policy making is understood by stakeholders (RQ3), how it might be enabled and obstructed (RQ4) and how it may be improved (RQ5). Such data typically lack detail and transparency across the policy documents and should hopefully become clearer and more explicable during the semi-structured interview phase. At this early stage, however, emerging themes and challenges for youth justice policy making are discernible, including the *dynamism* of policy contexts (for example, their rapidly changing nature, instability, insecurity), the dynamic and contingent nature of *power relations* and policy-making *identities* (for example the changing government–YJB relationship, government prescriptiveness) and the additional complexity of the partially devolved *Welsh* policy context.

4

Austerity youth justice as tentative policy 'progress'

The previous chapter outlined how the prevention policy focus of the Labour government was operationalised from 1997 to 2010 through an *expansionist* 'new youth justice' approach constituted by a series of neo-liberal and neo-correctionalist *strategies* (for example risk management, interventionism, responsibilisation, restorative justice) that expanded the purview of youth justice *systems*, *processes* and *practices*. This chapter examines the extent and nature of youth justice policy development from 2010 (post-Labour government) during a period shaped by significant socio-economic austerity and socio-political insecurities that rendered the expansionist 'new youth justice' approach to prevention increasingly infeasible – financially, politically, practically and evidentially. It will be argued that socio-economic austerity and socio-political insecurity have exerted a reconstructive influence on youth justice policy making since 2010 by motivating a more pragmatic *retraction* and *retrenchment* of policy and practice, supported by the *reimagining* of alternative, evidence-based, principled youth justice approaches. Therefore, Chapter 4 brings the qualitative data analysis of youth justice policy documents up to date by charting its evolution since 2010, from a consolidated and rebranded form of 'new youth justice' strategies for prevention into a more explicit strategic focus on integrating progressive 'Child First' principles to meet prevention goals. A conflicting and ambivalent mix of rebranded 'new youth justice' and Child First principles has characterised austerity-led youth justice policy 'development', evidencing macro-, meso- and micro-level constructive influences such as political power, organisational/occupational identities, academic evidence and practice discretion when 'making' youth justice through policy. Consequently, it could be argued that the '3Es' of expansionist youth justice policy (see Chapter 3), be they 'effectiveness, efficiency and economy' (Home Office 1998) or 'expedience, evidence and experience' (Smith, 2014), have been tentatively replaced by the '3Ps' of austerity youth justice: politics (change), pragmatism (necessity, rationality) and principle (Child First). For the purposes of coherent analyses, post-Labour youth justice policy trajectories are divided into two 'progressive' development periods:

- Coalition government policy: a 'newer youth justice' (2010–15)
  During the first half of the decade, the Coalition government (Conservatives and Liberal Democrats) consolidated and progressed prevention policy

through a rebranded and retracted form of 'new youth justice' in their 'Breaking the cycle' Green Paper (2010) and the independently commissioned 'Time for a fresh start' system review (2010). Thereafter, there was tentative policy progression away from 'new youth justice' strategies in the form of policy and strategy developments around diversion (a new out-of-court sentencing framework, for example) and assessment practice (for example a new assessment-intervention framework), although both were often pursued in practice through continued reliance upon 'new youth justice' strategies of interventionism and risk management. During this initial period of austerity youth justice, therefore, the socio-historical conflict and ambivalence of youth justice policy responses persisted.

- Conservative government policy: continued 'progress in principle' (2015 to the time of writing)
  Qualitative data documentary analysis (QDA) of policy literature identifies this period as one of notable policy progress in relation to the underpinning principles and strategic objectives of youth justice policy. This progress built on the Coalition's re-introduction of diversionary principles and a sweeping review of the Youth Justice System (YJS) in 2016, which catalysed developments in the trajectory of youth justice strategy (led by the Youth Justice Board [YJB]) away from the 'new youth justice' and towards 'Child First' as the guiding principle for youth justice policy, strategy and practice in England and Wales. It will be argued that these developments have represented 'progress in principle' for youth justice policy, as they have been 'progressive' in moving the policy debate forwards in principled, conceptual, evidential, strategic and practical terms. However, the policy and research literature indicates that progress thus far has been confined largely to areas of principle (reflected in legislation and strategy), rather than animated consistently or comprehensively in practice.

Coalition youth justice policy: a 'newer youth justice'?

In 2010, a coalition government (hereafter the 'Coalition') between the Conservative and Liberal Democrat parties came to power in the UK, with Conservative leader David Cameron as Prime Minister. The Coalition inherited a macro-level socio-economic and socio-political context beset by uncertainty, insecurity and volatility resulting from sweeping economic austerity. This presented them with a serious policy dilemma. There was an immediate political and public desire for significant and urgent policy changes (youth justice a prime candidate, as usual) as outlets for socio-political and economic anxieties. However, this initial political appetite for policy change, characteristic of new governments seeking to 'be seen to' effect sweeping change, was tempered by restricted and diminishing resources (political, financial, practical) and political will to realise change. An additional policy paradox lay in the government's inheritance of a seemingly successful and 'effective' YJS. Decreasing numbers of first-time entrants, reoffenders and children entering custody weakened the case for significant youth justice policy change while strengthening the case for austerity cuts to a policy area that was 'working' and so ostensibly needed less support or attention.

Notwithstanding the resultant inertia in youth justice legislation and policy making, associated social policy change was high on the Coalition agenda, with Cameron immediately outlining his 'Big Society' vision (Cabinet Office, 2010). The government committed to mending a 'societally Broken Britain' ridden with crime resulting from social problems such as 'family breakdown, welfare dependency, debt, drugs, alcohol abuse, inadequate housing and failing schools', themselves the apparent results of the "choices that people make" (Cameron, 2011: 3–4). The Big Society policy mantra was neo-liberal/responsibilising in its emphasis on individual action/responsibility and communitarian in its focus on nurturing people's sense of community, citizenship and civic duty (Evans, 2011). The government would 'empower' individuals, families and communities "to take control of their lives so we create avenues through which responsibility and opportunity can develop" (Cameron, 2009: 2). Herein, Labour's responsibilisation strategy was redolent through assigning primary responsibility to individuals for addressing/meeting their own welfare needs (Kisby, 2010) and situating primary responsibility for society's problems with communities (not government), to justify the empowerment of these communities (by government) to solve the problems they faced. As such, the Big Society's strategic emphasis on responsibilisation translated seamlessly from the 'new youth justice'.

Policy point: political policy paradoxes

The Coalition government took power in a macro-level context of unforeseen and atypical socio-economic austerity and socio-political insecurity. These contextual influences immediately presented the new government with two policy dilemmas regarding youth justice: the desire for policy change in a successful policy context and the perceived need for action in the context of diminishing resources and service retraction. It could be argued, therefore, that policy change at that time was both inappropriate and could not be afforded.

Policy question: policy change as political agenda?

Do new governments tend to default towards effecting change in key policy areas, even when the policies of their predecessors have evidenced a degree of success? When this does occur, can a self-serving political agenda trump evidence, or are there other potential influences on changes in policy direction?

Early Coalition youth justice policy: political rhetoric and conflicting legislation

Initial Coalition policy statements regarding youth justice indicated moves away from the punitive policy and strategic direction of the previous government (see Hopkins-Burke, 2016). In 2010, Home Secretary Theresa May proclaimed that the Big Society would tackle 'the root causes of poverty and criminality' (May, 2010: 2) through an approach to dealing with youth offending that was 'rehabilitating and restorative rather than criminalising and coercive'. However, despite this political rhetoric, initial legislative statements offered a conflicting reality by seemingly reaffirming a governmental commitment to 'new youth justice' strategies and the dominant prevention agenda in the YJS.

'Breaking the cycle': diversion, discretion and default to 'new youth justice'

In 2010, the Ministry of Justice (MoJ)[1] published a Green Paper entitled 'Breaking the cycle: effective punishment, rehabilitation and sentencing of offenders' (MoJ, 2010), which outlined five key objectives for improving the YJS (MoJ, 2010: 67):

1. Prevent more children from offending and divert them from entering into a life of crime, including by simplifying out-of-court disposals.
2. Protect the public and ensure that more is done to make young offenders pay back to their victims and communities.
3. Ensure the effective use of sentencing for young offenders.
4. Incentivise local partners to reduce youth offending and re-offending using payment by results models.
5. Develop more effective governance by abolishing the YJB and its freedoms and flexibilities for local areas.

'Breaking the cycle' was progressive in the sense of recommending improvements to the rigid, inflexible and escalatory out-of-court sentencing system imposed by the CDA 1998, which was characterised as criminalising children and deprofessionalising practitioners. The Green Paper recommended a policy/strategy of *diversion* from formal disposal, asserting that 'informal intervention could be more effective' (MoJ, 2010: 68). It also recommended more systemic and professional *discretion* to use expert judgement (by extension, less prescription from the centre) by asserting that 'trust in the professionals who are working with children on the ground' should be encouraged in order to 'determine the most appropriate response, depending on the severity of the offence and circumstances of the young offender' (MoJ, 2010: 69). Indeed, 'Breaking the cycle' went further than simply affirming and extending 'new youth justice' strategies of old by recommending that police, prosecutors and Youth Offending Teams (YOTs) be allocated far more local discretion to administer out-of-court/pre-court diversionary disposals, so moving away from the explicit system-based managerialism and interventionism of the CDA 1998. Furthermore, the Green Paper recommended localising the funding and governance of youth justice, including incentivising local authorities/YOTs to reduce demand on the YJS through a 'payment by results' model. The localisation and decentralisation – withdrawal of the state – agenda was extended with a recommendation to abolish the YJB, a recommendation reiterated in the Taylor Review in 2016 (see later in this chapter).

Contrary to this progressive (rhetorical) intent, however, 'Breaking the cycle' largely constituted an extension of the 'new youth justice' by reaffirming the government's commitment to prevention through risk-based early intervention and responsibilisation through parental responsibility (for example, via YOT parenting work, Parenting Orders) and more restorative justice. Despite its progressive, diversionary intentions, 'Breaking the cycle' privileged a prevention aim, framed as risk-based early intervention, asserting that 'intervening early in the lives of children at risk … [is] our best chance to break the cycle of crime' (MoJ, 2010: 68). Consequently, 'Breaking the cycle' illustrated the perennial conflict, ambivalence, 'cyclical' nature (Bernard and Kurlycheck, 2010) and 'messy complexities' (Goldson and Hughes, 2010) of youth justice policy making. Its espoused challenge of and progression from the perceived negative aspects of these strategies (for example criminalisation, interventionism, managerialist prescription) aligned with a 'rhetorical' mode of policy making, yet its simultaneous consolidation/extension of 'new youth justice' strategies in practice recommendations was more akin to 'implementational' policy making (see Fergusson, 2007).

'Breaking the cycle' also revisited a common trope in contemporary youth justice policy-making contexts, namely threatening the role, *identity and status of the YJB*, thus subjecting an already insecure organisation to further insecurity. An important addendum to this debate is that subsequent to 'Breaking the cycle', the YJB's proposed abolition was downsized into recommendations for maintenance of its current functions but in a reduced capacity (Public Bodies Act 2011) and a reduction of the YJB's independence to make it more accountable to ministers (Triennial Review – MoJ, 2012). The government had argued that the size and political importance of the YJB's functions required it to be brought directly under ministerial control and that these functions should be transferred to a new Youth Justice Division situated within the MoJ. Consequently, the YJB's abolition was presented as a simple restructuring of government bureaucracy, moving a non-departmental public body into a departmental unit (Souhami, 2015b). However, a vociferous rebellion in the House of Lords (notably from Lord Tom McNally, former Chair of the YJB – also interviewed for this project) resulted in a reprieve for the YJB[2] on the final reading of the bill (Souhami, 2015b).

'Time for a fresh start': blueprint for reform or more 'new youth justice'?

'Breaking the cycle' was consolidated by the publication of a government-commissioned independent report, 'Time for a fresh start', that purported to offer 'a blueprint for reform' of the YJS (D.J. Smith, 2010: 1). The objectives of the report, produced by the Independent Commission on Youth Crime and Antisocial Behaviour (hereafter 'the Independent Commission'), were deliberately framed as implicitly critical of previous youth justice approaches under New Labour in order to implicate the need for reform. These reforming objectives were:

- to identify a set of principles for responding fairly, effectively and proportionately to antisocial behaviour (ASB) and offending by children and young people and reduce the harms caused by these behaviours;
- to evaluate existing responses to ASB and offending through evidence gathering, consultation with key stakeholders and local visits;
- to investigate and identify alternative approaches;
- to devise a blueprint for an effective, just, humane and coherent response to children's and young people's ASB and offending;
- to propose sustainable and evidence-based reform of services;
- to influence policy through a report and an academic text.

(Independent Commission, 2010: 2)

'Time for a fresh start', its title indicative of the desire for policy reform (like 'Breaking the cycle'), criticised the YJS of England and Wales for the 'questionable nature' of its underpinning youth justice policy (nb under the watch of Labour governments) and its alleged unimpressive record of 'deep-rooted failings' (Independent Commission, 2010: 17). Contemporary 'new youth justice' responses were castigated for their 'lack of coherence', 'adultifying' tendencies (treating children as adults), criminalisation of children from deprived backgrounds, 'inflated use of penal custody' and for wasting money on 'expensive and ineffective and probably harmful' youth justice responses (Independent Commission, 2010: 23). The report concluded with a series of recommendations for reform based on prioritising prevention, early intervention and restorative justice (central planks of 'new youth justice') by reintegrating 'young offenders' into mainstream society through limiting the use of punitive measures such as ASB management and custody (ostensibly new, progressive strategies).

A related edited volume entitled *A New Response to Youth Crime* (D.J. Smith, 2010) was released, drawing on academic expertise to provide the 'framework of evidence and detailed analysis that supports the Commission's proposals' (D.J. Smith, 2010: 6) through a series of invited chapters reviewing literature, evaluating research evidence and outlining current thinking in the field. The key youth justice themes it addressed included patterns and causes of youth crime and ASB, responding to youth crime and ASB, preventing youth crime, family and parenting, models of youth justice and public opinion. Smith concluded the volume[3] by setting out a number of recommendations for reform that reflected the key themes of the invited contributions and the three key reform principles established in the 'Time for a fresh start' report: prevention, restoration and integration, and, moreover, the need for more intensive versions of these established strategic objectives.

Critical commentary: a fresh start for youth justice policy?

The degree to which the Independent Commission's recommendations represented policy 'reform' in relation to existing (new) youth justice strategies is debatable. Goldson (2011) argued that the report had failed to provide the promised degree of critique, instead uncritically accepting and adopting existing social constructions of 'crime', 'ASB' and 'young offenders' as harmful and threatening. Additionally, the reform recommendations regurgitated established risk management positions, exemplified in the conclusion that 'an understanding of "risk" and "protective" (or "promotive") factors provides a valuable basis for planning and implementing prevention strategies' (Independent Commission, 2010: 39). The report was also criticised for perpetuating 'new youth justice' responsibilisation through its continued commitment to individualising forms of restorative justice over broader considerations of universal prevention and children's rights agendas (Goldson, 2011).

Despite soliciting the (previously marginalised) expert perspectives of critical academics, non-governmental organisations, progressive practitioners and children's rights organisations, the report and its recommendations retained faith in much 'conventional youth justice apparatus' (Goldson, 2011: 7), resulting in a somewhat ambiguous and disparate set of well-rehearsed criticisms of the 'new youth justice' and recommendations based on the same 'new youth justice', ultimately settling on recommending a slightly modified version of the YJS (see Case, 2018/21). Therefore, rather than the promised 'blueprint for reform', the recommendations for policy reform were, at best, illustrative of a conflict and ambivalence in how to construct youth justice and, at worst, simply extrapolations of existing strategies of 'new youth justice'.

Policy question: making a newer youth justice?

What were the realities of the policy-making contexts, identities and relationships that influenced the content of 'Breaking the cycle' and 'Time for a fresh start'?

Coalition prevention plus: the paradox of financial commitment in an austerity context

Even in the context of economic austerity and service retraction, a trajectory of financial investment in the prevention agenda continued, albeit framed as strategic funding for time-limited programmes and schemes[4] rather than permanent increases in core investment into youth justice structures such as for YOTs.

The Coalition's policy commitment to prevention (typically conflated with early intervention) was formalised in 2010 by the establishment of the Independent Commission on Early Intervention to identify best practice models of early intervention which 'ensure that children at greatest risk of multiple disadvantage get the best start in life … to help fulfil their potential and break the cycle of underachievement' (Department for Education [DfE] website, August 2010). The Commission's recommendations for 'effective' early intervention practice were supported by the DfE 'Early Intervention Grant' (in England only – education remained a devolved policy area in Wales), a new funding stream to subsidise local authority provision of early intervention and preventative services and to replace funding streams for existing early intervention initiatives (for example Sure Start Children's Centres, Youth Opportunities Fund, Children's Fund, Positive Activities for Children). The government allocated £2,222 million to the Early Intervention Grant initiative in 2011/12 and £2,307 million in 2012/13, but spending on the initiative decreased to £1,709 million in 2013/14 and £1,600 million in 2014/15, largely due to service funding cuts during the period of economic austerity. The Early Intervention Grant was used predominantly to fund targeted services for children and families in need of intensive support (such as Sure Start, support for children with multiple problems, targeted mental health provision in schools), programmes that had previously suffered from implementation difficulties and a lack of evidence of their effectiveness. In the youth justice sector specifically, from 2010 new funding streams were made available, primarily to YOTs, for targeted youth crime prevention work (£31 million), Youth Inclusion Programmes (£10 million), Youth Inclusion and Support Panels (£11 million) and parenting services (£4 million). In 2011, the government Under-Secretary of State for Prisons and Youth Justice, Crispin Blunt, argued that most existing prevention programmes in England and Wales should 'target' children on the cusp of offending, justifying the need for even more investment in early intervention (CYP Now, 2011). The Coalition youth justice policy commitment to prevention was reinforced in the following year by the Prime Minister, who asserted that "prevention is the cheapest and most effective way to deal with crime. Everything else is simply picking up the pieces of failure that has gone before" (Cameron, 2011, speech to the Centre for Social Justice).

Policy point: a 'newer youth justice'

The first two years of the Coalition government witnessed the 'Breaking the cycle' Green Paper and the Independent Commission review recommendations for improving the YJS, with both packaged as policy 'reforms'. However, these recommendations were largely consolidations of the established strategic trajectory of the 'new youth justice' through continued political and financial commitment to responsibilisation (for example the low age of criminal responsibility, prioritising restorative justice), prevention through risk-focused early intervention(ism) and enhanced local discretion, albeit with a diminishing emphasis on centralised performance management. Therefore, it is possible to characterise early Coalition youth justice policy activity as constructed and driven by a 'newer youth justice' – an updated and rebranded version of the 'new youth justice' of the previous government yet represented as a distinct political/policy identity for the new government.

Later Coalition youth justice policy: tentative progress in principle

Two years on from 'Breaking the cycle' and the Independent Commission, there *was* a significant policy progression from the 'newer youth justice' through the formal reintroduction of *diversion*, a previously dominant youth justice policy/strategy in the UK in the 1980s (Allen, 1991). This was soon to be followed by AssetPlus, a significant revision to the Asset risk assessment tool and the Scaled Approach assessment and intervention framework used to explain youth offending and to plan and deliver appropriate youth justice responses.

Legal Aid, Sentencing and Punishment of Offenders Act 2012: re-enter diversion

In 2012, the Coalition passed the Legal Aid, Sentencing and Punishment of Offenders Act 2012 (hereafter 'LASPO 2012'), which represented a step change for youth justice policy and strategy by mandating reforms to the existing escalatory, criminalising, out-of-court sentencing process (reprimand–final warning–court-based referral order) through a revised, three-stage framework underpinned by diversionary principles:

1. Community Resolution – a police-administered out-of-court disposal requiring the child's agreement to participate, incorporating victims' perspectives; typically adopts a restorative emphasis and does not assign a criminal record.
2. Youth Caution – a second stage disposal administered locally in police–YOT partnerships and requiring assessment and intervention by the YOT, with criminal record assigned.
3. Youth Conditional Caution – a tertiary, pre-court disposal with proportionate rehabilitative, punitive and reparative conditions, with criminal record assigned. YOTs monitor compliance, while non-compliance results in prosecution for the original offence.

The new diversionary out-of-court system was more flexible than its predecessor, allowing children to move up and down between stages, to receive the same disposal on multiple occasions and even return to the out-of-court process following a previous court sentence. Consequently, by prioritising out-of-court diversion, LASPO 2012 progressed youth justice policy beyond previous punitive and inflexible systemic responses and towards non-criminalising, systems management-led responses and early support mechanisms to replace formalised interventions (Hart, 2014; Bateman, 2016). Accordingly, explicit reference to 'prevention' was limited, and the reorientation of pre-court processes suggested a tentative progression from risk-led targeted prevention cum early intervention (at least for first-time offenders) and towards the prevention of entry into the formal YJS (Haines and Case, 2015). As such, LASPO 2012 began a process of reconstructing youth justice by employing diversionary practice to serve policy-focused preventative goals.

From Scaled Approach to AssetPlus: a reconstructed assessment–intervention framework

Coalition revisions to youth justice out-of-court processes (and their related diversionary and minimal necessary intervention-related *principles*) were built upon through YJB revisions to the pivotal mechanism/processes of assessment and intervention for children entering the YJS. Early in his tenure as YJB Chief Executive, John Drew initiated consultation exercises with expert stakeholder groups (policy makers, practitioners, academics, children, families) to evaluate the utility and appropriateness of the Scaled Approach. The consultations were motivated by ongoing academic and professional criticisms of the framework's interventionist, expensive nature and its risk-focused, negative portrayals of children (see for example Case and Haines, 2009), its encouragement of disproportionate, stigmatising and potentially criminalising interventionism (see for example Bateman, 2011), its neglect of the voices of children (for example Case, 2007) and its capacity to deprofessionalise practitioners (for example Pitts, 2003). Drew intended this as a genuine, open-minded consultation exercise (in Case, 2018/21), unlike previous examples of YJB 'consultation', where practitioners were essentially presented with preformed policies and required to discuss the optimal ways to operationalise them in the real world (Case, 2007). The academic consultation in 2010 at YJB headquarters in London brought together a group of critical academics who had previously been blacklisted or marginalised by the YJB and prevented from entering into a constructive dialogue in relation to improving the YJS (Drew in Case, 2018/21).

Critical commentary: reflection on the Scaled Approach academic consultation

I attended the academic consultation session alongside a group of academics who had been highly critical of the YJB (for example Pitts, Bateman, Goldson, Phoenix, Haines, Smith), sharing a room with senior YJB strategic and operational managers and the creators of the 'Asset' risk assessment instrument. I recall three hours of detailed criticism of the theoretical, methodological, ethical and practical weaknesses of the Scaled Approach, all welcomed by Chief Executive Drew, who embraced critical and reflective dialogue, while the response from other YJB staff and the pro-Asset researchers in the room was a mixture of intrigue, shock and anxiety. I also recall that certain senior YJB staff expressed deeply held support for the widely published damning critique of risk management/Risk Factor Prevention Paradigm (RFPP) and much enthusiasm for identifying a replacement assessment and intervention framework. Such high levels of support appeared incongruent with longstanding, deep-rooted, documented YJB resistance to critique of policy and reluctance to engage with critical academics to that point, including rumours of an academic 'blacklist'.

A cynic or perhaps pragmatist may argue that this apparent 180° shift exemplified the realities of the political agenda and identity as policy-making influences, such that senior policy makers were acutely aware of the prevailing socio-economic, political and institutional climates (which included an appetite for policy and practice change) and were taking ownership of the processes of change by reconstructing their explanations of and responses to youth offending. This typified the political expedience, survival instincts, opportunism and instrumentalism of governmental youth justice policy making and policy makers since 1997 (see also Chapter 7). Furthermore, the newfound openness to radical new ideas, change and system improvement among previously intransigent senior staff (whose tenure pre-dated that of Drew) coincided with 'Breaking the cycle' recommendations for abolishing the YJB and so may have been motivated (justifiably in my view) by a degree of self-preservation and the desire to carve out a new identity and sense of value in the eyes of government, for example as experts complementing generalist civil servants (see also Chapters 1 and 3).

An associated lesson I learned from this exercise was that while there may be 'churn' over time in the political and policy stakeholders influencing the reconstruction of youth justice, with key individuals leaving an organisation and being replaced (see also Chapter 5), there may also be within-individual/organisation churn in relation to agendas and prevailing ideas. In my experience, dramatic and sudden changes to the views and agendas of individual professionals and organisations can be driven by political expedience, opportunism and self-preservation but also by access to new evidence, expertise and cultures of critical reflection.

The outcomes of the expert consultations informed the introduction of the AssetPlus revised assessment and intervention framework that replaced Asset and the 'Assessment, planning interventions and supervision' Key Element of Effective Practice and the Scaled Approach (YJB, 2013, 2014). In contrast to the risk management of the Scaled Approach, AssetPlus prioritised holistic, contextualised and dynamic assessment–intervention that emphasised or at least intended to emphasise: accessing children's voices (not adulterising assessment), identifying children's *strengths* and *promoting positive behaviours* and *outcomes* (claiming to eschew neo-correctionalist, deficit-based models) and exploring *interactions* between different elements of children's lives (not reduced to the deterministic influence of psychosocial risk factors). The intention was for a greater strategic and practical focus on *needs over risks*, more scope for *practitioner discretion/expertise* and improved *self-assessment* for children and their parents/carers (YJB, 2013, 2014). Consequently, AssetPlus promised a culture/paradigm shift away from the neo-correctionalist RFPP and towards more holistic, prospective and appreciative constructions of and responses to the lives of children who offend (see Haines and Case, 2015).

Policy question: what influences policy reconstruction?

How and why did the proposed reconstructions to youth justice policy implementation mechanisms evidenced by AssetPlus come about? For example, what were the respective constructive influences of political/governmental agenda, organisational (YJB) identity and academic expertise and critique?

Coalition prevention policy: a 'newer youth justice' of interventionist diversion?

The Coalition adopted a revamped approach to prevention in their policy rhetoric and legislation, which was animated by risk management/risk-focused early intervention, later evolving into a progressive focus on diversionary principles to pursue prevention within a retracted YJS. According to critical commentators, the Coalition ushered in a 'new era of diversion' (Creaney and Smith, 2014: 83), which was something of a curate's egg. On the one hand, it set out to subsume the New Labour emphasis on diversion from crime (through prevention) with a new approach to diversion from prosecution, linked to evidence that formal system contact can be labelling and criminogenic (see, for example, McAra and McVie, 2007). On the other hand, the new diversionary focus retained the interventionism of the 'new youth justice' to the extent that it has been labelled 'interventionist diversion' (Kelly and Armitage, 2015). For example, 'Breaking the cycle' established the Coalition's intention to simplify the existing out-of-court disposal framework by making it less rigid/escalatory, more flexible and offering more discretion to youth justice staff in the YJS in relation to sentencing and intervention planning. Simultaneously, however, the government prioritised the use of diversionary initiatives that had been piloted nationally under Labour, including the Youth Restorative Disposal (the forerunner of the Community Resolution), the Youth Conditional Caution, the Youth Justice Liaison and Diversion Scheme (A. Haines et al, 2012), the Triage model (Home Office, 2012) and the Welsh 'Bureau' model (Haines et al, 2013).

The prioritisation of diversionary interventions represented a continued policy desire to retain an element of centralised control over local practice, couched as the empowerment of local areas. The outcome, however, was further conflict and ambivalence around how out-of-court diversionary interventions should be implemented, what their focus should be and what structures, systems and processes children should be diverted *away from* and diverted *into* (Richards, 2014). Interventionist diversion raised a serious dilemma over how to offer support via intervention without a child acquiring a criminal label or identity through associated risk-based assessment and informal contact with youth justice agencies. While LASPO 2012 provided the space for 'dialogue around costly, net widening, criminalising, counterproductive and damaging institutional practices' (Yates, 2012: 5), the limited official guidance given to YOTs regarding the implementation of the new out-of-court system recommended they prioritise existing diversionary programmes (MoJ and YJB, 2013) and that assessments of children prioritise prevention, operationalised as preventing/reducing risk of reoffending, harm to self and harm to the public. The Coalition was so committed politically, financially and pragmatically to a diversionary form of prevention (in a diversionary sense) that the statutory self-assessment element of AssetPlus was modified into a 'prevention' tool for pre-court use (YJB, 2014) simply by removing the term 'offending' from within it, indicating that government/YJB thinking around diversion had barely moved from the interventionist and risk-based prevention focus of the 'new youth justice'.

Welsh youth justice policy (2010–present): dragonised principles, strategies and structures

> 'The political and organisational context in Wales, with partial devolution of relevant issues ... and a distinctive policy orientation for children (rights- and entitlements- focused), provides conceptual and practical space for progressive youth justice.'
>
> (Case and Haines, 2012: 40)

Since 2010, there has been a proliferation of political and scholarly arguments relating to a distinctively progressive Welsh youth and social justice agenda (see Case and Haines, 2021; see also Chapter 3), employing the concept of 'dragonisation' as shorthand for conceptualising how the Welsh Government has used its powers within a range of policy areas that intersect with the UK government's formal responsibilities for justice (Haines, 2010; Evans et al, 2022). Social policy for children in Wales has continued to espouse a distinct identity, promoting the principles of children's rights/entitlements, universalism and collective responsibility (Drakeford, 2009, 2010), compared to the perceived English tendency towards strategies of risk reduction, conditional rights (no rights without responsibilities, for example), targeted early intervention and individual responsibility/responsibilisation (see earlier in this chapter). Similarly, youth justice policy and strategy in Wales has retained the 'children first' principle as central and distinct from the risk-based prevention agenda in English youth justice and social policy (Case and Haines, 2015).

In 2011, the Welsh Government produced a cabinet briefing paper entitled 'Devolution of youth justice', which established 'a vision for increasing Welsh Government influence over the delivery of services to children and young people who are offending or at risk of offending' (Welsh Government, 2011: 1). The cabinet briefing recommended a key philosophical distinction in how youth justice should be constructed and administrated in Wales, namely through an entitlement/rights-based approach to supporting children as 'children first', not offenders first (after Haines and Drakeford, 1998): 'The principle is a focus on the needs of the children and young people, rather than on their offending behaviour' (Welsh Government, 2011: 4). The following year, the Welsh Government published a Green Paper entitled 'Proposals to improve services in Wales to better meet the needs of children and young people who are at risk of entering, or are already in, the Youth Justice System' (Welsh Government, 2012). The Green Paper progressed discussion regarding how the Welsh Government should employ its existing powers to develop a distinctive rights- and entitlements-focused youth justice that benefitted children in the YJS. It was consolidated by the recommendations of the Silk Commission on Devolution in Wales (Silk Commission on Devolution in Wales, 2014). The Silk Commission advocated that key youth justice stakeholders in Wales should be given more responsibility and influence over how Welsh youth justice is constructed and that youth justice decision-making powers should be devolved through a new Government of Wales Act.

Concurrent to these strategic, policy-focused developments in Wales, a series of bespoke structures were introduced to mobilise this espoused 'dragonised' approach to Welsh youth justice. In 2011, the Wales Youth Justice Advisory Panel (WYJAP) was formed to provide expertise, challenge and scrutiny on a range of strategic, policy, practice and research issues relevant to youth justice in Wales. The WYJAP was to contain representatives from the Welsh Government, YJB Cymru, Welsh YOTs, the Secure Estate in Wales, the courts, probation service, police, voluntary sector and academics from the Welsh Centre for Crime and Social Justice. YJB Cymru reports to each meeting on the standing item of 'Wales youth justice performance'. The primary purpose of the WYJAP was 'to assist the Welsh Government and the YJB to implement policy that prevents offending and reoffending by children and young people in Wales' (WAG and YJB, 2014: 1). A further significant structural move towards constructing a distinct Welsh youth justice through distinct policy-making processes was the formation of 'YJB Cymru' in 2012 as a 'division' of the YJB for England and Wales to sit alongside the other divisions (Corporate Services, Effective Practice, Community, Secure Estate) on the YJB Executive Management Group and to complement the Welsh representative on the YJB. YJB Cymru was created to monitor and manage the implementation of centralised youth justice policy and practice prescriptions in the Welsh context, acting as a policy mediator advising the UK government, the YJB and the Welsh Government and monitoring, supporting and advising the practice of Welsh YOTs (YJB Cymru, 2012; Case, 2014). This official role was set out in the 'Blueprint for promoting effective practice and improving youth justice performance in Wales' (YJB, 2012). YJB Cymru provides expert, Welsh-centric, expert advice to the YJB on youth justice matters, including contributions to the 'Issues for Wales' standing item within every 'Informational Decision Paper' produced by the Executive Management Group (Case, 2014). At ground-level (structurally), a committee for the YOT managers across Wales, YOT Managers Cymru, was created to work with the YJB to consider the implications of legislation, government guidelines and youth justice policy for Welsh YOTs and to determine effective responses to youth offending in Wales (YOT Managers Cymru, 2013).

In 2014, the Welsh Government and the YJB updated the 'All Wales youth offending strategy' (2004) (see Chapter 3), producing the 'Children and young people first' strategy (Welsh Government and YJB, 2014). Its vision statement reiterated the Welsh commitment to a 'children first' approach to youth justice in Wales, stating: 'Children and young people at risk of entering, or who are in, the YJS must be treated as children first and offenders second in all interactions with services' (Welsh Assembly Government and YJB, 2014: 3).

This vision statement set out five priorities for youth justice practice in Wales, which broadly mirrored the prevention approach favoured by the UK government (Welsh Assembly Government and YJB, 2014: 3): (1) a well-designed partnership approach; (2) early intervention, prevention and diversion; (3) reducing re-offending; (4) effective use of custody; and (5) resettlement and reintegration at the end of a sentence. These priorities were linked to specific 'children first' principles and objectives relating to the appropriate treatment of children in the YJS, with a context-specific focus on: children first engagement, actively seeking children's voices, helping children to access their rights and promoting diversion – all distinctly 'dragonised' forms of youth justice. The strategy also emphasised prevention and early intervention, challenging offending behaviours and enabling victim participation (through restorative justice, for example) and delivering youth justice through accountable multi-agency partnership working – all strategies of the more anglicised 'new youth justice'. Therefore, the priorities and objectives of the 'Children and young people first' strategy were arguably bifurcated or even polyfurcated, pursuing 'dragonised' youth justice through children first principles while simultaneously committing to strategies aligned with the English 'new youth justice'.

Dragonised youth justice in Wales: rhetoric or reality?

The political and practical desire to resolve the tensions between English-centric youth justice policy prescriptions and the identity of social policy for children in Wales (2010–15) has fuelled the construction of a distinct form of Welsh youth justice in rhetorical, principled, strategic and structural terms, evidenced by bespoke Welsh-centric youth justice bodies and 'children first' strategies to reconcile these policy tensions. However, there is a degree to which these bespoke bodies (such as YJB Cymru), key individuals (the Welsh representative on the YJB, for example) and Welsh youth justice strategy ('Children and young people first') have remained constricted in practice by the non-devolved youth justice requirements of the CDA 1998. For example, it is possible to view Welsh youth justice developments (certainly from 2010 to 2018) as often constituting little more than add-ons to mitigate the negative excesses of the 'new youth justice', informed variously by national strategy, local mediation and/or charismatic YOT managers, rather than functioning in practice as stand-alone, distinct and consistent approaches to delivering youth justice (Kennedy in Case, 2018/21).

There is an ongoing debate about the extent to which youth justice in Wales has evolved a dragonised identity in practice as opposed to being Welsh-centric predominantly in policy and strategy rhetoric but constrained by the statutory requirements of the CDA 1998 and its 'new youth justice' strategies. For example, in the light of the Commission on Justice in Wales 2019 recommendations that youth justice be devolved to Wales,[5] Evans et al (2022) re-examined the central claim that (partial) devolution had created the space and conditions for progressive justice policy to flourish in Wales. By reviewing policy developments and conducting empirical research (interviewing key stakeholders), Evans and colleagues revisited 'dragonisation' to assess the extent to which Welsh youth justice policy had diverged from its English counterpart since the formative years of devolution (Evans et al, 2022). The focus was less macro level than previous cross-national comparative studies and more of a meso- and micro-level examination of how localised forces (for example local penal cultures) govern and shape penal policy. The researchers raised doubts over whether Wales, as yet, had really adopted a more progressive approach to youth justice than England, instead identifying a range of local jurisdictional differences. They concluded that policy divergence between the nations had narrowed in recent years and that differences *within* the same system were often greater than the differences that existed *between* England and Wales. As regards the macro-level, socio-political context, it was concluded that although Welsh policy makers enjoy a considerable amount of autonomy over key planks of social policy (Jones and Wyn Jones, 2019), officials are still unable to influence many of the key drivers that shape policing and criminal justice in Wales. This has meant that Welsh Government officials are unlikely to 'advance more liberal or progressive' approaches when confronted by UK government control over key policy areas (Brewster and Jones, 2019) and have frequently been thwarted in their efforts to alter the direction of UK government criminal/youth justice policy (Welsh Government, 2018). Therefore, while 'dragonisation' has provided Welsh policy makers, practitioners and academics with a framework to pursue distinct approaches to policy and to think more critically about Welsh youth justice policy within Wales' highly anomalous constitutional arrangements, it remains more of a rhetorical device than practical reality at present (Evans et al, 2022). Notwithstanding these issues, it remains informative to examine the unique youth justice policy-making context in Wales in more detail to avoid uncritical, patronising and idealising generalisations that it simply mirrors that of England. For example, in smaller jurisdictions (such as Wales), the relationship between policy makers and practitioners is often more clearly discernible, while changes in policy and practice can be implemented and evaluated relatively quickly (Scott and Staines, 2021). Therefore, useful lessons can be drawn from the way justice is done in 'small places' (Evans et al, 2022), not least because they cast new light on the policy-making assumptions assigned to 'big places' (such as England).

Policy question: Welsh youth justice policy identity as rhetoric or reality?

Were the differences in the nature of youth justice policy making in Wales more rhetorical (see Fergusson, 2007) than real? If the differences were real, were there any specific contextual and relational influences (beyond those reported) driving the Welsh capacity and appetite for this policy reconstruction?

Conservative policy: continued 'progress in principle' (2015–)

The Conservatives replaced the Coalition as the UK government in May 2015. The socio-political context of uncertainty, instability and heightened economic austerity was exacerbated in June 2016 when the UK voted to leave the European Union in a move dubbed 'Brexit', resulting in the resignation of Prime Minister Cameron. In a bid to stabilise the chaotic political fallout from Brexit by establishing a larger political majority/ mandate and so stronger policy-making powers, new Prime Minister Theresa May called a snap General Election, which took place in June 2017. The outcome of this was a political disaster – a dramatically reduced majority and an enforced alliance with the Democratic Unionist Party of Northern Ireland. This chaotic socio-political and socio-economic context compounded the youth justice policy paradox faced by the new version of the existing government, namely the desire to carve a fresh identity through invigorated policy making in a context of significantly diminished political and financial power and capacity to effect change.

The subsequent period of youth justice policy making has been arguably most notable for building on the Coalition's re-introduction of diversion and for heralding the emergence of a new progressive guiding principle entitled 'Child First', which has functioned as a constructive influence on policy formulation and implementation – although it must be emphasised strongly that Child First policy/strategy has been driven by the YJB independently of government input or explicit support. Youth justice policy under the Conservative government's watch has thus far demonstrated 'progress in principle', in that key developments have been explicitly guided by principles, rather than practical and technical concerns reflected by the 'new youth justice'. This period has also been notable for diminishing political interest in youth justice policy making in a context of increased political instability and dynamism, illustrated by the rapid 'churnover' of key policy actors such as justice ministers (nine since 2015) and prime ministers (three in a six-week period in late 2022), along with churn in organisational agendas and arrangements (the transfer of YJB sponsorship from the Home Office to the MoJ in 2010, for example). In this context of heightened political insecurity and diminished profile for youth justice, the policy-making influence of non-governmental actors such as the YJB and practitioners has discernibly increased (see Child First discussion in this chapter).

The 'Taylor Review'

In September 2015, a thorough 'Review of the Youth Justice System in England and Wales' (hereafter the 'Taylor Review') was commissioned by Justice Secretary Michael Gove. The review was spearheaded by Charlie Taylor (interviewed for this book), a former headteacher and government special adviser on working with children with behavioural difficulties. Although the 'considerable success' in youth justice outcomes (Taylor, 2016: 2) inherited from the Coalition government had continued in the first year of the Conservative government, Gove maintained that reoffending rates (the proportion of identified offenders who reoffended, not the number) remained problematic. This served as the official government rationale for the review, rather than government admitting any political agenda as motivating a review of an ostensibly 'successful' system.

Further to constructing this reoffending issue as a problem, the government asserted that although fewer children were entering the YJS (Bateman, 2017), those who did so were disproportionately likely to present with personal and social disadvantages such as multiple complex needs, mental health problems, learning difficulties, looked-after care experience and coming from working-class and/or Black and minority ethnic groups (Taylor, 2016). This led Taylor to identify the question that would constitute his review rationale: '[W]ith fewer children requiring youth offending services, are the current arrangements for dealing with them the right ones?' (Taylor, 2016: 2). To populate the review, Taylor gathered performance and outcome data and consulted with staff (for example YOT workers, police, managers) and children during site visits to YOTs and secure establishments across England/

Wales and in youth justice organisations elsewhere (Scotland, Northern Ireland, Spain). He concluded his review with a set of recommendations for building on the established trajectories of success in the YJS and simultaneously addressing the concerns regarding reoffending rates, notably by prioritising:

Child First, education-focused youth justice

The central review recommendation was to reform the guiding principles for youth justice policy towards those of 'Child First' and education. Taylor recommended a reformed YJS where 'we see the child first and the offender second [and where] education needs to be central to our response to youth offending' (Taylor, 2016: 3). The report encouraged a progressive, principled 'children first' approach to youth justice, mobilised through changes in the language/narrative used to re-define 'young offenders' as 'children'. Taylor also proposed two new *structures* to animate Child First, education-focused youth justice:

- Children's Panels – panels constituted by specially trained magistrates working alongside the child, parents/carers, local authority key workers, lawyers and other relevant professionals should investigate the causes of youth offending (with due consideration of welfare, health and educational issues) and decide upon appropriate youth justice responses.
- Secure Schools – education-focused custodial institutions prioritising qualifications, skills and knowledge development, commissioning support services (for example health, mental health, speech therapy) should operate as and be governed and inspected as schools (replacing Young Offender Institutions in the Secure Estate).

Integrated service provision

Taylor recommended that health, education, social care and other services should collaborate in more integrated ways to facilitate multi-agency partnership working in the YJS. His rationale was that a more holistic systemic response to the problems of children who offend would avoid the risk of criminalising and 'othering' (labelling, marginalising, stigmatising) those children and would avoid compartmentalising 'youth offending' as a stand-alone behaviour that should only be dealt with through the siloed, youth justice-focused practice of YOTs. To this end, Taylor identified innovative local structures and integrated systems of youth justice delivery (such as Surrey Youth Support Service), wherein children who offend are given access to the same range of provision as children demonstrating other personal and social problems such as welfare needs, being 'NEET' (not in education, employment or training) or homeless. He concluded by emphasising the need for a more welfare-oriented approach to (integrated) youth justice, stating that 'our aim should be to create a twenty first-century system that moves away from justice with some welfare, to a welfare system with justice' (Taylor, 2016: 49).

Local devolution and discretion

The third key review recommendation was simultaneously *structural*, *strategic* and *procedural* – that the centralised prescription and bureaucracy of youth justice policy making should be stripped back through increased local devolution and practitioner discretion in decision making, assessment and planning and delivering youth justice interventions. The MoJ were encouraged to abolish the centralised, routine performance management of YOTs exercised by governance organisations (YJB, HMIP), and it was recommended that local authorities be given the freedom to develop their own diversion schemes, assessment systems and models/locally appropriate partnerships to 'make' youth justice. Attached to this recommendation was the (recurrent) proposal that the YJB be abolished and replaced by a new 'Office of the Youth Justice Commissioner' as an expert committee offering the government 'independent advice and challenge on its approach to youth justice' (Taylor, 2016: 55).

The government response to the Taylor Review

The official government response to the Taylor Review recommendations (Taylor, 2016) was partial, accepting some recommendations wholly or in part and ignoring others (SCYJ, 2017). This partial response inevitably reflected a number of potential political and economic practicalities and biases (that is, policy-making realities), including austerity-induced reticence, diminished capacity to enact big policy change and lack of fit with the current political agenda. The government acknowledged the 'successes' of the YJS while reiterating the problematic reoffending outcomes that had prompted the review (distancing itself from these inherited problems). The government offered rhetorical support for a more education-focused and integrated youth justice sector by committing to 'implementing his [Taylor's] key recommendations by putting education at the heart of youth custody' (Taylor, 2016: 3), including expressing strong support for the new Secure Schools structure.[6] Elsewhere, there was only limited acknowledgement of the recommendations regarding a greater focus on children's mental health and welfare. Recommendations for increased local devolution and professional discretion received some support through tentative commitment to exploring how local areas could be given greater flexibility to improve youth justice services, but no more detail was provided. However, in direct contrast to recommendations for more decentralisation and less centralised performance management of youth justice (consolidating an existing policy), the government promised to work with the YJB to set clear, robust performance standards for youth justice practitioners.

Despite tentative government support in a number of key areas, the central progressive and principled recommendation for a 'children first' approach to youth justice was completely ignored, as was the associated structural recommendation for Children's Panels. Indeed, the main thrust of the government response appeared to be a reinforcement of the risk-based prevention policy agenda by supporting early intervention (akin to the 'new youth justice'), illustrated by their claim that the most effective way to reduce crime is 'to intervene early and to prevent children and young people from committing offences in the first place' (Taylor, 2016: 4). The risk basis of this early intervention (risk management) approach to prevention was illustrated, according to the government/MoJ, by 'robust assessments which will enable interventions to be properly matched to the offending-related risks of individual children' (Taylor, 2016: 31). This assertion appeared to support exhuming the Scaled Approach, while it bore only limited resemblance to the operating principles of AssetPlus and ran counter to Taylor's recommendations for a positive and empowering children-first, education-focused YJS. In a subsequent twist, in April 2017, Taylor was appointed as the new Chair of the YJB. Thus began a rapid and radical policy reform journey towards 'Child First' justice, despite government and MoJ (civil service) ambivalence.

Policy question: what are the practical realities of policy reform?

What were the key political, strategic, practical and evidential influences that shaped the partial government/MoJ response to Taylor's recommendations? What influences may have dominated government thinking and decision making about how best to address the practical realities of the Taylor recommendations?

'Child First' youth justice policy: challenging the 'new youth justice'

Taylor's appointment to Chair of the YJB enabled him to drive forwards his recommendation for a 'children first' *principle* to shape the trajectory of youth justice policy, despite a lack of governmental support. Soon after Taylor's 2017 appointment, the YJB adopted 'Child First' as the central guiding principle for youth justice to underpin its five strategic objectives – their plan for realising policy and organisational objectives in practice (YJB, 2021). An initial YJB 'Board information paper' (YJB, 2018) outlined the YJB commitment to 'Child First', operationalising this principle as comprising the central features of the 'Positive Youth Justice' model: child friendly, diversionary, promotional, legitimate, engaging, responsibilising adults (Haines and Case, 2015) and the 'Constructive Resettlement' approach – constructive, co-created, customised, consistent, coordinated (Hazel and Bateman, 2021). Subsequently, Child First has been operationalised by the YJB as four interrelated 'tenets' (YJB, 2021: 10–11; see also Case and Browning, 2021a):

1. See children as children: prioritise the best interests of children, recognising their particular needs, capacities, rights and potential. All work is child focused, developmentally informed, acknowledges structural barriers and meets responsibilities towards children.
2. Develop a pro-social identity for positive child outcomes: promote children's individual strengths and capacities as a means of developing their pro-social identity for sustainable desistance, leading to safer communities and fewer victims. All work is constructive and future focused, built on supportive relationships that empower children to fulfil their potential and make positive contributions to society.
3. Collaboration with children: encourage children's active participation, engagement and wider social inclusion. All work is a meaningful collaboration with children and their carers.
4. Promote diversion: promote a childhood removed from the justice system, using pre-emptive prevention, diversion and minimal intervention. All work minimises criminogenic stigma from contact with the system.

To further contextualise and rationalise the introduction of Child First, the YJB has utilised its 'Strategic plan' to formally reject the previously dominant risk management approach/model for animating prevention policy, making a bold, progressive and evidence-based statement that

> [p]reviously, perspectives of children's involvement in the youth justice system focused on managing a child's offending behaviour and the risks they were considered to pose. However, in recent years, evidence has demonstrated that effective prevention is driven by focusing on children's needs; identifying their strengths and creating opportunities that realise their potential. Evidence also tells us that contact with the youth justice system can increase the likelihood of children reoffending. (YJB, 2021: 10–11)

In the context of this emerging strategic commitment to the Child First principle,[7] the MoJ and YJB published 'Standards for children in the justice system' (MoJ and YJB, 2019), which provided a 'framework for youth justice practice' and the 'minimum expectations for all agencies' to ensure that positive outcomes for children align with the Child First guiding principle for practice (MoJ andYJB, 2019: 4). The revised 'National standards' for practitioners were intended to enable the faithful translation of the Child First principle/strategic objective into practice (see Chapter 1). They were 'indicative of a clear distinction between the philosophy now espoused by the YJB [Child First] and that which informed the previous iteration of the standards [risk management]' (Bateman, 2020: 4). The new expectations for 'Child First' youth justice practice were consolidated in revised 'Case management guidance' (YJB, 2019), which outlined how practitioners and managers can work effectively with children at different stages of their journey through the YJS. Therefore, the 'National standards' and their associated 'Case management guidance' offer a 'guide to strategic and operational services' which emphasise that the delivery of policy requirements in practice should be both evidence-led and Child First (YJB, 2022). The centrality of the Child First principle as a constructive influence on youth justice policy has been reinforced in the annual 'YJB business plan 2020/21', which has committed to 'promote the implementation of the child first guiding principle' (YJB, 2020: 5). This commitment has been further reflected in the 'Vision statement' of the 'YJB strategic plan 2021–2024', which espoused the YJB's view that 'we want to see a Child First youth justice system' (YJB, 2021: 3).

Child First policy into practice: implementation as policy making

The Child First principle is now established in the documented strategy and formal practice guidance of the YJB. However, the extent to which the principle for enacting policy has been translated into documented and evaluated practice remains contentious and under-developed. That said, there is an emerging evidence base suggestive of shifting policy frameworks and distinctive models of youth justice in England and Wales since 2018, including nascent Child First-related models. Following a qualitative review of the youth justice plans of YOTs in England and Wales, Smith and Gray (2019) identified a typology of strategic and operational frameworks for the delivery of youth justice. Three main strategic and operational models were identified:

- Targeted intervention ('new youth justice') – responses to resource and structural constraints are geared towards specialised rather than minimal intervention. In other words, YOTs view themselves as having a role in identifying and addressing those aspects of children's circumstances (risk factors) which are linked with their offending in order to develop tailored early intervention programmes focusing on these specific areas of concern (see also Kelly and Armitage, 2015);

- *Offender management* ('new youth justice') – emphasis on delivering services according to national policy targets, meeting agreed objectives and demonstrating efficient and effective management of offenders. However, this model is consistent with the principle of 'minimum intervention' and the idea that diversion should be used to clear the space to devote limited time and money to working with children who are seen as a higher priority in terms of the problems they represent;
- *Children and young people first* (Child First) – where YOTs are closely aligned with more holistic understandings of children and their offending, viewing them as critically intertwined with contextual factors and their underlying social circumstances. There is often a clear commitment to developing interventions to avoid unnecessary prosecutions and criminalisation and to support children at the point of initial contact with the YJS.

Despite Smith and Gray's findings, however, the extent and nature of the implementation of Child First in practice remain nascent and inconsistent in England and Wales (Case and Browning, 2021b; Day, 2022; Hampson in Case and Hazel, 2023; see Appendix 3).[8] This implicates a degree of policy implementation failure or, more accurately, a 'policy implementation gap' (Gunn, 1978) in youth justice policy contexts. As discussed earlier, such gaps are often attributed by governmental policy actors to practitioners rather than to failures of agenda setting or policy formulation/decision making on the part of governmental actors (Hudson et al, 2019; Case et al, 2020), for example the absence of government and MoJ buy-in to the Child First principles established in the Taylor Review. Relatedly, Western governments are increasingly interested in how policy implementation can be 'strengthened and supported in order to ensure the policy intentions are turned into practice results' (Hudson et al, 2019: 2). Accordingly, there is increasing political and academic emphases on the *complexity* (a key theme going forwards), unpredictability, non-linearity and adaptability of policy-making processes designed to ensure that policy intentions are met in reality (Braithwaite et al, 2018), a focus underpinning the rationale for this book (see Introduction and Chapter 1).

The incongruence of Child First in a risk management context

Any discernible policy implementation gap or 'rhetoric–reality divide' (Haines and Case, 2008) related to the realisation of Child First practice in YOTs has been exacerbated by incongruence (incompatibility, contradiction, confusion) in the practice guidance provided to staff by governance organisations (YJB, HMIP). This incongruence has been redolent in the bifurcated pursuit of Child First forms of youth justice alongside existing risk management approaches, itself further illustration of the conflict, ambivalence and 'messy complexities' of youth justice policy.[9] For example, the 'AssetPlus' assessment–intervention framework rationale is incongruent. It asserts that 'theoretical debates … [and] perceptions and experiences of practitioners' (YJB, 2014: 4) regarding risk management have influenced moves away from the previous Scaled Approach framework by providing 'new ideas' regarding more holistic, integrated and collaborative processes for understanding and responding to children who offend. These new ideas include mechanisms for increasing practitioner discretion and children's meaningful participation, while tackling interactions between a wide range of criminogenic influences, not just between stand-alone risk 'factors'. However, the rationale maintains that 'assessment will involve identifying risk and protective factors' (YJB, 2014: 4–5), illustrated by the focus on practitioner judgements on risk (impact and likelihood of reoffending) and intervention emphasis on the reduction and management of risk (YJB, 2014: 3–4).[10]

Furthermore, HMIP inspection criteria for YOTs exacerbate this climate of incongruence through their contradictory mix of support for Child First tenets and risk management principles. For example, 'Organisational delivery' criteria (HMIP, 2022) encourage YOT management boards to promote evidence-based, multi-agency partnership working in child-friendly delivery environments (Child First). However, the same criteria also encourage the targeting of 'desistance factors', criminogenic needs (risk factors) and risks posed to others, identified using the 'Risk–Need–Responsivity' model, which matches intervention to risk level, identifies and targets criminogenic needs (risk factors) and tailors interventions to individual attributes and learning styles (Andrews and Bonta, 2010). The 'Case assessment rules and guidance' criteria (HMIP, 2022: 42) guide YOTs to employ assessment to support desistance by addressing strengths, structural barriers, diversity and developmental sensitivity (Child First) alongside attitudes/motivations for offending, personal, family and social 'context' (risk management). Incongruence persists in 'Supporting the desistance of children subject to court orders' section (HMIP, 2022), which promotes children's strengths, positive identity development, positive outcomes, constructive relationships and collaboration (Child First) alongside 'desistance factors' (risk factors). Despite this thorough-going incongruence, however, HMIP inspection criteria, guidance and evidence bases consistently privilege risk management and relegate Child First to the status of one of several possible 'models and frameworks' for practice (HMIP, 2022: 8) rather than recognising it as a principled framework for using the evidence from practice models (Case and Hazel, 2023).

Policy question: Child First in a risk management context?

What are the origins, drivers and operational realities of the perceptible incongruences in the strategy, practice and inspection guidance provided to 'street-level' practitioners by governance and monitoring organisations seeking to realise the government's prevention policy priority for youth justice? Can risk management strategies and Child First principles co-exist, or are they contradictory and oppositional?

Conservative policy 'progress in principle'

Youth justice policy developments under the Conservative government in the UK since 2015 have been indicative of 'progress in principle', in the sense of progressing principled youth justice (for example Child First), but more in principle (rhetorically in policy and strategy) than in practice reality. Building on the diversionary intent of LASPO 2012 and catalysed by the progressive Taylor Review recommendations, youth justice policy has undergone a slow evolution/progression away from the alleged negativity of 'new youth justice' strategies and towards more positive 'Child First' constructions of offending behaviour and appropriate responses to it. A trajectory of progressive policy has been extended through the formal YJB commitment to Child First as the guiding principle for youth justice policy, strategy and practice in England and Wales. At present, however, this trajectory remains largely confined to rhetorical, documentary evidence in the strategic publications of the YJB, tentative additions to HMIP inspection criteria and strategic-rhetorical commitments by policing and court sentencing organisations. Child First is yet to be formalised in government legislation, and this remains unlikely in the continued context of socio-economic and socio-political insecurity, anxiety and uncertainty (which itself may leave Child First vulnerable to abolition), compounded by associated practical and financial restrictions/realities and personnel churn.

As discussed, Child First still lacks a detailed, long-term trajectory of evidence in practice (see Bateman, 2020), although this might be expected because, as a principle and strategy, it remains relatively young and is still developing. Furthermore, documented examples of effective 'Child First' practice are steadily emerging across England and Wales (through the YJB-funded Pathfinder projects and successful HMIP inspections, for example), and the YJB continues to monitor, manage and critically reflect on how it can most effectively facilitate the faithful practice implementation of Child First (see subsequent analyses of YJB stakeholder feedback).

Conclusion: austerity youth justice as tentative policy 'progress in principle'?

This chapter has reported on the findings from the second half of the QDA of youth justice policy documents from 2010 onwards that informs this project. The chapter has outlined the extent to which reconstructions of youth justice since 2010 have constituted continued 'progress in principle' through a modernised and distinctive approach to policy development based on principles, with other 'developments' better understood as updated and rebranded versions of 'new youth justice' strategies.

Initial analyses suggest that Coalition youth justice policy (2010–15) was shaped by a responsibilising and communitarian 'Big Society' agenda, reflected in the youth justice sector by the 'Breaking the cycle' Green Paper, the 'Prevention matters' report and the 'Time for a fresh start' independent review recommendations for emphasis of 'new youth justice' strategies of responsibilisation and risk management as vehicles for actualising an early intervention-focused prevention policy. Subsequent revisions to the out-of-court sentencing process under LASPO 2012 and to the assessment and intervention framework through AssetPlus (circa 2013) illustrated conflict and ambivalence in Coalition youth justice policy, between building on 'new youth justice' strategies and constructing contrary, progressive, principled approaches driven by diversion, participation, eliciting children's voices and enabling practitioner discretion.

Analyses indicated that the youth justice policy of the Conservative government (2015 onwards) has been characterised by political/policy ambiguity and a degree of inertia, shaped by continued macro-level socio-economic and political changes, insecurities, anxieties and restrictions linked to austerity and Brexit. The most significant youth justice policy development under the Conservatives thus far has been the Taylor Review, which offered progressive recommendations for improvement, including children first- and education-focused youth justice, diversionary Children's Panels, Secure Schools and more local devolution and discretion in the delivery of youth justice. However, with the exception of Secure Schools, these recommendations were largely ignored in the government response to the report in favour of a reiterated commitment to the 'new youth justice' strategy of *risk-focused* early intervention in the pursuit of prevention, reintroducing conflict, ambivalence and uncertainty regarding the future of contemporary youth justice. The Taylor recommendations *have* been animated, however, in the evolution of a new strategic direction and identity for youth justice policy in the form of the Child First guiding principle. Since its inception in Welsh youth justice strategy, Child First has been driven forwards strategically by the YJB in England and is slowly being evidenced in professional practice.

With this in mind, it is interesting to reflect on the recent policy-making implications of the YJB's strategic position statement that

> Child First is a journey for the YJB. … We are not alone on this journey. … We realise that the change we want will be years in the making. Meanwhile, we are committed to exploring with others how the evidence base might be applied. … Working with practitioners, policy makers and academics alike in doing so. (YJB, 2021: 8)[11]

Analysing austerity youth justice (2010–2024)

So now that the policy analyses phase is complete, what can be concluded in relation to the research questions (RQs) that frame this project?

What is youth justice 'policy'? (RQ1)

The identification and analyses of policy-related documents, grey literature and critical scholarship since 2010 continue to implicate youth justice 'policy' as framed politically as a stated intention and a present or proposed course of action (Levin, 1997), typically defined by the incumbent government (although it should be noted that this continues to be inapplicable to the influential 'Child First' strategy driven by the YJB). In the period analysed, *prevention* remained the dominant policy narrative, but other emergent youth justice policy agendas from 1996 to 2010 gained more traction. In particular, diversion and children first (now 'Child First') have increased in prominence since 2010, a period more notable for *pragmatic* youth justice policies than its *punitive* predecessors (see also Goldson, 2017) and for the retraction of youth justice policy making rather than its expansion.

Who are the 'makers' of youth justice policy? (RQ2)

Analyses continue to implicate governmental actors as the primary 'makers' of youth justice policy in the early years of the Coalition government, particularly in terms of problem emergence/agenda setting and policy formulation/decision making. However, as the decade progressed, diminishing (documented) government interest in and influence upon the youth justice agenda was palpable, potentially for a raft of socio-economic and social-political reasons (for example insecurities, anxieties), allied to the ostensible successes of the YJS. The insecurities and anxieties impacting the youth justice policy-making capacity and appetite of government were illustrated by 'churnover' of key decision-making staff and organisational responsibilities.

The dynamic context of youth justice policy making from 2010 has been further illustrated by the growing policy-making influence of the YJB as an independent, expert, strategic policy adviser (influencing policy formulation/decision making) and policy into practice guidance (for example influencing policy implementation and evaluation in the developing Child First context). These discernible changes in the nature of youth justice policy 'making' since 2010 tentatively indicate the constructive influence of contextual elements such as professional and organisational *identities* and *agendas*, *expertise* utilised to generate *evidence* and *relationships* within and between policy-making organisations.

Elsewhere across the analyses (as in Chapter 3), there are some latent yet discernible indicators of how youth justice policy making is understood by stakeholders (RQ3), how it might be enabled and obstructed (RQ4) and how it may be improved (RQ5). However, such data lack detail and transparency across the policy documents and should become far clearer and more explicable during the semi-structured interview research phase.

5

Exploring youth justice policy-making contexts and mechanisms

This is the first of three chapters examining the semi-structured interviews (see Chapter 2), which produced data to analyse the research questions (RQs) guiding this project:

1. What is youth justice 'policy'?
2. Who are the 'makers' of youth justice policy?
3. How is youth justice policy making understood, re/constructed, experienced and made meaningful by policy makers working in different contexts?
4. What are the barriers, challenges, enablers and opportunities for policy making?
5. How can youth justice policy making be improved?

The qualitative documentary analyses (QDA) presented in Chapters 3 and 4 began to address the first two RQs from an official, documented/published and legislative policy perspective. A series of potentially important constructive influences emerged from these initial analyses, such as the complexity, dynamism, contingency and contested nature of policy-making contexts (for example nationally, locally, organisationally), power relations, policy-making agendas, organisational/professional identities, expertise, the application of evidence and relationships between and within stakeholder organisations. Analysis of the semi-structured interview data affords more situated and privileged insight into the constructed, dynamic nature of policy making by eliciting the perspectives and experiences of expert stakeholders actively involved in youth justice *contexts* that shape the mechanisms of policy making. The overarching aim of the interview data analyses, like the QDA of policy literature, is the identification of policy-making coherence and meanings from a necessarily complex and ostensibly chaotic (unpredictable, non-linear, random) set of interacting contexts in order to better understand youth justice policy making and how it can be explained and reformed.

The chapter begins by asking 'What is youth justice policy making?', analysing interview data to identify expert stakeholder perceptions of the complexity and lack of consensus around understandings of policy and policy making. There follows a discussion of the multi-layered, multi-systemic and fragmented nature of policy-making structures and processes, which can foster conflict and role ambiguity within and between stakeholder organisations but can also be cohered through multi-agency collaboration promoting universal policy, shared objectives and seeking alignment of agendas.

The following section, 'Who makes policy?', identifies the broad contexts of youth justice policy making and focuses on the key stakeholder policy makers across the Youth Justice System (YJS). It begins with the category of governmental policy actors, exploring the general policy-making roles of politicians/ministers, senior policy advisers (SPADs) and other civil servants, with an additional focus on the interactions/relationships between these groups and right-wing media and think tanks. The subsequent sub-section examines the policy-making role of non-governmental actors, with particular focus on the Youth Justice Board (YJB) for England and Wales and the Office of the Children's Commissioner (OCC). There is a focused discussion of the contested and ambiguous identity, role and status of the YJB in policy-making contexts, alongside discussion of the OCC's unique influence at the problem emergence/agenda-setting stage of policy making. These discussions cohere by identifying the soft power of non-governmental organisations in youth justice policy-making contexts.

The third thematic section asks 'HOW does youth justice policy making happen?', framing its analysis in terms of the stability and change discernible in policy making since 1996, which can be understood as indicative of the messy complexities and conflict and ambivalence of the social construction of youth justice. The stability of youth justice policy trajectories is illustrated by discussions of their cyclical nature and contexts of gradual development that are encouraged by mechanisms of consensus, clarity and consistency of approach, contexts within which policy changes in different directions at differing speeds can be understood as populated by commonly identified mechanisms of change. These dynamic mechanisms include 'churnover' of key staff and policy and chaotic, often sudden and unpredicted/unpredictable policy making resulting from structural changes, critical events, opaque and incoherent policy influences, political and financial short-termism and opportunistic, instrumental policy making. The chapter ends with a general overview of the implementational 'mode' of policy making and the role of managers and practitioners in policy-making contexts, including their responsibility and culpability (relative to governmental actors) for policy implementation failures/gaps, which are discussed further in subsequent chapters.

What is youth justice policy?

QDA of key academic commentaries on the fields of social policy and youth justice (see Chapters 3 and 4) implicated 'policy' as a contextualised social construction that is complex, dynamic, contested and contingent (see

Chapters 3 and 4). The QDA indicated that policy is typically understood by experts who make policy (for example the authors of policy documents) as a proposal carrying commitment to future action, whether this be stated intention, current/past action, organisational practice, indicator of formal/claim status for a course of action or all of these (see also Levin, 1997). Notably, policies are often framed in deliberately broad, generalised ways (for example 'prevention', 'diversion') to allow flexibility and discretion in their translation into policy 'action' (for example legislation, strategy, practice). Additionally, the opening chapters identified policy 'measures' as 'things done to implement the policy', typically manifesting as policy 'products' (see Souhami in Case, 2018/21) or 'instruments' like government legislation (such as Acts of Parliament) and Green and White Papers, concluding that 'policy is something much wider than this' (Souhami in Case, 2018/21). These contested representations of the nature of youth justice policy and policy making will be explored in the interview analyses, with the overarching goal of 'understanding policies and the sources of their complexity and contradictions' (Ferguson, 2007: 10).

Complexity and lack of consensus

Expert stakeholder feedback supported the view that youth justice policy making is experienced as complex, contested, multi-layered and fragmented within and between policy-making contexts (for example organisations, systems). Commenting on the complexity and lack of consensus about what youth justice policy actually is and how it is understood across the sector, an Association of Youth Offending Team (YOT) Managers (AYM) Chair reflected:

> 'I'm doing a piece of work where I've asked for a number of different policies. Some people have sent me policy, some have sent strategies and some have sent what I would call practice guidance. They're all using different language. What's a policy meant to do? There isn't necessarily that understanding across the system.'

Building on this professional view of the complexity and lack of clarity of roles and responsibilities within youth justice policy making, a senior His Majesty's Inspectorate of Probation (HMIP) official stated that

> '[t]here isn't that one route to policy-making. There isn't one clear process. It's all very muddied. A lot of it depends on hobby horses. A lot of it is about politics and some of it is about relationships. But sometimes there is a real lack of understanding and lack of clarity about who fits where. We have evidence. The YJB works with YOTs and sees in detail what goes on and has more expertise than policy

colleagues. Then there's the lobby groups like the AYJ [Alliance for Youth Justice], the AYM or its Welsh equivalent. It's not clear to me what all those roles are and who has the say, so it's all very soft.'

Multi-layered policy making

Several stakeholders commented on the *multi-layered* construction of youth justice policy making, with these layers understood variously as levels of the social system and the different contexts within which policy making takes place (for example, occupational/organisational, systemic, geographical, national/local):

> 'I see layers of policy. I've always understood policy to be the direction and intention to achieve something and the means by which you do it. In a political sense, I've always felt that regarding decision making on direction of policy, the role for people like me [YOT managers] is to advise bureaucracy on how they shape policy, then to implement it as best I see fit. How well does it fit with my worldview and that of my colleagues and that of my locality?' (YJB board member, YOT manager)

> 'Policy exists at lots of different levels and lots of different people have an important role to play – the guy who maybe puts the flagpole up or pulls the rope that puts the flag at the top of the pole. They have a greater prominence … people's importance as policy makers exists at lots of different levels.' (YJB Chief Executive)

Fragmentation of policy-making roles and responsibilities

A range of stakeholders reflected that complex, multi-layered youth justice context/s lead to *fragmentation* between and within systems and organisations/agencies, which in turn fosters *role ambiguity* and *contested responsibilities* for different professional stakeholders in the making of youth justice policy. According to a senior HMIP official:

> 'One of the biggest things for strategy and policy is the children that we work with and straddle so many different government agencies, government agendas and also inspectorates. As a practising YOT manager, it's really difficult to understand who's prioritising what. This bit's from Ofsted, then this bit's from HMIP. Then you've got the YJB saying something different than the Youth Custody Service and the MoJ [Ministry of Justice]. So there's so many different bits and it feels very disparate at a national level.'

Reflecting on his professional experience of the multi-systemic context of youth justice as contributing to fragmented policy making, a former YJB board member observed:

> 'There is a fragmentation of the policy picture. The YJS goes well beyond a single government department's portfolio. Different policies may counteract one another. There's no golden thread through the different portfolios of government. There isn't a single point in government that owns the various different constituent parts that make an impact. For example, MoJ isn't interested in safe, healthy, happy childhoods, that is somebody else's portfolio. Creating the conditions for change within youth justice won't just come from YJB or MoJ.'

A senior academic consolidated this view of a fragmented, disconnected, disparate and chaotic policy landscape by highlighting their experiences of the influence of external policies and systems for supporting children:

> 'If you were a Martian, you would be astounded about the way that [youth justice] policy formation happens. You've got to look at all the other policies for children across the piece. But it's important to recognise that what's happening in other areas of services for children is influenced by what happens within the justice system and also has an influence on children who come into the YJS. But again, there's a disjuncture between different policies and the inconsistencies, the lack of joined-up connectedness and the darkness of policies across children's services, because they don't talk to each other.'

The issue of fragmentation and ambiguity of youth justice policy-making responsibilities was reinforced by a senior leader from the third sector:

> 'So in the MoJ, you've got the Youth Justice Policy Unit and they have a really big churn of staff and it's incredibly frustrating, but at least you know that you're going to be handed over to somebody's successor when they leave. Whereas in the Home Office, half of the task at the AYJ is to try and understand who it is that's leading on a particular initiative ... a specific place responsible and accountable for producing policy around children. That makes policy much more challenging to influence.'

Conflict and role ambiguity

Several senior YJB officials made particular reference to *conflict between government departments* engendering *role ambiguity and contested responsibilities* in the context of youth justice policy making, which exist across macro-level structural/political contexts and in terms of meso-level relationships with the YJB:

> 'Beverly Hughes [Department for Children, Schools and Families (DCSF)] once made a bid for youth justice, arguing that its policy shouldn't sit under MoJ, it should come across to the DCFS, because really education was the answer to everything. By then, Jack Straw [Justice Secretary] had come back to the MoJ and was really interested in picking up youth justice again. So ultimately, they decided they would split the sponsorship of YJB between education and justice. It was a complete farce.' (YJB Chief Executive)

> 'Government has different departments, with no-one necessarily taking responsibility for children. We [YJB] had Ed Balls [DCSF] in Education and Jack Straw in the Home Office, with all of these policy ideas popping up from different places. We invited them to the YJB and had all the board members around the table with them and their junior ministers. We were trying to say where we think they should be taking their policy thinking, but there was quite a lot of competition between those two. But what happens when the **** hit the fan and there's another child murder on the streets? Who owns the risk then?' (YJB Chair)

A similar experience of *fragmentation through internal conflict* and *lack of consensus* engendering *role ambiguity* was recounted by a senior YJB official:

> 'When I got to YJB, we had staff working on three floors and they never spoke to one another. We had the custodial people working on one set of things. We had the research people working on another set of things. There was no coherence across the piece and no engagement. That was a consequence of how YJB had been set-up, so I spent years trying to get people connected and to ensure we wouldn't just end up doing a set of policies or practice guidelines over there and something over here that didn't connect to it, then fighting about who's guidelines were gonna have the upper hand.' (YJB Chief Executive)

Cohering fragmentation and reconciling agendas: collaboration and consensus

As suggested in the previous quote, expert stakeholders are able to identify mechanisms that promoted non-fragmented, joined-up, connected policy making in otherwise disparate and complex youth justice contexts. For example, a policy adviser from the OCC identified pursuing *universal policy* as a potential mechanism for cohering and reconciling competing agendas across systems and contexts, emphasising that "[t]hey're still children, don't forget that. It's not just youth justice. It's mental health policy, housing policy, legislation, safeguarding. When people talk about what policies impact on the YJS, we must consider the impact of the same policies for every other child."

Other interviewees recalled their experiences of encouraging *multi-agency collaboration* through *shared objectives*, *sense-making* and *seeking alignment* as a mechanism for reconciling different occupational and disciplinary agendas, objectives and practices between and within policy-making contexts and organisations:

> 'Policy should be influenced by systems and people's experience. We [in Wales] work with a range of policies, seeing where they contradict themselves or work well together, where they're unclear relative to other agencies, policies and guidance documents. We have to make sense of all of that and work together. You often take six steps forward and eight steps back, but because it makes the policy more aligned in the end, it's worth going back and forth. It's certainly a process.' (YMC Chair)

> 'It [the youth justice sector] was such a vortex of complexities, with some people not part of the YJS and others part of it. I perceived education as somewhat disconnected from youth justice. I did outreach work with the teacher unions to get them briefed. Articles in their professional journals, lots of conferences, a whole range of networks. Showcasing as often as possible where youth justice policy was effective. Gradually building alliances within the board with members who understood children's trajectories from different backgrounds.' (YJB Chair)

A summary of the key contexts and mechanisms identified when exploring the question of 'What is youth justice policy making?' is provided in Appendix 4.

Who makes policy? Identifying the contexts of youth justice policy making

> 'Youth justice policy … isn't made just by senior civil servants and ministers, but by all kinds of people working in government and in partnership elsewhere … if we want to understand youth justice policy making, we need to look at what youth justice policy makers do.' (Souhami in Case, 2018/21)

Having gained an initial, broad understanding from stakeholders about experiences of *what* policy making actually is, this section interrogates expert perspectives of *who* is involved in the making of youth justice policy (RQ2), in which contexts this takes place and how this is understood by policy actors (RQ3). The opening chapter distinguished between governmental and non-governmental policy makers, noting that policy 'actors' working in governmental contexts nationally and locally (for example politicians/ministers, SPADs,[1] civil servants) are often more visible and privileged in explanations of policy-making processes, particularly at the problem emergence/agenda-setting and policy-formulation/decision-making stages of the so-called 'policy cycle'. However, that same chapter emphasised the importance of acknowledging a broader range of policy actors/makers in analyses of policy making (see Souhami, 2015a), notably those located in non-governmental contexts (for example practitioners, academics, media) who are considered less visible and thus potentially less influential (Vergari, 2015). This consideration is reinforced by Fergusson's (2007) exposition of the multiple discourses and 'modes' 'of youth justice policy making, which concluded that no party/actor has unique or extensive control over all stages of the policy-making process and that policies are subject to constant mediation and moderation (reconstruction) by different actors. Indeed, Fergusson's conclusion that the roles and influence of a *broader range of policy makers* should be considered when seeking understanding of youth justice policy making was consolidated by the experiences of two senior managers of youth justice stakeholder organisations:

> 'Policy is not in the first instance made by ministers or their senior civil servants. It's made by strategic or operational leaders such as the Magistrates' Association or AYM. That's where the key makers of youth justice policy are and their insights and agreements then bubble up to the policy work.' (YJB Chief Executive)

> 'Who makes policies? It's stakeholders, lobbyists, specialised groups, for example, the Howard League, researchers, the world of academia as well, they all contribute. Policy comes from what is known, what is on the ground, your experiences, funding, as well as the amount of money that's available.' (YMC Chair)

Acknowledging the necessity for a broader analytical lens, the policy-making roles and influences of a range of governmental and non-governmental stakeholder groups are now explored, with particular focus on the relationships between and within these groups in meso- and micro-level organisational/occupational policy-making contexts.

Governmental policy actors: who are they?

According to the Institute for Government (2011), approaches to understanding policy making neglect or marginalise the constructive influence of politics, and thus the policy-making roles of governmental actors (especially politicians/ministers) are represented as merely contexts to be 'managed' that exist externally to the policy process. This allusion to the reductionism of policy-making explanations was consolidated by the recent research conclusion of the Higher Education Policy Institute and Loughborough University (2023: 7) that 'while the term "policymakers" can be nebulous, it is [typically] used to refer to the following three groups: political actors (such as Ministers and SPADs), those involved in parliamentary scrutiny and non-political actors such as civil servants'. Such reductionist understandings of the potentially constructive influence of politics and government (governmental actors) are unrealistic, undesirable and flawed for three key reasons: policy making can never be extricated from politics, politics adds value to policy making and evidence and analysis is never 'pure' or above politics (Higher Education Policy Institute and Loughborough University, 2023: 7). Therefore, it is crucial to examine the constructive influence on youth justice policy making of governmental actors working within political contexts, simultaneously acknowledging that their role and influence should be neither neglected nor privileged over other groups. Indeed, certain interviewees perceived a significant *political influence* on youth justice policy, often through the 'rhetorical' mode of policy, where the power of professional politicians brings to the fore the punitive discourses founded in conservative-authoritarian values (Fergusson, 2007).

Dead hand political influence of Number 10

Experts cited their experiences of a 'dead hand' political/policy influence and agenda emanating directly from 'Number 10', the Prime Minister's office:

> 'The real dead hand was the number 10 influence, because whatever the Secretary of State wanted to do was this overriding desire for number 10 to demonstrate that it was tough on crime. It made it difficult to take through or get support for policies that would bring the numbers of offenders down. The overarching power of number 10 to squash any kind of individual policy idea cannot be underestimated.' (YJB Chair)

> 'Number 10 or the Prime Minister's policy delivery unit will have a much closer relationship with policy teams in different government departments depending on their political agenda of the day. Once

number 10 start getting really involved in a particular policy area, once you've got them breathing down your neck as a policy team, then that completely changes the way that policy is developed and delivered. They start weighing in and saying we need a quick headline, we need a good story.' (AYJ Chair)

Dead hand media influence of right-wing newspapers

According to stakeholders, the dead hand political influence on youth justice policy does not occur in a vacuum. It can be significantly influenced by a less visible policy actor in the form of media, and more specifically the right-wing newspapers in the UK perpetuating a punitive, anti-child agenda that exacerbates the public's fear of crime. These relational and dynamic features of the right-wing media function as mechanisms shaping policy making (for example agenda setting) in political contexts:

> 'My experience of the dead hand of the *Daily Mail* or the right-wing *Daily Telegraph* is that they frighten the **** out of the Conservative Party. Very few politicians are willing to stand up to them. It's the dead hand approach, that paranoia about the negative opinions of the core role and core supporters in the media about anything that looks flexible or lenient.' (YJB Chair)

> 'People's perception is that teenagers are running around with knives and guns. That's perpetuated by the media. It creates fear in communities, who then say, all these bloody kids need locking up and the key throwing away and punishing and that's where it comes from. We don't value children and teenagers. What would the *Daily Mail* reader say?' (AYM Chair)

Importantly, it was also emphasised that media influence on government policy agenda can be born of reality, which can reflect actual events and emerging social problems. Drawing on the knife crime example, a former SPAD reported that

> '[i]t was driven by media focus, but the media focus represented a genuine underlying reality that teenage knife crime had gone up. So there was an underlying reality to the media focus on knife crime at that time … and the longer it's in the papers, the more the pressure comes to do something about it.'

However, it is not always the case that the political agenda has a basis in reality, as evidenced by the experience of a YJB Chair who reflected on the *distortive effect of media* on government rhetoric that can influence subsequent policy making:

> 'We [YJB] were trying to brief ministers to balance things about children getting into risk. One minister saw a quote somewhere that there were 189 gangs in London recruiting children. No idea what the basis of that was. I advised him strongly not to use that figure, but just to say, risk comes in different ways and the kids are being exploited and so on. But he didn't. The *Evening Standard* [local, London-based newspaper] got hold of it and that's something that immediately raises anxiety with the police and local communities and public.'

Interviews demonstrated a broad stakeholder consensus that politicians in government have been able to exert significant influence over the shape and nature of youth justice policy making, with a particular focus on the problem emergence/agenda-setting stage, albeit an influence moderated and reconstructed by the 'dead hand' of the right-wing newspapers. This conclusion leads neatly into discussion of the policy-making role of other governmental actors, notably SPADs and other civil servants, particularly in terms of agenda setting and as potential architects of policy formulation.

Government–civil service policy-making relationship

To reiterate the conclusions of Souhami (2011, 2015a) from her ethnographic studies of the YJB, civil servants are generalists whose careers are structured to provide the technical skills to support ministers with their policy-making goals. As a result, expert knowledge of policy areas such as youth justice is rare among both civil servants and the ministers they support. However, this view of civil servants as non-expert generalists who 'serve' and are steered by ministerial agendas has fostered reductionist assumptions that government bureaucracy is unconnected to policy formation and that its primary role is largely confined to policy implementation and supporting ministers, without political authority to define its own objectives (Klammer et al, 2021). Conversely, Souhami (2015a) argues that civil servants and other officials with whom they work closely (such as YJB staff) are often intrinsically involved in youth justice policy making. She argues further that the context of bureaucracy in which they work is a site at which policy ideas both *emerge* and are *formulated* through officials elaborating on ministerial decisions in order to put them into action (see also Page and Jenkins 2005; Cairney and Oliver, 2020). Indeed, rather than being passive and neutral arbiters of technical information, civil servants can perform dynamic, reconstructive roles by re/formulating criminal justice policy problems and solutions in terms of 'good stories' that can be presented to ministers

(Stevens, 2011). Therefore, central government officials can routinely be involved at the policy formulation/decision-making stage of policy making and can also shape how problems are constructed at the problem emergence/agenda-setting stage. In other words, while civil servants can be steered by ministers, they can also steer ministers in youth justice policy-making contexts. Thus, the institutional context of government administration is of central importance when seeking to better understand youth justice policy making (see Souhami, 2015a).

Civil servant role: being steered or steering?

A pivotal debate within the policy-making literature concerns the nature and direction of the relationship between government/ministers and their civil servants, particularly the prescriptiveness and degree and nature of 'steer' (power) exerted by politicians in policy-making contexts relative to the discretion of civil servants to challenge and reconstruct centralised policies. It has been asserted that ministers have to recognise the value of challenges to their policy proposals, as otherwise civil servants have few resources to raise important issues and will privilege the maintenance of a 'good relationship' with their minister over constructive challenge (Institute for Government, 2011). The report authors also acknowledged the complexity of the political context within which civil servants operate and the need for strategically 'picking their battles' by working out which policies can be challenged without seeming to be obstructive (Institute for Government, 2011). The autonomy, discretion and generalised, technical expertise of civil servants has been emphasised in policy analysis literature, with particular focus on their role as a political counterbalance, managing risk for their ministers and developing robust policy in the face of socio-political and socio-economic uncertainty (Cairney and Oliver, 2020). This view aligns with Fergusson's (2007) 'codificational' mode of policy, where civil servants steer government towards statutes that maintain continuities with the welfare traditions of the preceding era and secure the customary discretion for professional practitioners. With this ongoing debate in mind, the broader policy-making role of civil servants and their relationships with other political/governmental actors will be interrogated across the interview data.

Reflecting on the traditional view of government steering civil servants in policy-making contexts, interviewees commented that:

> 'I had a very good relationship with my civil servants and the MoJ and never had any problem with any of them. I think they felt they had a very strong steer from me and were happy with that and followed it through.' (Government minister)

> 'Ministers who have a clear idea of what they want to do can get their policies through, but they sometimes run into querulous civil servants who say "are you sure"? But if the minister has a clear idea, he can put it through ... the big field reforms that they carried through either by campaign groups or by individual ministers sticking to it.' (YJB Chair)

SPADs steering civil servants on behalf of ministers

Stakeholders discerned the role of senior civil servants (SPADs) as different in nature and influence from the 'standard' civil servant role of staff working in the Home Office or MoJ (in the Youth Justice Division, for example). They described a much closer relationship with government ministers, with *SPADs advising and steering* both ministers and external, non-governmental organisations such as the YJB:

> 'You [SPADs] basically get copied in on everything that goes to the minister ... you can comment on anything that's going to him. You get a ringside seat to the top of government.' (SPAD)

> 'The role is almost like the party whip of the manifesto. They make sure that the MPs stay true to the government's intentions. Any minister has got more than they can handle in terms of what they can pay attention to. The SPAD is making sure ministers don't get short circuited. They double check that this stuff's in line with the manifesto and look for ideas or ways of looking at the world from the outside.' (YJB Cymru Chair)

> 'Beverly Hughes had just been appointed [as Minister for Children, Schools and Families] and I asked to meet her as the responsible minister. We [YJB] had a list of ideas and it was clear she did not want that list. On reflection, I should have had a SPAD tell me what it is that the minister wants to hear about.' (YJB Chair)

Civil servants as policy-making 'architects'

In contrast to the perception of civil servants being steered by the government and their SPADs, some interviewees had experienced the non-senior civil servant role (with particular reference to the MoJ Youth Justice Policy Unit) as more steering and architectural – advising ministers and SPADs on how to re/construct preformed policy ideas and agendas at the formulation stage so that they would have the best chance of success at the implementation stage:

> 'The manifesto of the party is the policy. Civil servants are asked to think of ways of implementing that policy. To call a civil servant a policy maker is to mix up those two things. Civil servants are the architects of what government want their house to be like. So then the civil servant goes away and draws a design for this house that the politician wants. What you can't do is come back and say, I know you want a swimming pool, but you gotta have a pond, because it won't ride. But you could come back and say, you wanted a swimming pool that was gas-fired, well would a solar-powered one be alright? That's the wiggle room you've got as a civil servant. Even though the evidence might suggest the best way of treating kids in the YJS, politically, ideologically, it's not always going to ride.' (YJB Cymru Chair)

> 'There is a civil servant way of selling a certain thing to fit the politics. Which also makes it messy and it makes it hard to be able to establish where these ideas come from and where these changes start.' (YJB board member)

However, concerns were raised by stakeholders over the extent and nature of any civil service steer of/influence on government-led policy making, on the basis that civil servants are generalist *non-experts* with limited youth justice specialism/expertise, particularly when compared to staff in other advisory bodies such as the YJB (Souhami, 2015b):

> 'Civil servants advise and report to the ministerial team on all matters youth justice and deliver ministerial priorities through policy making. The job of the MoJ Policy Team is to come up with some policies to make that happen. But how can they do that if they don't know what the issues are? If they don't know what they're doing and are not working from evidence? It always feels superficial. Ministers are not experts, and they never will be. But they need a Policy Team that does get the issues and does understand what will and won't work. That is why we have so many failed policies, because they're flawed from the start.' (Senior HMIP official)

> 'A key point of conflict, misunderstanding and caution, even now, is where did these civil servants come from? They've never worked in the real world, never worked in local authorities. Having people who have been in the business adds authenticity. Instead, we have bright civil servants promising a lot and holding themselves hostages to fortune when ministers change. For example, rolling-out a measure from the adult world without any policy or evidence. It's just a bright idea a minister or a SPAD has come up with.' (Senior AYM official, YJB board member)

Despite concerns regarding undue and non-expert influence, the necessary role of civil servants in counterbalancing and mediating/moderating political power, agendas and decision making was acknowledged when reflecting on the service *retraction and deprofessionalisation* encouraged by austerity under the Coalition and subsequent Conservative government:

> 'The power and influence [over policy making] of civil servants has declined, and political influence has become stronger. In recent years, the government has stripped out the mechanisms whereby their political priorities get translated from policy documents and legislation into the operational. Deprofessionalising the civil service increases the power of politicians, yet it becomes harder for politicians to make things happen, because the civil service isn't there to do the dirty work. The skill in the civil service increases the power of politicians to do things over the longer term. Deskilling the civil service means that politicians can say whatever they want and there's no one telling them they can't, but their ability to implement policy actually declines.' (YJB board member, YOT manager)

A summary of the contexts–mechanisms relationships identified when exploring the question of 'Who makes youth justice policy?' in relation to governmental actors is provided in Appendix 5.

Non-governmental policy actors: who are they?

Having conducted an initial exploration of the policy-making role and influence of governmental actors – politicians, SPADs, civil servants – the next stage of analysis examines the role and influence of non-governmental policy actors. Interview data identify certain stakeholder groups as particularly significant in youth justice policy-making contexts:

- YJB – a non-departmental public body sponsored by the MoJ, with a statutory duty to advise government on policy development and to guide the implementation of policy in practice. The YJB is constituted by a 'board' of 12 members (political appointments ratified by the Secretary of State) and non-board member 'officials' who are public servants (not civil servants serving a minister). The YJB Chair is a board member, while the Chief Executive is not.
- OCC – a group of non-governmental organisations sponsored by the Department for Education in England, Wales and more recently in local areas. These offices promote the rights, views and interests of children in policies or decisions affecting their lives, in particular representing children who are vulnerable or who find it hard to make their views known.

- Welsh Government Crime and Justice Unit – a civil service department in the Welsh Government working with and reporting to the Minister for Social Justice on criminal justice policy matters in Wales.
- Manager/practitioner organisations – practitioner organisations in England (AYM) and Wales (YOT Managers Cymru) promoting the role and status of YOT managers and staff and agreeing policy initiatives that put children and young people at the heart of the YJS.
- Third sector organisations – groups such as the AYJ (formerly the Standing Committee for Youth Justice), a coalition of over 75 organisations (national charities and advocacy organisations, smaller grassroots and community organisations, AYM) and the National Association for Youth Justice, an individual membership organisation advocating for and with children to drive positive change in the YJS of England and Wales.

YJB policy making

> 'My interest in the YJB was simply that I suspected it was where youth justice policy making took place.'
>
> (Souhami in Case, 2018/21)

In relation to the YJB's potential policy-making role, Souhami (2015a) notes that its status as a non-departmental public body promotes sustained periods of staff employment in a single area of executive activity, which allows for specialisation and continuity of knowledge and thus offers a unique structural opportunity for the *expert* administration of youth justice. The sustained nature of this context of expertise contrasts with the more transitory and generalist context within which civil servants operate as policy advisers. As discussed in Chapter 3, the YJB's statutory functions[2] give the organisation a central role in shaping the YJS, although these functions are inherently ambiguous (such as 'advising', 'monitoring'), elastic and open to multiple interpretations, so the structural, 'arm's-length' relationships within which the YJB operates are intrinsically slippery. In particular, relationships between central government, YJB and YOTs are not situated within a conventional hierarchy, and the flows of power dynamics between them are in constant flux (see also Chapter 7). Ostensibly, therefore, its structural distance from central government, its privileged 'insider' status and its slippery and ambiguous identity and role give the YJB significant influence in shaping the direction of the YJS and a broad and flexible arena in which to act (Case, 2014; Souhami, 2015b, 2018). However, as a senior YJB official remarked to Souhami (2015a), this freedom is inherently limited: "At the back of all officials' minds are, if you step too far beyond what you know the minister believes, then they'll stop listening to you altogether. It's a trade-off."

According to certain YJB stakeholders, the extent and nature of the YJB's policy-making role and influence remain ambiguous and contested:

> 'Youth justice policies that have dominated the field in the last 25 years … some are at YJB level, some are at other levels. Sometimes the YJB is guilty of irritating people elsewhere in the food chain by implying that they are more responsible for youth justice than they actually are. You have a particular role.' (YJB Chief Executive)

> 'MOJ would say that the YJB does not do policy; that policy is owned by MoJ, that we've got statutory functions and policy doesn't feature there. We've got the oversight and advice and identifying and disseminating effective practice. All of that lends itself to policy. What's differed over time is MoJ's capacity to fill that policy space. YJB is aware that there's been this vacuum and we've stepped into that space. But where does guidance end? Where does policy start? It's an area where there is a lack of clarity at present.' (YJB senior official)

The contested nature of the YJB's role feeds into the ambiguity surrounding its identity, role and status (see also Chapters 6 and 7), itself encouraged by the broad, generalised framing of 'policy' within the youth justice field:

> 'We [YJB] have a lengthy list of statutory functions that can be interpreted in different ways. A classic example is oversight and monitoring of the YJS. We interpret it as oversight because we just don't have the resource or the capacity to be able to monitor in that in-depth way. Does it mean youth justice services and the Secure Estate?[3] Does it mean all the partnership organisations that make up a youth justice partnership? So there's lots of room for interpretation. Are we part of the YJS?' (YJB senior official)

However, some senior YJB leaders were more confident and clear about the organisation's advisory and supportive role and influence, especially when compared to the role of civil servants:

> 'We [YJB] are less tied to political priorities [than civil servants], so we can focus on the evidence and our experience. There's a bit more freedom to manoeuvre. We do have this relationship with the MoJ, an arm's-length sponsorship arrangement. So I can't say we're not influenced by cross-government approaches, but we're perhaps less intensively influenced than core departments would be.' (YJB senior official)

> 'The YJB job is to advise on policy and strategy in youth justice. I envisaged our role as providing expertise and advising ministers. My preference was for strategising in the longer term to be able to influence ministers. My worry was if we acted like a lobby group we would be treated as such and have little influence. We had to walk a careful line because what we didn't wanna become the policy-making function for the MoJ. Nevertheless, we would be involved a lot in discussions over policy and we would push, nudge, cajole and support the development of policy. It wasn't our job to devise policy or to sign policy off for ministers, but if we're actually in the room where policies are being discussed, we're able to have more influence. That was the sweet spot.' (YJB Chair)

OCC policy making

Reflecting on the unique and somewhat ambiguous and free-floating policy-making identity of the OCC (see also Chapters 1 and 6), an OCC senior policy adviser observed that

> '[w]e are not making policy. We're not a delivery or implementation department. We're not civil servants, although we draw on some of the same skills. We get to be the Gad fly, pushing the system into doing the things that it should be doing. We can identify problems or draw attention to problems that other people have identified. We're good at drawing attention to those bits where systems are failing children. We're not doing the detailed policy work and telling individual government departments they have to do this. We often do end up writing a lot of policy that departments should have come up with for themselves.'

Stakeholders offered their professional lived experience of exercising *soft power* in policy-making contexts, for example in the partially devolved Welsh context:

> 'The intersection between being a policy maker and making policy gives us that sense of soft power. There is a recognition that we need to work differently. When you build the right relationships with operational colleagues, that stuff starts to flow quite naturally because these are often operational policy decisions in terms of how you want to make things work as opposed to lofty policy decisions. It takes cooperation, joint work and shared vision and a shared sense of what the evidence base says.' (Welsh Government senior civil servant)

> 'One of the nice things about this office [OCC] is no-one's exactly sure who we are. They know that we're official, but they're not really sure what

we do [see also the YJB's slippery, ambiguous role]. Some organisations have interacted with this before, but not all. That means that if they get an e-mail from us within an official context, they say, we'd better respond, which makes it very easy for us to reach out to a wide range of stakeholders, get them in a room and have a conversation.' (OCC senior policy officer)

However, others were more sceptical of the potential policy-influencing role of the OCC:

> 'People who do understand youth justice are not always in a position of power to make changes, for example, Children's Commissioners ... are they going to hold enough power to be able to make changes? Probably not because they'll be stopped by ministers. Ultimately ministers are doing what they think communities want, which is to punish children.' (AYM Chair)

Practitioner and third sector policy making

Understandings of policy making are traditionally shaped by a hierarchy within which policy formation is privileged over policy implementation (Hill and Hupe, 2015; see also Chapter 1). However, policy-making *contexts* are increasingly understood as much more complex, multi-faceted and multi-layered, particularly since early analysis of the 'policy implementation gap' (Gunn, 1978) has been supplemented by complex systems thinking informed by concepts of unpredictability, non-linearity and adaptability in policy-making contexts (Case and Haines, 2014). Consequently, it is essential to analyse youth justice policy making through a broader lens that considers the role of multiple different actors operating at different levels of the social system and YJS, including prioritising the much-neglected role and influence of practitioners. This analysis should not be limited to practitioner influence on the implementation of policy in practice, although understanding this stage remains essential, of course. For example, in the 'implementation' policy mode, discretion is exercised collectively (Fergusson, 2007) through *localised mediation and moderation of centralised policy prescriptions* by 'street-level bureaucrats' (Lipsky, 1980), typically practitioners and (practice/practitioner-led) third sector organisations,[4] as reflected by practitioner interviewees:

> 'Politicians may not be the only source of power. It's about the ability of managers and practitioners to help shape and put that policy into practice. We have some residual power in policy making. It's about minding the gap between national policy intention and localised practice. What goes on between is mediation and how things are interpreted, bastardised or improved by street-level bureaucrats and

> practitioners on the ground, interacting with young people.' (YJB board member, YOT manager)

> 'The work that AYJ does is that we're not pushing a particular service or intervention or [practitioner] organisations' ways of doing things when we do our policy influencing work. We're coming at it from the point of view of what is the right thing for children. Part of our work is actually recognising the fact that not everybody, there's not 100 per cent consensus about exactly the right way of doing things.' (AYJ Chair)

Adopting a broader, more holistic analytical lens for understanding *who* makes youth justice policy enables a move away from stereotypical, reductionist and dichotomised depictions of policy success as the responsibility of governmental actors and policy failure as the responsibility of practitioners. In particular, political cycles can contribute significantly to policy failure, with *politicians* not held accountable for policy outcomes because they have moved on/out (see also 'Churnover' section), being too easily attracted to the prospect of short-term results (see 'Political and financial short-termism' section), avoiding involvement in the messy, protracted and frustrating details of how policies work in practice and being more likely to get credit for legislation passed than for implementation problems avoided. As such, governmental actors can employ *mechanisms of governance* in policy-making contexts to avoid culpability for policy failure:

> 'I always liked the fact that if a policy looks good, it gets positive outcomes, then it's down to the credit of policy. If it goes wrong, it's down to implementation, it's just not implemented properly. My view about policy and ideas is any fool can have ideas, but it's actually how you translate those into practice.' (Senior academic)

A summary of the key contexts–mechanisms relationships identified when exploring the question of 'Who makes youth justice policy?' in relation to non-governmental actors is provided in Appendix 6.

How does youth justice policy making happen? Exploring contextualised mechanisms of stability and change

> 'Youth justice policy is this "thing" that's moving and fluid ... its more challenging by the nature of the environment.'
>
> (Senior HMIP official)

> 'When you ask the question, how does policy get made? The answer is it's a bloody miracle that anything gets worked through into practice.

You've got a legislative framework and various things that are set in stone, but then it just moves and shifts and migrates, sometimes at the behest of events.' (YJB Chief Executive)

Stability and change

The initial analysis of interview data in this chapter constitutes a scoping exercise, providing a general overview of the what, who and where of youth justice policy-making contexts framed as observable features: places, spaces, people and things (Greenhalgh and Manzano, 2021). What is now needed is a deeper dive into the *how* of policy making – the qualitative, explanatory, dynamic and relational features of these contexts that shape the mechanisms through which policy is made (Greenhalgh and Manzano, 2021). Stakeholder experiences of the nature of youth justice policy-making trajectories and processes indicate an ongoing complex, dynamic, contingent and often contradictory mix of stability and change (including change as instability) within and between policy contexts (macro, meso, micro). Interviewees experienced contextualised mechanisms promoting stability in the form of status quo, inertia, consensus and policy cycles (returning to previous constructions), alongside change manifested by policy cycles (as cyclical development, for example), gradual development, churnover and sudden, unpredicted and opportunistic change, all operating with varying levels of coherence, predictability and explicability in different contexts at different times. A senior academic articulated their view of macro-level political contexts characterised by simultaneous stability and change, indicative of the messy complexities and perennial conflict and ambivalence of youth justice policy making:

> 'The New Labour agenda wasn't particularly novel and, in most respects, was largely building on an emerging sense of punitiveness. The government recognised that it was a stick to beat the opposition with and something which was, at the time, popular with the media and certain sections of the electorate. They just determined to put some gloss on it and operationalise it in a way which would make it seem like it was completely new. Therefore, New Labour reforms were a bit contradictory. In one sense, they were simply a continuation of what was already happening. In another sense, there was a radical departure from the way in which the mechanisms of youth justice delivery changed and were mandated centrally.'

Gradual policy development as the practical reality of policy making

Senior stakeholders observed that the stability of youth justice policy trajectories was fostered by mechanisms of gradual development, reflecting the practical reality at the macro level. This finding is indicative of a discernible and explicable coherence to policy making, for example the cyclical nature of policy making and change (development):

> 'Bernard's cycle of juvenile justice[5] sees policy changes as circular. It's a reaction to what's gone previously and the problems that have emerged as a consequence of previous policy. It's at the heart of his idea of a cycle of justice because of the perceived problems of the current policy regime that leads to a perceived need for change in the opposite direction. So that gives policy making some kind of randomness.' (Senior academic)

In this sense, therefore, gradual policy development reflecting practical reality could be conceptualised as reflective of both continued stability and gradual change – a consistent and coherent mechanism of policy making operating across different contexts and levels of the social system. Taking Secure Schools as an example:

> 'There was quite a big ambition from the Policy Unit and the number 10 policy engine to scale up Secure Schools quickly. But this was where reality bit and we had to be honest about resourcing and about what they would look like. That's why in the end it was decided to consolidate the Medway School and if that was a successful model, to develop further Secure Schools. That was a really good example of ambition being tempered by reality … progress in development of youth justice policy is quite a gradual one.' (Government minister)

> 'The pace of decision making and the processes that we have to go through can feel quite painful at times, much slower than I've experienced in other departments. There's only so many bills that the government can take through Parliament in any given session. So Secure Schools took a couple years to find the right time and space and legislative vehicle for that to be possible. There is only so much bandwidth. We are trying to make a number of changes. We need to prioritise our efforts. We can't do everything.' (Senior civil servant)

Seeking common ground

The pursuit of *consensus* or, moreover, *common ground* between stakeholders within and between organisations (see also Chapter 7) presented as a mechanism facilitating gradual policy development. Stakeholders viewed this mechanism as promoting *collaboration*, *synergy* and *consistency* in (typically meso-level) contexts of stability, which ultimately encouraged change through gradual development:

'There's been a steady consensus as to how youth justice policy has developed over the last 10–15 years. The result of a lot of hard work by the YJB and others. We [government] had good ministers who understood the context of the issues. We didn't have any serious clashes on youth justice. A lot of the noisy politics has been taken out of youth justice, mainly because a lot of the policies are just working quietly in the background. If it ain't broke, don't fix it was my approach. We were very much on the same page. I hope that it withstands a change of government and change of party.' (Government minister)

'Put the foundations in place and hope they stay. The ideal is that they build and grow to enable a joint, agreed narrative and philosophy about making this place [YJS] the best place for children. Then there's a workforce that believes and does all of this stuff and drives it and works together … the foundation is the culture.' (Children's Commissioner)

Clarity and consistency

Similarly, clarity and consistency of approach and messaging was an identified mechanism for identifying common ground and reconciling tensions between stakeholders and different agendas in policy-making contexts:

'With Child First, the YJB Chair was worried about reputational impact. The government certainly wouldn't want to be in the space of talking about Child First. At the same time, they were talking about toe rags beating up old ladies. The YJB decided collectively that they wanted to go in the direction of Child First because it set out clearly what the aims of the overall system should be. Robert Buckland [Justice Minister] started to use that concept quite regularly. So it was a hook. We didn't push too hard but used it when there was a need to fall back on something. Then we just filtered it out from there. We got the pace right and we were ready just to row back if needed, but it has changed things. It is a mindset piece rather than a sudden policy shift.' (YJB Chief Executive)

'Churnover' of staff

A key mechanism influencing the short- and long-term pace, consistency and predictability of policy-making stability and change was identified by several key stakeholders as turnover and 'churn' of staff in policy-making positions (hereafter 'churnover'). Loss of key staff was identified as an enabler of, but mainly a barrier and challenge to policy stability and change/development and to consistent, consensual policy making. Churnover as a policy-making barrier could be predictable with a long lead-in time (for example, planned measures to address austerity, staff and governments reaching the end of their tenure, staff/organisational funding ending) or unpredictable and relatively sudden (staff resigning, being sacked, being moved into and out of policy-making positions, snap elections, for example). Churnover was consistently highlighted as a mechanism influencing the pace and direction of policy-making trajectories, serving to stall, slow or speed up development/change. For example, churnover influenced policy-making trajectories through shifts in ministerial agenda (precipitating sudden changes) or the need to re/educate new staff (necessitating the stalling or slowing of progress). Consequently, staff churnover (like financial short-termism) contributes to youth justice policy-making contexts of discernibly 'stable change' (gradual development) and 'predictable unpredictability' (consistent and expected instability):

> 'Sometimes you take maybe three steps forward in conversations about development and policy growth. Then it's back to the drawing board because you're needing to reignite conversations with someone new and that's from senior level within ministry departments. In the time I've been involved, what has there been, five justice ministers?' (Senior civil servant)

> 'The lead-in time for a policy is at least six months just to get it out to consultation, it's crazy. Then probably some of those people will have moved on. Then somebody else picks it up and you get a different view again.' (AYM Chair)

> 'One of the things that's bedevilled justice youth justice in the last 20 years has been the turnover of ministers. When it comes to more serious changes in direction in policy, you need ministers to do that. The danger is if ministers aren't in post for long enough, you haven't got anyone there to understand the policy.' (YJB Chair)

Several current and former YJB officials highlighted the impact of ministerial churnover and agenda change on the YJB,[6] most notably on its ability to fulfil its statutory advisory role to government in a consistent, coherent and impactful way:

> 'When you see a change of minister, you can't guarantee they're gonna have the same appetite and interest as the previous minister. Civil servants say that when the minister changed or was reshuffled, they went around looking for projects to kill just because if you kill a project, you free up resources for the new minister to play with, because they will have their own interests and own concerns. I call it the murder of the innocents every time there's a new minister.' (YJB board member)

> 'The turnover of ministers is hugely frustrating because you can only make limited policy progress. I don't think I'd really appreciated how much policy is driven by the whims of ministers and what their particular interest or cute pet projects might be. We're constantly having to navigate that and second guess where the opportunities might lie, depending on what those ministers want.' (Senior YJB official)

Other stakeholders expressed the contrasting view that ministerial churnover could actually benefit (or at least, not harm) YJB policy making because it served to insulate them from intense and unnecessary scrutiny. In turn, any negative impact could be moderated by *consensus of policy agenda and approach* within government and through the *stability and continuity of the YJB* in relation to both agenda and staffing:

> 'Swift turnover meant less pressure on the YJB because ministers just didn't have time; no sooner had they bedded in, than they were off again. We [government and YJB] benefitted from the fact that there was a consensus actually. Go back to the Ken Clarke [Justice Secretary]–Tom McNally [YJB Chair] relationship, then the Davids [Lidington, Gauke], Truss and me, we all had broadly similar views about youth justice, which meant a period of continuity in that area. I don't detect my successor has decided to radically depart from that.' (Government minister)

> 'I had an introductory meeting with the Youth Justice Minister a couple of weeks ago. It was in his first week of office and he's no longer the minister. His question to me was, what do you give me that my departmental civil servants can't? I said that we [YJB] give longevity of perspective because we are building our view from an evidence and practice base. Our advice develops incrementally, so it won't suddenly change or be driven by fiscal events, parliamentary time scale, the appointment of a new minister or a general election.' (YJB Chief Executive)

An AYJ Chair viewed stability and relative *lack of churn in the civil service as beneficial* to their organisation's development of constructive, empathetic and consistent policy-influencing relationships:

> 'Over the last few years where there's been such kind of political turmoil from a government perspective, so it's been crucial to us [AYJ] for being influential to maintain really strong relationships with senior officials [SPADs]. You still get a churn, but it's not in such a rapid, unplanned way as mood changes in ministers. We have regular catch-ups with

> the head of the Youth Justice Policy Unit [MoJ] and other officials, where we try and emphasise how we can be helpful to them. We're not just there to critique what they're planning to do. We try and get kind of ahead of the curve. Rather than responding to a consultation document once it's already part-baked, we will try and get wind that they're working on something and we'll say we might be able to help you with that.' (AYJ Chair)

Chaotic youth justice policy making? Macro, meso, micro, messy

Youth justice policy making can be understood as chaotic in the sense of it being sudden, non-linear, unpredictable, unstable, messy and even random and inexplicable (see also Case and Haines 2014). Analyses of the interviews identified several contexts and mechanisms indicative of chaotic policy making in the YJS, for example sudden change in government/ministerial agenda, the impact of external events, political and financial short-termism, opaque policy drivers/incoherent policy making and opportunism/instrumentalism. The challenge in this context of chaotic complexity remains that of the book as a whole – to discern a sense of coherence and explicability to youth justice policy making … to identify 'patterns in the noise'.

Sudden and random policy change

Experts recounted their experiences of sudden policy change as indicative of *instability* in policy-making contexts following *changes of government* and as *responsive to ministerial agenda*:

> 'The change of policy can be just overnight with a change of government. The slate can be wiped clean. Following the 2010 election, when the Coalition came in, I remember being in the Welsh government with quite a big Home Office crime team there doing face-to-face work with community safety partnerships. The day after the election, they started clearing their desks. They were gone! Their policy of doing things was just swept away.' (YJB Chair)

> 'New Labour established governance. Ministers and governments came and went, but there was a recognition that although they could set the key direction of travel, they didn't know the mechanics or the history. But they could introduce new policies because there were people around them [civil servants] who stayed in their job. Expertise in the subject area was replaced by a civil service much more responsive to the whims of politicians, which increased the potential

for politicians to determine what happened in particular policy areas very quickly. Policy became more random and could change more quickly.' (Senior academic)

Sudden change due to external events

A significant flaw in the reductionist, linear and deterministic 'Policy Cycle Model' (see Chapter 1) is that the construction of policy can be influenced by unpredictable/unpredicted external events, rendering policy making inherently uncertain and unstable. Often, these events can be beyond a government's control and outside of its agenda, leading to sharp discontinuities and illogical decisions (Institute for Government, 2011). A notable example of a macro-level 'event' that undermined the UK government's coherent position on youth justice policy is the *socio-economic austerity* that engulfed the industrialised Western world around 2010, necessitating sweeping and immediate change, such as service and resource retraction and rationalisation (see Chapter 4):

> 'Austerity had a massive impact on YOTs. So while perhaps children's services or health and probation would have seen a cut in their funding because they were all the statutory funders to a YOT partnership, the YOT felt it five times because we had five statutory partners because we were a multi-agency partnership … losing great swathes of practitioners and certainly losing our more specialist roles.' (Senior civil servant)

> 'One thing we [YJB] did in terms of changing our approach was we slimmed down massively. I inherited an organisation of 230 people, and I left an organisation of 100. Some of that was because we've moved some work into the custody service, with significant efficiencies in there. Also, we've concentrated on getting money out to the frontline, so money was being spent on children rather than on bureaucratic overhead. And we focus some of our attention on a number of priority projects.' (YJB Chief Executive)

A more recent, unpredictable macro-level event was the global coronavirus (COVID-19) epidemic, which exerted an extremely significant influence on the nature of youth justice, most notably at the operational level:

> 'COVID threw a blanket over everything. The fact is that crime rates were suddenly totally different [dramatically reduced]. … Government eyes were totally elsewhere, which meant that we didn't have the terrible incident that then would evince a punitive response or quite sudden changes in policy. My role as Lord Chancellor changed almost

overnight from being largely strategic to being mainly operational. I had no choice other than to become an operational Secretary of State, which meant that I had to have a day-to-day understanding of what was going on in the estate.' (Government minister)

Political and financial short-termism and precarity

The sudden, unpredictable and unstable nature of youth justice policy-making contexts can be catalysed and exacerbated by political and financial short-termism (see also 'cyclical policy-making' discussion earlier in this chapter), a view articulated by stakeholders from different policy-making contexts:

> 'When something happens, an individual event or general climate or bidding war between politicians, you suddenly find that although you were achieving short-term gains by doing things under the radar, you weren't actually altering the fundamental climate within which policy is shaped, and your own achievements are like houses built in sand, they get washed away terribly quickly. That's the fundamental conundrum.' (YJB Chief Executive)

> 'You get a whole separate policy-making cycle around fiscal events. When there's a spending review, the department will be asked about their spending plans and say what it is they would like to achieve in return for the spending settlement. What kind of policy can we give them that will be appealing to the spending review teams in the Treasury. It's not really very strategically aligned. It tends to be much more, much more kind of transactional than that.' (YJB senior official)

The instability of policy making engendered by political short-termism and governmental cycles is exacerbated in non-governmental policy actor organisations (for example in practice contexts) by financial short-termism and precarity, whereby funding available to organisations working in policy-making contexts is often unpredictable in amount, frequency, duration and certainty. This situation has become so commonplace across the youth justice sector, particularly since austerity hit and support services retracted, that it can be characterised as a 'stable instability' or a 'predictable precarity' that constrains ambition, long-term planning and organisational resourcing/capacity:

> 'Finances drive a lot of policies, so if you're wanting to push things that are going to cost money or which stop people making cuts, you're gonna have a hard time. In times when there isn't that pressure, people become more open to change. But they close down in times of crisis.' (AYM Chair)

> 'In terms of policy, money may give you the authorising environment to do things, but what stops us is the fact that those outcomes are not going to be seen in the political four-year period. It takes political will to take a risk … harder in the prevention and early intervention space because you can't prove the things you've stopped. We had to shift the thinking of politicians from statutory must does to show that you can spend money in different ways and achieve the same outcomes.' (Children's Commissioner)

Political and financial short-termism can affect the *quality of the policy-related output*, according to professional experiences:

> 'The money is only guaranteed for a certain amount of time. For example, we [YJB] had to produce 15 Key Elements of Effective Practice guides and only got two years to deliver those and do a quality assurance process, because the money then dries up and I don't have the project after that. If I was given more time, I would have done a proper consultation, having more conversations with those who had to deliver it.' (YJB board member)

> 'We're not resourced to be able to take the step back and do the thinking and that's why all of our work is often about playing that brokering role, making sure that people who do have the time and space and specialism are the stations in the main. To do that requires a lot of sustained investment and support and resilience and hope and not giving up.' (Senior civil servant)

Opaque and incoherent policy making

The *opacity and incoherence* of policy-making processes and the influences upon them, which can have the appearance of chaos and randomness, was emphasised by stakeholders with direct professional lived experience of a range of policy-based, strategic and practice development:

> 'Policy initiatives and new directives … it's not always clear what the driver is, what the principles are. This is something we [HMIP] and the YJB need to get a grip of. If you were to ask ten YOTs, for example, what's the policy driver behind out-of-court disposals, you'd probably get ten different answers. That can't be right, because if it's a different policy driver, then that means they're doing different things. Policies can be introduced, often without the rationale for that being clear and that then can lead to a real messy landscape.' (Senior HMIP official)

> 'Reductions in custody for children … at different times there have been deliberate articulations of that, but equally there's been government policy quite antithetical to and at odds with the policy. Home Office and MoJ policies and guidance have gone against that, and you get these contrasting, bifurcated messages and systems. It's Janus-faced policy making at the government-level and is fairly incoherent.' (YJB board member, YOT manager)

> 'You had all these different policies [circa Crime and Disorder Act 1998] and where they came from … there's lots of different routes. I can't remember any of them being carefully thought through apart from the construction of YOTs. The rest of them were very hand-to-mouth. Referral Orders popped out of left field. There was a lot of chaos. The [YJB] policy-making process was just compromise. Make it up on the hoof. Policy making was reactive and unplanned.' (Senior academic)

Opportunistic and instrumental policy making

Experts perceived seemingly chaotic, random and opaque policy making as driven by opportunism and instrumentalism in certain instances, thus having discernible and coherent strategic foundations and objectives ('patterns in the noise'), without necessarily being predictable:

> 'I'd love to say there was a beautifully worked up strategy as to how we're [YJB] gonna effect change, but that would be a lie. Where there's a direction of travel, it's a lot of grabbing an opportunity such as when there was a new Prime Minister.' (YJB Chief Executive)

> 'I had an opportunity at the YJB, completely spontaneously with a minister who was doing his rounds talking to staff. I took the opportunity to ask him a question about a particular issue and as a result of that conversation, just off the cuff, not planned, he went away, made a couple of calls, talked to a couple of people. He telephoned me the following week and said just let me check I've got this right, is this the issue? And it was done, and there was a new set of guidance and new policy went out. So a new policy being introduced to another department as a result of something that had been identified in the youth justice practice field. It was a quick win.' (YJB board member)

The chaotic and unpredictable nature of policy-making contexts was perceived as beneficial at times (like governmental churnover), especially when it drove mechanisms of opportunism and instrumentalism that facilitated relationship building, networking and associated policy making. For example, several stakeholders discussed the instrumental importance of 'picking your moments' and identifying 'windows of opportunity' and 'fertile periods' in policy-making contexts, particularly in terms of relationships with government:

> 'On 24 hours' notice, Gordon Brown had become Prime Minister, and I'm sitting beside him in a round table in Downing Street with a range of folks, the parents of children have been murdered, children's charities, police etc. It's performative politics because nothing of policy substance particularly came out of it. But that opportunity to sense where alliances might emerge, the relationship building that went on was important, recognising that we could be allies of what they needed to do and they could be allies of what we needed to do.' (YJB Chair)

> 'There are fertile periods within the relationship [with government and MoJ]. Some things are harder to land now, and some might be easy to land in a month's time or a year's time. There are points where there is no point labouring a particular policy area that you would like to see delivered because it's not going to happen and you're better off not spending the capital on an area that is not going to get a landing. An example of that would probably be about age of criminal responsibility. The trick is being able to recognise and gauge when to have which conversation with whom and when not to.' (Senior YJB official)

> 'You could see government being preoccupied by events. That was our [YJB] window of opportunity where we were able to articulate Child First without any undue interference from government change and chaos in government has enabled us to drive that.' (Senior YJB official)

A summary of the key contexts–mechanisms relationships identified when exploring the question of 'How does youth justice policy making happen?' is provided in Appendix 7.

Conclusion: contexts–mechanisms relationships in policy making

This chapter began the analyses of the expert stakeholder interview data in relation to the project RQs[7] (see also Chapter 2) and sought to gain a better understanding of youth justice policy making. The detail and nature of the expert feedback make it both undesirable and infeasible to address each RQ in isolation. Instead, it has become more appropriate and informative to consider interrelationships between the questions and how they can be responded to in terms of the relationships between the contexts and mechanisms of youth justice policy making.

In the opening thematic analysis section addressing 'What is youth justice policy making?' (RQs 1, 3, 4), experts reported their understandings of policy and policy-making contexts as complex, contested, multi-layered, multi-systemic and fragmented. These policy-making contexts were characterised and populated by mechanisms of conflict and ambiguity in organisational and professional identity, role and status, which functioned as barriers/challenges to policy making. However, contexts also contained mechanisms to address these barriers, including universal policy, shared objectives and seeking alignment, thus serving as enablers/facilitators to policy making.

When offering their perceptions and experiences of 'Who makes youth justice policy?' (RQs 2, 3, 4), experts identified influential policy-making contexts as inhabited by governmental actors (for example government, ministers, politicians, SPADS, civil servants) and non-governmental actors (such as YJB officials, OCC officials, youth justice managers/practitioners, third sector coalition professionals). In governmental contexts, the dead hand influence of Number 10 and right-wing newspaper media was identified as a mechanism that served as a barrier and challenge to effective policy making, as was the retraction of civil service power (for example through governmental agenda, resource constraints and deprofessionalisation). The steering of civil servants by politicians and SPADs was seen as both a barrier to and an enabler of policy making, while governmental receptiveness/openness to being steered, advised and challenged was identified as a mechanism enabling and facilitating youth justice policy making. Non-governmental actors attested to experiences of policy change through relationships characterised by more equitable power dynamics wherein they felt able to exercise soft power, broker policy-making relationships and advise, support and challenge governmental policy (strategically and diplomatically), such as through the localised mediation and moderation of centralised policy. A consistently identified barrier/challenge to non-governmental policy influence, however, was the contested, ambiguous and often threatened identity and role of the YJB, although this ambiguity was also seen to offer opportunities for policy-making influence.

The final thematic analysis section explored the contexts and mechanisms around how youth justice policy is made (RQs 3, 4, 5). Stakeholders again perceived and experienced complex contexts of policy making characterised by simultaneous stability and change, persistent conflict and ambivalence and frequent instability, short-termism and precarity. In these contexts, mechanisms of policy making were characterised as cyclical and gradual, often mediated and moderated by political and practical realities. Certain mechanisms were identified as enabling/facilitating more effective policy making in these contexts, notably the pursuit of consensus and a common ground and adopting clarity and consistency in the policy-making approach and messaging. Policy-making contexts (such as political agendas) were also frequently viewed as chaotic, random, unstable and/or liable to sudden change, for example due to a change in government, staff 'churnover' or unpredicted external events. These contextual characteristics tended to precipitate barriers/challenges to effective policy making such as political and financial short-termism and opaque and incoherent policy-making processes. In contrast, however, they also produced more strategically designed responses that could enable policy making, such as encouraging mechanisms to re-educate (new) colleagues and those grounded in opportunism and instrumentalism during fertile policy-making periods, particularly for non-governmental actors.

6

Professional identities, expertise and evidence

The previous chapter identified the general contexts and mechanisms of youth justice policy making, exploring what youth justice policy is, who makes it and how it is made. Analyses established that youth justice policy develops in socially constructed contexts that are complex, contested, multi-layered, multi-systemic and fragmented. These complex contexts foster mechanisms of policy making characterised by conflict and ambiguity of identity role and status, alongside attempts to cohere complexity and fragmentation through universal policy, shared objectives and seeking alignment. In terms of who is involved in youth justice policy making, stakeholder feedback indicated central roles for *governmental policy actors* (government ministers, politicians, senior policy advisers [SPADs], civil servants), adopting roles that oscillate between steering and influencing others based on agenda and expertise and being steered/influenced by other governmental actors and external dead hand influences from Number 10 and right-wing newspaper media). Stakeholders also identified roles of policy influence for *non-governmental policy actors*, most notably the Youth Justice Board (YJB) and third sector coalitions employing mechanisms of advice, support and soft power, the Office of the Children's Commissioner (OCC) identifying problems, brokering solutions and utilising soft power and managers/practitioners mediating and moderating centralised policy to fit local contexts. Finally, analysis of how policy making occurs identified an overarching context of stability–change and conflict–ambivalence promoting mechanisms of change characterised by gradual development, a cyclical nature and clarity and consistency of approach. The context of constant staff 'churnover' necessitating agenda change and re-education of colleagues typified broader policy making that was often chaotic, random and sudden in their trajectories of change. Mechanisms identified as operating in these chaotic contexts included changes of government (influencing agenda change), unpredicted and influential external events, political and financial short-termism and precarity, opacity and incoherence and opportunity and instrumentalism in policy making.

This chapter builds on these lessons by exploring the contexts and mechanisms of youth justice policy making in more detail, focusing on the *relational* nature of contextualised policy making. It focuses on how *relational contexts* influence the identities of policy-making organisations and professionals, including the *expert identities* often prioritised when soliciting and generating *evidence* and implementing evidence-based policy and practice in the Youth Justice System (YJS).[1] Analyses implicate identities and associated expertise as complex social constructions that are dynamic (also contingent and contested) in their trajectories and interpretations by identity holders themselves and by others assigning identities to them, as always, within and between macro-, meso- and micro-level contexts. As such, organisational and professional identities can be relational and dynamic constructive influences on youth justice policy making. This chapter identifies macro-level *policy discourses* as representing the identity of governments, with analyses of the sustained populist punitiveness discourse contrasted with the hybrid and conflicted prevention–support–diversion discourse emerging from the 'new youth justice' and the distinct 'dragonised' identity of youth justice policy in Wales. This is followed by discussion of governmental open-mindedness and receptiveness to civil servant influence in meso-level relational contexts when making youth justice policy, which challenges dominant discourses of governmental prescriptiveness and agenda as shaping policy. The chapter moves on to a detailed exploration of the policy-making identity, role, status and influence of the YJB, exploring the organisation's role as a policy influencer and as a strategic influencer. There is particular focus on the evolution of the YJB's policy-making identity from managerialist prescription to engaging with and *empowering practitioners as experts*. The penultimate thematic section explores the policy-making role of *practitioners as experts by experience* in the youth justice sector and as 'street-level bureaucrats' engaged in bottom-up policy making through the *localised mediation and moderation* of government policy. Finally, there is an exposition of the broader role of *experts, expertise and experience* in youth justice policy making, including discussion of the central role of evidence in shaping policy.

Identities as constructive influences on youth justice policy making

A range of expert stakeholders[2] suggested that organisational and professional/individual identities situated at different levels of the social system exert a contextualised, constructive influence on youth justice policy making. As such, identities functioned as both dynamic, relational *contexts* within which mechanisms of policy making operate (for example mechanisms of open-mindedness, insecurity, resilience, challenge) and as dynamic *mechanisms* of policy influence in their own right (such as where ministerial personalities influenced political agendas). For example, in the political sphere, it is possible to discern the constructive influence of macro-level *political identity* of government, illustrated by *policy discourse* (see also Chapter 3) and *political agenda*, and meso/micro-level individual *ministerial identity*.

Policy discourse as governmental identity

Several experts acknowledged the strategic/instrumental, dynamic and contested nature and influence of policy discourse on youth justice policy making. This influence was often typified by *conflict and ambivalence* (see Case, 2018/21) between the political pull of populist punitiveness and polyfurcated 'new youth justice' policy-making trajectories of prevention, support, diversion and alternatives to custody (see Chapters 3 and 4). For example, senior YJB officials reflected on the punitive–prevention discourse, conflict and bifurcation, notably in relation to political pressure being placed on the police:

> 'When the two major political parties started battling for the high ground of law and order policy [in the 1990s], Labour introduced a good model alongside a lot of punitive rhetoric, which was hard to resist. There was a political culture of pressures during that period for more emphasis on being tough on crime rather than tough on the causes. The drift was all wrong. Operationally, the police were paid bonuses if they hit their numerical targets. Could anyone be surprised that would have perverse consequences?' (YJB Chair, senior academic)

> 'There was a very clear policy change later [circa mid-2000s] in terms of police being instructed to increase arrests and prosecutions. The easy way to do that was to prosecute all youngsters they encountered to improve their statistics. In the early days of the Coalition [circa 2010], there was a move in the opposite direction, building on Labour policy change from about 2007 onwards, when there was a real focus on what can we do practically to reduce the number of outputs? Everything had to be pitched in terms of support and prevention. Government moved towards investing in diversion and tentative thinking about alternatives to custody.' (YJB Chief Executive)

Other experts noted the disconnect/rupture between political discourse and evidence in youth justice policy-making contexts, reflective of the dominance of political and media agenda and instrumentalism over evidence-based policy:

> 'In terms of youth policy, two or three strands of political thought knocking around in British politics trace their roots back to liberalism, conservatism and socialism. Whichever party of the day is in power, they tend to base what they want the world to look like on one of those flavours. But there are tendencies, and the evidence can take a back seat.' (YJB Cymru Chair)

'One of the frustrating challenges at the moment [2023] is that politicians still assume that the public and victims wanna be tough on crime, whereas I don't think that evidence suggests that. People have enough common sense that they want us [YJB] to adopt an approach that works. The ridiculous scenario with politicians is that they guess and misjudge what they think the public wants. Then you throw in the media. It's not in the media's interest to get rid of crime.' (YJB senior official)

The dynamic, contested and contingent (socially constructed) nature of political discourse in youth justice policy-making contexts was further reflected by a YJB Chair who had experienced within-party divergence in the political/governmental/ministerial identities and agendas of different Conservative justice secretaries:

'One of my Conservative colleagues [Grayling, Minister of Justice] said, as long as there was one more prisoner in prison at the end of Parliament than at the beginning, that is my job. Conservatives are frightened to death of any reform which seems soft on the criminal. It makes it very difficult to get almost any reform through. However, I worked with Michael Gove as Minister of Justice, and he was keen on education as one of the key counters to recidivism and failure.'

Government open-mindedness and receptiveness to civil servant influence

The perceived (micro-level) constructive influence of individual ministers on the nature and direction of youth justice policy introduces the possibility that political identity and discourse is neither intractable nor deterministic at the macro level of politics. Indeed, civil servant experts reported experiences of governmental and ministerial open-mindedness/receptiveness to external, expert influence (see also the discussion of civil servants steering government in Chapter 5) and a relative *lack of predetermined political agenda* during policy formulation processes. However, the policy-making influence of this open-mindedness was always tempered by political and practical realities, including established political agenda, policy direction and resource constraints. When recounting his experience of conducting his review of the YJS in 2016, Taylor stated that

'[i]t was an incredibly open-ended review really. The Secretary of State Gove said, we'd like you to evaluate the YJS because bits of it don't feel right to me, but I don't know enough about this to know what to do about it. I was gonna need to talk to an awful lot of people and get people's views to really build up a body of evidence and interest.

> But I had a remarkable amount of freedom in terms of what I could propose. Also, instinctively, I had to take into account that this was a Conservative government, so going with the grain of government was important. Making proposals and using language that Conservative politicians will find antagonistic had to be avoided, because that won't land, so there is a political aspect to it.'

The degree to which this political open-mindedness could be tempered and constrained by political, financial and practical realities was elucidated by a former SPAD who had been instrumental in formulating the government's official response to the Taylor Review:

> 'We had a pretty free reign to decide what advice we put up to ministers. We could give an honest view. I saw a lot more mileage in the idea of Secure Schools, and we gave that a positive write-up. Perhaps the rest of the agenda didn't get the same degree of attention. In order to translate a set of recommendations by an independent reviewer into official government policy, that needs a commitment to government spending, potentially to new legislation, to new guidance. It needs activity by government to make their recommendations happen.'

Expert reflections on the Taylor Review indicated that civil servants can have a degree of policy-making influence through the nature of their relationships with government, which can oscillate between *steering and being steered* instrumentally by the political agenda (see also Chapter 5). This constant underlying tension and dynamic, contingent and fluctuating relationship was reported by a senior Ministry of Justice (MoJ) civil servant when explaining that

> '[u]ltimately, the way big things [policies] happen is through advice to ministers and ministerial decisions. Submissions go to ministers setting out options for changes, with advisory recommendations. More time than I'd care to think about is spent working with my team to hone advice and make sure it's as clear and sharp as possible.'

Welsh youth justice identity: child-centred policy discourse

The dynamic nature of political discourse and policy-making identity is illustrated by the so-called 'dragonised' context of Welsh youth justice (see Chapters 3 and 4). Wales has a unique, partially devolved policy context and disparate youth justice ideology and identity (compared to England) due to an embedded national commitment to social justice and children's rights-based social policy for children (see also Chapter 5). The Welsh experience exemplifies how a localised[3] (actually national) youth justice policy-making identity can evolve in contexts within and outside of the YJS through mechanisms designed to seek consensus and common ground among like-minded professionals. For example, in the expert evaluations of two senior Welsh professionals, there is a discernible difference between the *national youth justice policy identities* (for example approaches, discourses) of the English-based (UK) and Welsh (devolved) governments:

> 'In Wales, the YJB in England [circa 2010] was seen as more part of this punitive neo-liberal managerialist "thing", whereas the experience of in Wales was more part of the fabric of society and part of all chipping in to try and help kids. I describe it as a bridging translation role for youth justice. Or another bridge between UK policy and Welsh government.' (YJB Cymru Chair)

> 'We [Welsh policy makers] are conscious that from a youth justice point of view we don't have a political leg to stand on in terms of driving change, but there's a need for doing things differently and Wales because the context is different. The devolved elements that sit in the Welsh government are so fundamental to the delivery of justice systems across the entirety of the criminal justice sector. Welsh government has a clearly articulated position that is child centred. There's a clear values base for us to draw on when we think about how to apply that in the youth justice space, in particular, when we report into the [Welsh government] Minister for Social Justice.' (Welsh Government senior civil servant)

These views were supported by the experiences of a Children's Commissioner (also a YJB board member) regarding the development of the Child First principle, who believed that "Welsh government are comfortable with Child First. It speaks to the Welsh government's commitment to the UN Convention on the Rights of the Child [UNCRC]. I don't get the same sense from the UK government about what we're doing."

Cohering policy agendas in Wales

According to a representative of the OCC, the evolution, sustainability and clarity of the Welsh youth justice identity and vision is a product of a universal children's rights policy that engendered shared agendas/understandings (see Chapter 5), which then help to reconcile inter-agency tensions:

> 'The children's rights framework that we all operate within Wales really helps to bring [policy] cohesion. Children need the right support,

> as well as maintaining their other rights under the UNCRC. The measure [Rights of Children and Young Persons (Wales) Measure 2011] is helpful in terms of actually refocusing the vision on children. It is unique. They don't have that in England.'

Mechanisms of *consensus* and *seeking common ground* (see also Chapters 5 and 7) were consistently cited as helpful, consolidating constructive influences for fostering shared understandings, agendas and identities across a range of youth justice policy-making contexts in Wales. The constructive influence of pursuing consensus and common ground as a mechanism of policy development and change was seen as facilitated in Wales by bespoke national, multi-context, multi-agency structures such as the Wales Youth Justice Advisory Panel and strategies such as the 'All Wales youth offending strategy' and the 'Blueprint' (see Chapters 3 and 4):

> 'The Youth Justice Blueprint materialised at the end of the [Welsh government/YJB] Children and Young People First strategy. But the Blueprint is the first time that we were proactive as opposed to reactive in policy making. We were very clear from the start that it needed to be a joint approach that took that joint alignment and formalised it. It would never work if it was the Welsh government saying is, here's our vision, do you agree?' (Welsh government Crime and Justice Unit senior civil servant)

The unique, bifurcated Welsh context of youth justice policy making

Mechanisms of seeking consensus/common ground enabled the development of a national shared policy identity in Wales, facilitated by the Welsh policy-making context itself, notably its unique, poorly understood, geographically small and marginalised nature relative to the English context. Stakeholders perceived this nuanced Welsh political/policy context as facilitating *closer working relationships* between stakeholders and, ultimately, creating *relational contexts* within which shared identities, agendas and ownership of youth justice policy could flourish, sometimes *under the radar* in a context largely ignored by the English-based UK government (see Chapter 7 for further discussion):

> 'The YJB is an unusual beast because it's not like most quangos and it's got this strategic element. But they didn't like it "when Taffy gets too big for his boots". So you [Wales] can do what you want to be honest, as long as you're not making too much trouble. It gave us a lot of freedom to pursue policy change, but in ways which make the YJS work well in Wales.' (YJB Cymru Chair)

> 'The policy direction Charlie Taylor wanted to go in was to raise everything up from operational to strategic engagement. He felt that the YJB was far too in the weeds. A lot of that stuff had been going on in Wales at the time. Innovative, different things were being driven forward and tensions existed. Wales was maybe seen as a maverick, doing its own thing. Maybe there were things that Wales was doing that could be a benefit to the wider organisation and there wasn't that synergy with it.' (YJB board member)

A summary of the key contexts–mechanisms relationships identified when exploring the issue of 'Policy discourses as governmental identity' is provided in Appendix 8.

YJB policy making: identity, role and status

> 'We [YJB] have got the body [YJS], and we are at the heart or the brain of that body. Every time it beats, it has an instant impact on us. As you go out towards the other government departments, out to the MoJ, out to practitioners, you'll feel the effect of that beating heart, but it's not gonna be as instant as when you're next to it and feeling every single oscillation.' (YJB Chair)

Chapter 5 identified differences in the ways that the YJB and its staff self-identify as 'experts', particularly in comparison to the perceived non-expert, generalist and transient status, role and identity of civil servants. This expert identity, dynamic in its trajectory over time since the YJB's inception in 2000, exists at the individual professional (micro) level and the broader organisational (meso, macro) levels. In particular, it encompasses how the YJB's advisory role and identity as an arm's-length, independent non-departmental public body organisation is perceived by itself and others. Accordingly, the YJB's policy-making identity is now analysed in more depth, initially focusing on the organisation's general *policy-making role*, then exploring its specific role as both a *policy influencer* (for example during the contentious period of *managerialist prescription* in the first decade of the 2000s) and as a *strategic influencer*, before concluding with an evaluation of whether the YJB's policy influence is *waning or changing* in extent and nature.

YJB as policy maker: steered or steering?

> 'The YJB is an arm's-length body. It's an influencer of YOTs [Youth Offending Teams] and an influencer of policy.'
>
> (YJB senior official)

A former YJB Chair recalled his experiences of the early, independent policy influence of the YJB, alongside his perceptions of *civil servants being led/steered by* the political agenda as a possible barrier to policy making:

> 'I made it clear that I was in the job as long as I was able to function properly and do what Parliament asked me to do. But I can't honestly say that I was never directly influenced on what we did in terms of policy. I had regular meetings with SPADs, who I found cautious and conservative, but it may have been that for the individuals involved there was a certain element of dealing with permanent stuff. However, that was difficult to drive at government-level and to reconcile with the sense of urgency for [policy] change at YJB-level.'

When analysing the nature of the YJB's policy-making role subsequent to the tenure of the previous interviewee, a YJB Chief Executive offered his perspective of the YJB role as a policy-making bridge:

> 'One vision was that the YJB should be a buffer between the youth justice sector and central government. I replaced it with my idea of the YJB being a bridge between the whole series of different systems that actually needed to work more closely. A bridge between children's services and criminal justice services, a bridge between England and Wales, a bridge between the frontline and policy making.'

Another expert (YJB Chair) viewed the YJB's policy-making role as strategic, instrumental and YJB agenda-driven, rather than politically steered:

> 'I saw my role as an opportunity to push forward the agenda from the Taylor Review. The YJB shouldn't exist for the sake of it. It should exist in order to fulfil certain functions. The starting point should be the needs of the children and the functions and structures that need to be in place in order to support those children.'

A YJB official and senior academic suggested that there is a degree of bias and a *lack of expertise* among current (circa 2023) board members, contributing to a *lack of clarity* in the organisation's policy and strategy direction (see also later in this chapter):

> 'The most senior people in the YJB have come from a secure background. They've not come from a community background, yet the YJB is a community-facing organisation. I don't think the way that things can operate in custody, where you might move people around into different roles, works to the same extent in an organisation where

you need depth of expertise to effectively engage with strategic and operational partners. Immediately pre-COVID, the annual report was a bit more philosophical, visionary, but it didn't actually say anything very much about what the YJB was doing, what it thought or the direction it wanted to go in.'

YJB as policy maker: managerialist and prescriptive

According to Whitehead and Arthur (2011: 476), 'the Government's insistence on micro-managing the YJS was viewed as counter-productive; as over-riding practitioner discretion with an excessively prescriptive, inflexible and graduated (escalating) approach'. Consequently, any detailed analyses of the YJB's policy-making identity and role would not be complete without examining the initial period (context) of 'new youth justice' managerialist prescription regarding how policy should be realised in practice that was introduced by the Crime and Disorder Act 1998 (CDA 1998) (see Chapter 3). As with all constructive influences on youth justice policy making, the impact of managerialist strategies and prescriptive mechanisms was experienced in dynamic, contested and contingent ways by expert stakeholders. Experts perceived the YJB–government policy-making relationship and the YJB's prescriptive role and subsequent identity as itself prescribed and steered by government:

> 'For the first decade of the YJB, the government was like God. The YJB were there to make sure the local authorities and youth justice practitioners would be tamed. The selection of the first Chair and the first Chief Executive was influenced very heavily by government, based on who they could trust. The YJB role was to take the policy outlines developed by New Labour and operationalise them in a way which used the discretion for local players and mechanisms for ensuring the targets determined the way the interventions were delivered.' (Senior academic)

Reflecting on this growing YJB prescriptiveness as constraining practice expertise and discouraging a new influx of expertise, Professor Kevin Haines told me that

> '[p]eople were entering YOTs to work with no previous experience of youth justice and were just doing what Asset told them to do. Experienced YOT workers were being constrained by the Key Elements of Effective Practice. Movement away from this prescriptive working culture was difficult, very much against the flow of the stream.' (Haines in Case, 2018/21)

However, expert YJB stakeholders who had worked in the formative years of the YJB and YOTs emphasised the *necessity of managerialist prescription* for evolving the newly reconstructed YJS. They also pointed to this managerialism as both indicative of the YJB's early *policy-making influence* within government and fostering early YJB resistance to challenge from practitioners:

> 'Norman Warner [first YJB Chair] was the big reformer who was going to see the YJS bedded in through a policy-making structure animated in the YOTs. He did that in a very firm and efficient manner, encountering a good deal of opposition in some respects from youth justice managers at a local level because he ran the YJB and its edicts to the local teams as if it were a single organisation, as opposed to a guiding body that was providing analysis of data research and other support mechanisms. Norman's position was entirely understandable. He was advising Jack Straw [Home Secretary]. They were formulating the policy that they implemented shortly after the election with remarkable speed.' (YJB Chair, senior academic)

> 'YJB at its most influential had a seat at the table and carried the agenda on behalf of a Labour government, albeit a managerial and legislatively trigger-happy government.' (YJB board member, YOT manager)

A YJB Chair reflected on this resistance in relation to the degree of governmental steer (often via civil servants) that the organisation was subject to in the mid-2000s:

> 'Louise Casey is the most effective civil servant that I've ever encountered, because she was so effective at delivering the punitive message. She came to a YJB meeting and just laid into us, me in particular and my challenging the criminalising use of ASBOs [Antisocial Behaviour Orders]. But within a year of me departing, it had all been swept away. Either I was hopeless at achieving what I was seeking to achieve or there was delayed victory for the arguments I'd been pursuing without the public at large or the *Daily Mail* [right-wing newspaper] noticing. I never fully appreciated the way you get things done when it comes to shifting the balance of policy.'

Other stakeholders expressed the view that managerialist prescription by the YJB as sector experts was a necessity to *mediate against poor practice* stemming from unchecked discretion while simultaneously empowering practitioners by increasing the *legitimacy and expert status of YOTs* within local authorities:

'The first period of managerialism, exemplified by YJB gatekeeping, was actually designed to get children out of custody, rather than to restrict children and the work of social workers. I don't have a particularly romantic view about what wonderful things social workers or youth workers would come up with if left to their own devices, because I know from practical experience that this can produce shockingly awful work. The consequence can be large numbers of children sucked into the system and cast away.' (YJB Chief Executive)

'The YJB could never say "you have to do it like this", but there was real advantage of prescription from a YOT manager perspective. When you're in a YOT management board and you're trying to fight for something that you believed should be the way of working and you have YJB support, you are not a lone voice. You've got the whole of the YJB behind you when you're having that conversation with your YOT Management Board or head of children's services or the police. The YJB gives a level of legitimacy in the eyes of local authorities.' (Children's Commissioner)

YJB insecurity and threatened identity

Interviewees reflected on the ongoing legacy of YJB prescriptiveness as indicative of a persistent lack of political leverage and the result of constant feelings of *insecurity*, *threat* and *powerlessness* due to the organisation's ambiguous and consistently threatened sustainability, identity, role and status (see also Souhami, 2015b):

'The YJB Chair went to see the Prime Minister to ensure the future of the YJB [circa early 2000s], saying keep your Home Secretary in line. But the more chairs of the YJB along the chain, the distance between YJB and government became quite significant. There wasn't the political leverage that previously existed, and civil servants can now push their weight around a lot more with the YJB and keep it in its box. It doesn't help when you've got rogue YOT managers who've got the ear of their local politicians, slagging off the YJB. It's ducking the bullets in the crossfire while walking on eggshells. Maintaining the autonomy and independence of the YJB in the political environment in London.' (YJB board member)

'The YJB always felt quite vulnerable, fragile, lacked a bit of teeth, because it doesn't really have any sanctions. What can it do? It's a bit soft and fluffy. In some ways, the inspectorate [His Majesty's Inspectorate of Probation (HMIP)] has more teeth because of their ratings.' (YJB board member)

YJB lack of policy direction and re-emerging managerialist prescription

Other stakeholders reflected on the extent to which constant political and practice threats to the YJB's identity and status have contributed to a *waning policy influence* (see later in this chapter) characterised by *retraction of prescription and oversight*, a *lack of clear policy direction* and, ultimately, a creeping *re-emergence of managerialist prescription* in the organisation in recent years:

> 'There was a pulling back. You can see the contraction of the YJB in those years [post-2010 austerity]. All the monitoring and sanctions largely fell away. There was a very routine regular threat of do this or we withdraw your grant. They would be laughed at. You're gonna be abolished next year anyway. This tacit understanding that there's not much they could do. I questioned how much authority I would have had to stop it, but who knows. That's the ambiguity of the YJB role.' (YJB board member, YOT manager)

> 'The YJB has been more controlled [by government and the MoJ] in recent years. When the Coalition came in, when the board's [YJB's] demise was proposed in one of the bonfire of the quangos, that relationship has certainly changed, and the board is less active now.' (YJB board member, YOT manager)

> 'I wonder about the direction of the YJB now. Is it clear enough where it's going and what it's trying to do? Could more have been done to help the wider world understand Child First? It's a YJB shop window that should be telling you something about what it is, but I'm just not sure about direction elsewhere. I'm not sure what sort of policy context that sat within. This move back to more prescription, more oversight. To what end?' (YJB board member, senior academic)

YJB as strategic policy influencer

Expert stakeholders have suggested that the YJB, particularly since the 2016 Taylor Review, has had an explicit *expert role and influence* upon policy making. However, others were more equivocal, representing the YJB's role as ambiguous, slippery and fluid (see Souhami, 2015a) and situated in the grey area between strategy and policy where less formal 'soft power' is exercised. For example, several experts who have occupied senior YJB positions constructed the YJB as more of a policy *influencer* than policy *maker*, an influence realised through *relationships with civil servants* (such as those in the MoJ), which themselves can be based on steering or being steered (see earlier in this chapter; see also Chapter 5):

> 'It [YJB] does help inform policy, but in a quasi-policy role through case management guidance and the youth justice plans that ultimately gets signed off by the ministers and agreed ultimately by the MoJ Policy Unit. It's really important that YJB is one of those influencers because of the fact we've got a unique role. We sit alongside government, but we're not part of government. We're an independent body, but we're actually submerged in the workings of government and helping to influence that. I believe that this influences changes over time and oscillates backwards and forwards.' (YJB Chair)

> 'The YJB doesn't write formal policy as such, but we develop guidance documents, include requirements for youth justice plans etc. I see this as multi-track. You've got the formal policy ownership which rests with the MoJ Youth Justice Policy Unit. What we seek to do is influence policy. We develop our own positions, which follow a classic policy-making [cycle] playbook around identifying a problem, looking at what the evidence base is for that problem, trying to identify potential solutions and then we seek to use those positions to influence policy making by government.' (YJB Chief Executive)

> 'The YJB should be a strong voice in terms of shaping policy delivery through YOTs, but as a board member, I had different experiences depending on who was in charge. John Drew [Chief Executive 2009–13], for example, I always felt was effective at finding a way in for particular areas of policy that we might want to influence. But others were more about delivering policy that was set. There isn't a clear process or necessarily clear roles for all of the different agencies involved in terms of where they fit and what they bring to the party.' (YJB board member)

When drilling down to examine the nature of the mechanisms through which the YJB develops and exerts its policy-making influence in the YJS, certain stakeholders perceived these to be *strategic* due to the YJB's explicit role/identity as a *strategic policy adviser to government* (see Chapter 3). In this case, strategy was understood as the process of *identifying emerging problems* and *animating/realising policy in practice*. Interview feedback demonstrated the YJB's self-identification as *strategic policy-influencing expert* by employing mechanisms such as scanning the environment for emerging problems, formulating these into strategic objectives and using data and expertise to inform policy:

'Our starting point is what our strategy is. We identify what it is we're trying to achieve and then each year as part of our Business Plan we identify areas of concern where we feel that there are weaknesses through a mixture of using data and strategic environmental scanning and analysis and then judgement, because we have a board with significant expertise and experience. We're constantly looking around at what's going on to identify whether there's work that we need to be picking up on, identifying what's getting in the way of achieving what we want to achieve, and then sort of like hypothesising about what solutions might work. Looking at the evidence and understanding the strategic choices that the system should be making in order to reduce offending by children, that's the overarching objective of the YJB.' (YJB Chief Executive)

'My argument with the board was even if you think this is the wrong policy, we are gonna end up butting heads with government if we set ourselves up in opposition like a lobby group. Actually, we're gonna be better off if we're able to influence the way in which this policy is actually delivered and developed.' (YJB Chair)

Advising and engaging with colleagues

Other experts perceived the YJB as exercising strategic (policy) influence through mechanisms of *advising* ministers, *engaging* stakeholders across multiple contexts and *supporting* practice improvement:

'A mixture of people have ideas and kick them around. The ministers then make decisions based on the advice they receive. If you're not at the table, you can't give your advice and your voice isn't heard. The prime source of advice is the policy official [civil servant], but actually there are all these other people, and I was trying to make sure that the YJB was more than just a lobby group. We were an independent adviser that looked to the whole system.' (YJB Chief Executive)

'Charlie Taylor was very clear as Chair that he wanted the YJB to be less meddling in the day-to-day delivery by local authorities [policy implementation] and more strategic in supporting improvement rather than delivering itself. And that was quite helpful to me. How do I get the staff to think differently?' (YJB Chief Executive)

YJB policy influence: waxing, waning or changing?

'As a reaction to the consequences of innovations and policy decisions, the role of the YJB has changed dramatically [from 2008 to 2023]. You

> had new personnel involved, and it became substantially bigger and less easy to control. But it also changed as a consequence of policy suddenly veering off in a different direction as a reaction to the failures of New Labour policy making. Suddenly, the YJB became a champion for doing policy different, whereas under New Labour, their role initially was as a transmission belt from politicians down to practice.' (Senior academic)

From the expert perspective, the nature of the YJB's policy-making influence has waxed and waned since 1997 rather than maintaining a consistent, centralised trajectory over this period. For example, qualitative documentary analysis (QDA) of policy documents and thematic analysis of the semi-structured interview data indicate that the initial trajectory of managerialist prescription or YJB influence did not last following the early expansionism of the CDA 1998.[4] Consequently, the nature of the YJB's self- and externally perceived *identity and power* (see Chapter 1) as policy maker has been dynamic, oscillating between independence and steer and between prescribing practice and consulting with and empowering expert practitioners. According to experts, the dynamic nature of the YJB's identity and its associated power dynamics/relationships with other stakeholders (see Chapter 7) have been cyclical and dynamic, shaped by a series of micro- and meso-level mechanisms.

Shifting trajectories of YJB policy influence

The dynamic trajectory of a *changing and cyclical* policy-making trajectory since the CDA 1998 was reflected upon by a senior academic:

> 'Policy has been driven from above, and practitioners have effectively responded to what they've been told to do. With the New Labour reforms, local discretion was severely cut and constrained. People who thought differently or who had cultural and practical expectations from the previous period were encouraged to leave and were replaced by people with no idea what youth justice was. That was deliberate and had quite an impact on the extent to which the practice base were able to influence policy themselves, rather than simply do what they are told. But again, that varies over time, partly because of the more progressive nature of top-down policy in recent years and partly because when government try to eliminate or reduce targets, the scope for different approaches in different local authorities is considerably greater. There's a cycle there. You've gone from practitioners having very little impact on policy to having the scope for doing things differently at the local level.'

Experts shared the view that the YJB's own degree of *organisational discretion and autonomy* as a policy influencer has changed, for example due to youth justice becoming less visible and politically important as a policy area in recent years. The view of the YJB's changing identity as policy influencer was consolidated by the experiences of the board member quoted in the following excerpt, who evaluated this trajectory of change as one of *waning policy influence* due to a *lack of government legislation* and a relative *policy vacuum* in youth justice:

> 'The YJB are arm's length from government and working in a policy area that the government doesn't see as a priority, dealing with relatively small budgets and with a relatively small proportion of the child population. So it gives them quite a lot of discretion and influence for the current period because no-one's influence is great, but that could change very quickly.'

> 'If you look at the early days of the YJB, it created and wrote absolutely everything, legislation, a whole new range of orders, different ways of working. Over the last few years, that's significantly dried up in terms of what the YJB actually produce about what the system is and how it should be. This has waned because there has been less major policy change since 2010 and less new legislation because we went through a period in the 2000s, where there were continual changes of legislation. What would the last big piece of legislation be? LASPO [Legal Aid, Sentencing and Punishment of Offenders Act] 2012?'

However, the same expert stakeholder also identified a shift (rather than retraction) in direction for the trajectory in YJB policy influence through placing more emphasis on facilitating *policy into practice pathways*:

> 'Around 2010, it became the job of the YJB to think about how we guide the YJS to put what it needs in place. From a YJB point of view, it would be producing guidance, consulting with the sector, looking for evidence of good practice. Around Taylor's time [2016 onwards], the YJB became less prescriptive, less in the weeds, gave practitioners more discretion, more flexibility. YJB would speak to all relevant government departments, the inspectorate, the sector. They would put something together that they believed to be right and then put it out to consultation, really to test, have we got this right? Are there any areas that need to be tweaked? They then reflected it back to the ministers to say this is what we've done and this is why. This is the support it's got, now implement it.'

A summary of the main contexts–mechanisms relationships identified when exploring the YJB's policy-making role and influence is provided in Appendix 9.

Experts, experience and evidence in youth justice policy making

This chapter has highlighted the constructive influence of *relationships between experts* and the use of *professional expertise* and *experience* as a 'resource' to shape policy outcomes in youth justice contexts (see also Rose, 1996), a set of mechanisms operating in relational contexts of policy-making. Interviewees identified the policy-making period from 1997 to around 2009 as one in which the expertise of certain 'experts' was privileged in policy-making contexts, notably government ministers with political agendas, civil servants with generalist knowledge, YJB officials offering continuity (stability) of expertise in a complex and volatile policy area (Souhami in Case, 2018/21) and criminologists with a partiality for risk management (Case, 2022). Additionally, interview data highlighted the centrality of expert-produced *evidence*, consolidating findings from the QDA regarding New Labour's commitment to modernisation and good-quality, evidence-based policy as a mechanism for mobilising expertise.

Experts also reported, however, that the contextualised expertise and experience of non-governmental actors (such as practitioners, professionals working in Wales, critical academics) during this policy-making period was relatively marginalised and often rejected (see also Smith, 2014; Creaney, 2020), despite these groups self-identifying as credible, like-minded experts pursuing common ground and shared agendas. The perceived marginalisation of practitioner (and other expert) perspectives aligns with the conclusions of Souhami (2015a) that the construction of the YJB and YOTs introduced a new series of uncertainties and ambiguities to the practice field. These uncertainties/ambiguities placed at issue the nature of professional expertise itself, such that youth justice social workers were required to relinquish ownership of their work, and professional expertise and experience were initially seen to count for nothing. However, this situation has changed in recent years according to the author of the 2016 Taylor Review, who acknowledged the constructive influence of *credible expert practitioner voices*, including his own:

> 'I appeared in front of a Select Committee with whom my school had a good reputation. We had very positive Ofsted inspections, so I had credibility as someone who knew about children's behaviour. That was where my appointment came from. For YJB, if you've got someone like Tom McNally [as Chair], a former Coalition minister with lots of credibility, he was able to do things with the YJB that it wasn't always able to do because it didn't always have that credibility or clout with ministers.'

A YJB board member during Taylor's tenure as Chair went further by asserting that the organisation should do more to use its own *in-house expertise*, rather than deferring to or functioning like short-termist and generalist civil servants:

> 'Harnessing the expertise of the right people in the organisation is crucial. You've got people with good knowledge and understanding of youth justice, people experienced at working within the sector. Drawing on their experience to shake things and actually listening to them and recognising what they've got to say can strengthen the arguments the YJB can make to others. The YJB needs to value its staff and to recruit more from the sector, because otherwise you just dilute and then you don't have a unique selling point, do you? You start to look like a government department who parachutes people in to do a certain job.'

Using expertise to generate and challenge evidence

Interview feedback indicated that expert evidence is both a context (for example, the professional 'evidence mindset' for supporting evidence-based practice) within which policy is constructed and a mechanism for mobilising expertise in organisational/policy-making contexts and occupational contexts. However, at the same time, its influence should not be overstated and must be contextualised as one influence within multi-faceted policy-making processes that can be superseded at any point by other constructive influences such as political/professional agendas or critical (often unpredicted and sudden) events.

Twin-track evidence generation and utilisation: academic evidence and YOT data

During interviews, experts drew the distinction between *data* employed as evidence (typically understood as performance information/statistics) and expert *evidence* (represented as explanatory knowledge and understanding), typically generated from empirical research or the expert analysis of data. There was a particular focus on the evidence-generating expertise and professional experience of two traditionally marginalised but increasingly recognised expert groups: *critical academic researchers* (predominantly evidence) and *practitioners* (predominantly data):

> 'We think of evidence as either from academia or from the [performance] data that we [YJB] collect. Our central data team was putting together a performance information and evidence pack that went regularly to the board to inform our priorities. We used the annual [YJB] Convention to build a lot more input from academic colleagues.

We brought an academic in as part of the board and that changed the nature of the discussion at board level significantly, because he'd say there's some evidence that backs this up or you need more analysis of what's going on here, more research. We used quite a lot of academic stuff to push the Child First agenda. We'd say to ministers, this piece is written by academics. That made a real difference and helped us. We've used evidence in that way.' (YJB Chief Executive)

'There's a twin track approach [to evidence generation and utilisation]. We [YJB] spent a fair amount of money on commissioning academic research to analyse the data and to look at the practice on the ground to feed that to the YOTs in the form of guidance notes on particular operational options. The other thing in advance of getting better quality data as to what was happening on the ground was to reach out to the YOTs locally to hear what they were saying about how they thought it was working. Operationally, by talking to people to find out what their operational problems were, we could see how we could better support YOT managers who weren't managing very well.' (YJB Chair)

A senior HMIP official espoused the importance of *data and evidence quality* for effective inspection practice to inform policy development, reinforcing the 'twin-track' approach to using evidence generated by practitioners and academics:

'Quality of evidence is very important if I'm thinking about how a new programme should work. Pulling together all of the current evidence, we're looking at what the evidence base is and taking the learning from this current programme of inspection. Our head of research is putting together a wealth of the evidence in terms of academic research. What's out there? We commission various research analysis bulletins. Our [YOT] inspection framework is based on an evidence-based model. It's designed to give us a much firmer foundation, really, in terms of what it is we're looking at and what we're doing.'

Using an 'evidence mindset'

Stakeholder experts identified having an *evidence mindset* favourable to the generation and use of expert evidence as a mechanism for effective policy strategy and practice development. The evidence mindset context was mobilised by mechanisms of open-mindedness and boldness to challenge existing evidence and boldness to create new evidence. According to a YJB Chief Executive:

> 'There isn't always very good science deployed around a policy question, but people need to seek that. It requires a certain attitude towards evidence, an understanding that it may not be possible to get perfect evidence on a particular issue, but you need openness to the work of researchers. That doesn't necessarily mean a huge research programme, but you need to have a state of mind, a mindset willing to challenge its own presumptions. It needs senior people to be bold enough in whatever their setting is to say to the people above them, it's not like that at all. YJB have to be able to engage with politicians. You need a youth justice service manager to say, now here's the evidence that this doesn't work and here are some things that we could try because we've learned of this from other places. The only way we can engage with that is through debate and through having at one's fingertips the refutation of those sorts of arguments. You have to have an appetite for the battle in youth justice.'

The advocacy of adopting an *evidence mindset* that encourages *collaboration with experts* to enhance policy influence at YJB level was supported by a more recent Chief Executive and by a current senior official, who argued:

> 'To inject a new sense of purpose into the YJB, we increased not just our evidence capability, but also our evidence mindset. Recognising that there may be opportunities for us to influence choosing the right subjects for research and how researchers might want us to amplify their research findings. We now have a much stronger emphasis on looking at the evidence and talking to the sector, building upon existing policies, looking at wider government approaches, listening to the political steer. The evidence and the experience of experts working in the field, including children themselves, are far more important in shaping our approach. Child First is a particular ideology. It is very much about what the evidence tells us is effective in working with children in the YJS and beyond. That strengths-based, future focus applies to all of us, not just children. You could encapsulate it as an approach to practice and probably policy.' (YJB senior official)

The utility of expert evidence as a mechanism for localised, contextualised and practitioner-led policy implementation through *practice innovation and challenge* of existing, ineffective policy-making approaches was advocated by Association of YOT Managers (AYM) and YOT Managers Cymru (YMC) Chairs when reflecting on their experiences (as YOT managers) of translating policy into practice:

> 'Evidence is really important. You have to marry your evidence with your local context. Evidence gives you the direction that if you do these

things, you're likely to achieve an outcome because your evidence shows it. Then you think I could do that in my local context. Do we have the resources in the right places? Do we have to adjust things? Recognising that it might not work out how we want it to work out, but if I've taken on board the evidence and made a decision. I encourage that creativity, that dynamism, that willingness to try different things.' (AYM Chair)

'We had to have independent research and empirical data and evidence about whether we were doing the right thing. We could have been self-deluding and thought that we were doing the right thing for all the right reasons. But we could have still come up with the wrong results, and the only way that you can actually do that is by having an independent arm which has access to all the available information and is able to determine where things are actually going. It's an enabler, a foundation stone.' (YMC Chair)

The dynamic influence of evidence in policy making

According to experts, the *role and status of evidence* in policy-making processes is dynamic, fluctuating, fragile/precarious and relative in its influence when compared to compelling narratives, the dead hand of political influence and the political agenda:

'Data and evidence and analysis goes into a policy-making pot, which then gets lost in the mist of time terribly quickly.' (YJB Chair)

'There are other drivers [of policy] which owe nothing to evidence.' (YJB Chief Executive)

'Evidence was a big part of it [local policy development] for sure, but I would also say that it was the narrative that I needed to sort of, not twist, but you need to tell a compelling story.' (Children's Commissioner)

The dynamic and fragile nature of evidential influence was illustrated by expert experience of a series of (often interconnected) challenges and barriers to its effective use. These include the *dead hand influence* of political *agenda* (for example governmental, ministerial) and strategic agenda (such as that of the YJB) and the generation of evidence that may be viewed as *partial* (biased and incomplete), *policy based* and/or (politically) *inconvenient*. For example, the dead hand influence on evidence generation exerted by ministerial agenda, reflective of political agenda, short-termism and sudden policy shifts (see Chapter 5), was reported by a YJB board member when reflecting on the introduction of the Knife Crime Prevention Programme:

> 'Me and a colleague, an experienced YOT worker, were given 20 minutes to design a policy for the MoJ to tackle knife crime. I read our Key Elements Effective Practice notes and said, here are seven things that ought to be in a knife crime programme. We took 15 minutes on a white board in my office. We wrote them down, typed it out, sent the e-mail to the YJB Chief Executive. That was the basis for the government's Knife Crime Prevention Programme. The minister needed to know now because he's going into the house [Parliament] in two hours. Because they're responding to either press or incidents, events. As a YOT manager, I'd never spend my research budget because I knew a Home Secretary or Minister of Justice could be faced with a sudden challenge that would need immediate [policy-based] research evidence.'

The challenges of *short-termism* and *sudden/immediate policy development* were further reflected by the Chair of the Alliance for Youth Justice (AYJ) third sector coalition:

> 'The four pillars that we try and incorporate into all of our policy work [examining children's rights implications, seeking evidence, consulting practice experts, consulting children] are difficult to address when being reactive. The challenge is going back to government departments or the relevant Select Committee and asking for more time. That's partly because they don't really want any genuine consultation and quite often, by the time you hear that there's a consultation open, they say you've got six weeks to get something back to us, which when you're working in a small team and you want to go through that careful, evidence-based process, that doesn't necessarily leave you enough time to do that.'

Using evidence from academic experts

> 'For a while, there was no place for academia in YJB and MoJ in terms of policy making.'
>
> (YJB board member, YOT manager)

As part of my monograph *Youth Justice: A Critical Introduction* (Case, 2018/21), I interviewed Professor John Drew (YJB Chief Executive 2009–13). We explored his rationale for addressing the knowledge– and evidence–policy rupture in youth justice post-CDA 1998 that had developed into a fractious YJB–academia relationship bordering on disconnect and active hostility (see also Chapter 4). John told me:

> 'One of my first objectives upon taking post in 2009 was to try to establish new relationships with academics. We [YJB] were already

starting to build alliances with practitioners, but we were very resistant to working with academics. They were the best thinkers in youth justice and having debates was critical to developing youth justice. It was about ideas not personalities. You definitely want your best brains and biggest critics to get involved in youth justice to explain their criticisms and to develop new systems.' (Drew in Case, 2018: 249–50)

Upon its inception in 2000, the YJB of England and Wales was charged with 'commissioning research' to inform the development of 'effective practice' and consequently 'committed to developing and expanding [academic] research … to provide evidence that can constructively influence central policy decisions [and] enhance the existent knowledge base' (YJB, 2009: 1–2; see also MoJ, 2012). The espoused intention was that academic research take precedence in populating the youth justice evidence base, as opposed to allegedly 'less robust' practitioner-generated evidence grounded in knowledge from training, prejudice and opinion, practice experience, anecdote, fads/fashions and advice from senior colleagues (Jones, 2001: 15; Stephenson et al, 2011). However, according to some, the role and constructive influence of academic experts in generating evidence to shape policy has been under-utilised due to YJB resource constraints, rather than necessarily due to resistance to challenge or lack of an evidence mindset: "We [YJB] were really grateful for the space that you [academics including the author] stepped into because we've not got the resource to be able to do that. It's about building that partnership and trying to form a collective. Hashtag stronger together" (YJB senior official). Indeed, YJB representatives were keen to acknowledge the influence of *academic expert evidence* on the evolution of the Child First guiding principle as an evidence-based priority for youth justice 'policy' (in the form of strategy developed and espoused by the YJB rather than policy developed by government/MoJ) and practice (see Chapter 4):

'Child First has been a terrific system achievement and the biggest contribution that the academic community has given to the YJS. It's by a long way in the last 25 years the most important initiative that academia has given to youth justice. What were the most important policy initiatives? Child First would be one.' (YJB Chief Executive)

'Quantifiable evidence is crucial and so it made sense to look in this direction around Child First. We [YJB] ask ourselves, what are we going to do in relation to doing the right thing around children and victims and safer communities around this big policy idea? What's the evidence behind it? We're gonna get challenged about it. The fact was that yourself [author] and others [academic experts] were able to offer independent rigour around the evidence for what we're doing. In order to look at a system change, the evidence for what you're doing needs to be as tight as it can be.' (YJB Chair)

The challenge of inconvenient evidence

The centrality of *political agenda* and *political realities* for shaping policy was illustrated by stakeholder reports of the challenges experienced when *inconvenient evidence* was produced, that is, evidence that challenged or at least did not sufficiently support pre-existing political policy directions:

> 'In the early YJS [immediately post-1998], there was no methodical approach, so you're gonna have to rely on promising, rather than evidence-based approaches. The Home Secretary [David Blunkett] lost his rag because that wasn't what he wanted to hear. That's the heart of the problem. You're asked to tell a story and you tell the truth, but the ministers don't wanna hear that cause they want a solution. With evidence-led work in youth justice, there's not always a solution. My experience was telling the truth about what worked and saying this is promising and this is what should be invested in was always mitigated by politicians' desires to have a success story and to talk something up and say it will work. It's a silver bullet.' (YJB board member, YOT manager)

> 'The Home Secretary [Blunkett] said there is absolutely no way we can publish this [evidence counter to government youth justice policy], but we were committed to publishing. You couldn't hide it away because it was politically inconvenient. He did not want to see it publicised because he knew it was gonna hit the headlines of the *Daily Mail*. I remember going to see him about that and we had a very, very difficult discussion.' (YJB Chief Executive)

Building on the previously identified mechanisms of 'telling the truth' and using 'compelling narratives' (see Stevens, 2011) for challenging the political agenda and the rejection of inconvenient evidence, a YJB Chief Executive highlighted *respectful and proportionate discussions* (see also Chapter 7) reflective of *professional lived experience* (see later in this chapter) as mechanisms for addressing evidence–policy 'ruptures' (see Phoenix, 2016):

> 'Charlie Taylor's reports from 2016 have nuggets of gold in them and aren't referred to now on the whole. Sometimes we're data rich, but we don't have the time or the time is not taken by policy makers to think about, what do we know previously? Lived experience can help us think about what we do as a board when you get to contested evidence

and data. You need to have uncomfortable discussions with colleagues in a way that is respectful and proportionate.' (YJB Chief Executive)

Political and organisational agenda overriding evidence

The notion of *political agenda* as shaping the nature of the 'acceptable' evidence generation by experts to inform policy was reinforced by the experience of a YJB Chief Executive when detailing the origins of the Scaled Approach assessment and intervention framework (see Chapter 4):

> 'I was told that the Scaled Approach arose because the YJB had been beaten up by politicians in a Justice Select Committee. A senior official came back to the YJB and said we need something which makes this look a lot more hard-edged and research based, so there were policy drivers around that. But there are always charlatans in the research community, academic community and practice community who pretend that there are simple solutions.'

The YJB itself was not immune to criticism in relation to its own *organisational agenda* overriding independent and objective expert evidence generation, with a board member experiencing their early approach to procurement as highly partial towards experts with more acceptable, politically palatable evidence-generation approaches:

> 'In the early days, the Probation Unit [Oxford University] dominated. There was so much money and power in the board that their procurement processes and relationships with stakeholders were very different. I can remember being in the meeting with the YJB Chair saying, Probation [in the adult Criminal Justice System] have got OASys [risk assessment tool], so we want our version of that. That was a throwaway remark and there was no real thinking through. There was a commitment to that risk-based approach, and the Probation Unit and probation generally had a massive impact on the board's policy development. They weren't that bothered what they were putting forward. They wanted to win a whacking big evaluation contract to evaluate how Asset [the YJS risk assessment instrument] went. That was one key relationship.' (YJB board member, senior academic)

Partiality in the generation, use and evaluation of evidence to populate and justify 'evidence-based policy' in the YJS (including ignoring inconvenient evidence), was perceived by certain experts as a mechanism of *policy-based evidence generation* to self-fulfil preformed policy agendas:

> 'Policy tends to get written backwards. So if you introduce something like Youth Inclusion Programmes, depending on their outcomes, they [governmental actors] rewrite the objectives backwards from the eventual evaluation or just bin it and hide it. The policy gets rewritten according to how implementation went. Big multi-million-pound policies got buried and thrown away. The big problem with the public sector is you're not allowed to fail. So there's no learning that goes on about failure.' (YJB board member, senior academic)

> 'Quite often, there is evidence. One thing we tried to do in the YJB was seek the facts to justify the policy. But we were continually running up the down escalator in terms of central direction.' (YJB Chair)

Using evidence from practitioner experts

The other identified experts in the YJB's 'twin-track' approach to generating and using evidence (largely as data) were practitioners. The significance of *practice expertise and experience* in the production of evidence to inform youth justice policy making was consistently reflected by interviewees. AYM representatives attested to the importance of practitioner expertise, experience and evidence generation and believed that the organisation's influence was growing in the contemporary YJS, particularly as the MoJ becomes more visible, robust and muscular (in its own right and relative to the YJB) in policy-making contexts (see also Chapter 7):

> 'There is mileage in having those expert people who know what a policy should look like, but who should not be far removed from practice. We are a conduit to a lot of that expertise, experience, evidence.' (AYM Chair)

> 'You've got a wide range of [evidence from] experiences, bearing in mind that YOTs are different throughout the country. That's the beauty of the AYM, because it brings regional representation, it brings that diversity of practice. It's alright having a policy, but it's about the way it's played out in practice in different localities.' (AYM Chair, YOT manager)

> 'The ideas and evidence we as practitioners through the AYM are giving the board ... the dynamic is different now that YJB is a sounding board for current MoJ civil servants, rather than when it was a policy lead.' (YJB board member, YOT manager)

One AYM Chair interviewed highlighted the Turnaround prevention programme (see Chapter 4) as a cogent example of the growing identity of the *AYM as policy influencer* in the eyes of the MoJ:

> 'There was a decision made through the MoJ Youth Justice Policy Unit to give YOTs an additional grant [Turnaround] to beef up diversion and preventative early intervention. MoJ asked me to work with them on how they allocate the money to YOTs and how to draft guidance in terms of what this would mean. They came to me as a sort of acknowledged expert. We started to look at what they had originally put together, which was produced by people who didn't understand youth justice. So we [AYM] would advocate challenge, advise, suggest alternative wording.'

A summary of the key contexts–mechanisms relationships identified when exploring the policy-making influence of experts, experience and evidence is provided in Appendix 10.

Professional lived experience, expertise and evidence generation

The incremental shift towards the YJB self-identifying as a more consultative and empowering (less prescriptive) organisation enabling practitioner influence on policy making has extended into an evolving perception of the *practitioner identity and role* being one of expert able to inform policy development. Both YJB stakeholders and practitioner experts (along with stakeholders spanning both groups) attested to a changing perception of the policy-making capacity of *practitioner expertise*. Stakeholder feedback identified a series of themes that focused on both the YJB's identification and use of practitioners as experts and practitioners' own self-identification as experts in policy-making contexts. Professional experiences highlighted the YJB's previous *neglect of professional lived experience and expertise* in policy-making processes, despite an acknowledged need to use these qualities. Experts reported evolving trajectories of the influence of practitioner expert identity and credibility, characterised by *changing YJB–practitioner relationships* in local contexts, but some viewed this increased YJB engagement as *instrumental and self-serving* (that is, strategic). Practitioners also reported the widespread *localised mediation and moderation* of centralised policy prescriptions by 'street-level bureaucrats' and the utility of *resistance and challenge* of prescribed policies as mechanisms of evidence generation and practitioner influence. In turn, these mechanisms encouraged the evolution of *local penal cultures* through the central mechanism of *collaboration between like-minded, credible experts* and *advocates* in local contexts.

Evolving YJB–practitioner relationships and the practitioner expert identity

Early YJB prescriptiveness and the organisation's relative *neglect of localised and practitioner expertise* was reported by two former board members:

'At the YJB, I got more and more angry about the very autocratic, top-down framework being developed. I felt that there needed to be much more discretion at the local level to make judgements about what kinds of things need to be done and who should be doing them. The only person who really knows whether the young person is making progress towards compliance with the order or taking the **** is the YOT worker. Who else is able to make that judgement?

We should have an approach to national implementation without being too intrusive and recognising that people are professionals and know their own work. It's about giving clear and consistent key messages. That gets it on the agenda for conversations locally that local teams can then interpret. But don't prescribe that everybody does the same thing all the time, because you take away local context. There is that balance. Key messages are gonna be the same. Their interpretation and the application may be slightly different. People are professional enough to understand the concepts and principles, even with different interpretations.'

A YOT manager who sat on an early incarnation of the YJB expressed a contrary view, reporting that even during the peak period of YJB managerialism and prescription, practitioner expertise and credibility (at least, in-house expertise) remained highly valued by the YJB:

'I took ownership and sponsorship of the effective practice agenda. So you had a practitioner turned policy maker or policy influencer like me. The YJB was having people who've done the job in the role of developing and thinking and promulgating changes or adaptations to practice implementation. What makes the YJB effective is having those practice routes and links with those who have got a bit of dirt under the fingernails. We've done the job and understand how hard it is to take a bright idea and make it happen, which is something that civil servants don't understand. That's the key.'

This perception of the acknowledged importance of practitioner expert identity and credibility was consolidated by a YJB Chair, who claimed to have eschewed managerialist prescription in favour of prioritising more *localised, micro-level engagement* with practice:

'I took the completely opposite view [to managerialist prescription], that the innovative qualities of the YJS, like multi-disciplinary teams, could only be a good thing. If YOT managers developed a professional association and provided each other with professional support and expertise, we should facilitate that. I argued that instead of the YJB being at the apex of policy directing operational staff at the local level, it should rather be local teams developing innovative operational systems, being supported by the fairly substantial resources available to the YJB. It was more than inverting of the triangle.'

A Chair of the AYJ third sector organisation further advocated for *practice expertise*, along with utilising an *evidence mindset* and engaging with children as experts when outlining the organisation's strategic approach to exerting policy influence, which coheres around a children's rights framework:

> 'We designed a framework for our policy work, which was going to be underpinned by children's rights. For example, when there's a policy idea that's been developed by government and they put out a consultation paper, we look at the extent to which that upholds or particularly infringes on children's rights, using advice of members that have got particular expertise in that area. Secondly, we look at research and evidence to help us to formulate our positions on issues within our policy papers and positions. Thirdly, we incorporate the practice expertise of our members. Fourthly, we do the same with our young advocates and get them to discuss what they think the implications are for young people.'

Prioritising relationships with local practice experts

Changing governmental actor views of the expert identity and associated utility of engaging practitioners were reflected in the development of supportive, constructive and mutually beneficial policy-making relationships (see Chapter 7). They believed that their organisation had become more *engaging and supportive* of practitioner expertise situated in local contexts in recent years:

> 'We [YJB] seek faithful and effective policy implementation. We're trying to introduce proportionate ways of influencing and structuring practice, but what we've recognised is that this needs to be developed locally and requires a degree of individual expertise, skill and craft that needs to be nurtured. We have a constructive relationship with YOTs, but we haven't been present enough for them and that's partly because a strategic decision was taken very early on in our existence that this wasn't what our focus ought to be. We are currently somewhat reversing that and saying actually no, it's the place where we can add the most value.' (YJB Chief Executive)

> 'We [HMIP] are significantly increasing the number of people from the YJB who are in regionally based roles, having a clutch of YOTs

> that they have a primary relationship with. That's a good way of trying to increase our influence with YOTs as well as building a picture of their delivery and practice. They are more important stakeholders than they were. We're more visible, vocal and present.' (HMIP senior official, YJB board member)

The perception of a less prescriptive, more empowering and context-sensitive YJB receptive to practitioner expertise was reinforced by an AYM Chair. However, the nature of this apparently empowering and decentralised approach was also perceived as motivated by previous *lack of engagement* leaving *localised knowledge gaps* that needed to be urgently redressed:

> 'During Charlie Taylor's time at the YJB [2017–20] they had a phrase for it. Basically, it was taking away all the constraints and letting you [YOTs] get on with it. That's when they cut down their regional representation. Then all of a sudden, they realised that they hadn't got any data to demonstrate the things that they wanted to demonstrate. It was a good idea to give YOTs their freedom to get on with it. But of course, when ministers start saying, why are we giving all this money out and all of a sudden they haven't got the data. So it's all about them having to demonstrate that there is value for the money that they're giving to YOTs. YJB managers weren't coming to management boards, and they weren't meeting with the YOTs very often. And they were losing their ear on the ground.'

Following from this, an AYM official believed that YJB engagement mechanisms with practice could be perceived as *instrumental and self-serving*, designed to fulfil the organisation's strategic goals and to *address their lack of clear policy direction* as opposed to being the empowering objectives asserted by the YJB itself:

> 'MoJ are far more influential now than they've been. YJB is just a seat around the table with AYM and anybody else. The YJB conventions turned out to be a good social event, but when it comes to policy and strategic direction, they floundered. I always felt peed off by the YJB, because their approach was to extract as much information covertly from YOT managers and practitioners, then translate that into the voice of the sector or the YJB position.'

Practitioner self-identification as experts: local mediation and moderation

A counterpoint to the historical criticism of YJB managerialist prescription of youth justice practice is, of course, the mechanisms of *local mediation and moderation* influencing the interpretation and implementation (making) of youth justice policy in local contexts (see Chapters 3 and 5). For example, even during the early years of YJB prescriptiveness, practitioners were able to exercise a degree of discretion when interpreting and implementing centralised guidance such as risk assessment processes (Kemshall, 2008; Briggs, 2013). Notably, Bateman (2012: 46) observed that punitiveness remained the dominant ethos for youth justice policy in the first decade of the 21st century, but that it was mediated by various 'institutional frameworks, cultural constructions, national dynamics and local political or economic considerations'.

In this contentious context, it is instructive, therefore, to compare and contrast YJB perceptions of the centrality of practitioner expert identity with practitioners' own perceptions of their professional lived experience and its role/influence on policy making. Interview feedback continually evidenced practitioners' self-identification as 'experts by experience' (Creaney, 2020) in their often fragmented and nuanced professional and local contexts, exemplified by 'local penal cultures' (Goldson and Briggs, 2021). Practitioner experiences implicated a significant policy-making role for local contexts within which centralised policy prescriptions are moderated in a bottom-up fashion by practitioners operating as 'street-level bureaucrats' (Lipsky, 1980). These findings align with the concept of 'local universality' in policy making (Sausman et al, 2016), whereby centralised policy rules, guidelines or products are shaped and tailored to fit local contexts and practices (see also Allcock et al, 2015; Braithwaite et al, 2018). Interview feedback indicated that practitioners see themselves as operational policy makers in local practice contexts, shaping policy implementation through mechanisms of necessary challenge of and resistance to centralised prescription and the development of *local penal cultures* through collaboration between *like-minded individuals* supported by influential *advocates*:

> 'We underestimate the value of what the operational side of policy delivery should look like. Practitioners have a lot of insight, and they know how this [policy] is going to land with children, families and how is it going to be delivered. What we need to do at local level is to make sure practitioners are involved in the conceptualisation of how it's gonna happen.' (Children's Commissioner)

> 'Where you have policies, you have understanding, but it's interpreted very differently in practice. This is my experience, that lots of these things are agreed locally. We have systems in place to meet policy and support children, but we don't call them the same and the criteria are different.' (YJB Chair)

Practitioner resistance and challenge

A central component of practitioner professional identity that functioned as a policy-making mechanism in the testimonies of interviewees was the perceived *capacity and willingness to resist and challenge* centralised (for example governmental, MoJ, YJB) policy prescriptions at the local level. According to a YJB board member and YOT manager, practitioner resistance and challenge draws upon professional lived experience, expertise and discretion in *proactive and innovative* ways, rather than staff perceiving that they are helpless and victimised:

> 'We [YOTs] don't wanna get told off by HMIP and embarrassed, so YJB need to give us really clear instructions. But the most dispiriting experience you will ever have is going to a YOT meeting with staff dribbling and moaning about teeny aspects of process recording that the YJB have made them do. "We can't do this, nobody understands how difficult it is for YOTs." Grow up, go out and be proactive and change your situation. There's a real sense of victimisation by YJB and HMIP in the YOT management community and a sense of a lack of love and understanding within their own local authorities. "Nobody understands how difficult it is because we've got all this regulation and prescription." But you can either lay down or grab the reins and see this other vision for how youth justice can be incorporated into a bigger vision for children.'

The principle of *challenging prescription through innovation* and *valuing practice expertise* was reinforced by a professional operating within the Youth Custody Service:

> 'I'm in a very hierarchical organisation and that makes a difference for how policy is implemented, how it's designed, how it's discussed, being able to challenge and support each other as professional colleagues. It's a different way of working. For example, would a social worker feel confident going to a Director of Children's Services and saying, we might need to do something different in my experience or able to develop those relationships throughout the organisation? It's really important that people in senior positions are really valuing what practice can bring to policy and strategy development. Do things collaboratively with those who were implementing the practice.'

The ability of YOTs to successfully resist, challenge and subvert prescribed policy was espoused by an AYM Chair when recounting her experience of practitioners employing *negotiation and discretion* to challenge the risk management priorities and perceived incongruent guidance of governance organisations (see Chapters 4 and 5):

> 'HMIP always had a view on risk and the YJB had another view. We could be considered by the YJB as managing risk effectively, and the HMIP would come in and say you're not managing it effectively or vice versa. This became quite an issue for YOTs. We [AYM] were able to collectively go back and say, we really can't be working to two different viewpoints on this because it doesn't tell YOTs how to improve. YJB measures demonstrate that you're doing well, but HMIP will come in and say this needs to improve because we're not seeing what we need to see. But it's a lot better than it was. We did that through roundtables and seminars about inspections and called HMIP in to have discussions around those so that they could understand the viewpoints of YOTs and obviously the YJB.'

Bottom-up policy making by 'street-level bureaucrats'

> 'Youth justice has been shaped by a bottom-up policy making by committed individuals and organisations like the YJB. Committed people help to either reinterpret government policy or help shape future government policy.'
>
> (YJB board member, YOT manager)

Two AYM Chairs reported their perceptions of contemporary bottom-up policy making as practitioner generated and consolidated by YJB, academic and local professional *advocates*:

> 'If a policy comes and you think it doesn't make sense, then implementing it has its challenges. But if it's grounded in common sense, then it's easier. For example, the Child First policy that they're [YJB] pushing now has come from the bottom [practice]. We've been using Child First practice in YOTs, and it's been a bottom-up approach supported by academics. When you've got academia pushing it, people have to start to take notice.'

> 'You can change things locally, but f you get the Association of Directors of Children's Services, the Local Government Association and the Police and Crime Commissioner behind you to push things nationally, we can bring youth justice issues to those discussions. For example, I took the offences brought to justice issue [late 2000s] to the local Criminal Justice Board, outlining examples of children being inappropriately charged to court. The magistrates came on board because they didn't want to be seeing these children. By doing that

> locally, police forces decided not to pursue these low-level crimes and to take a stance, to the point where the Home Office started thinking, is this the right approach to take? Then the YJB came on board, things changed and we saw the drop in first-time entrants across the country.'

The importance of *advocacy* was reinforced at the local level by a YOT manager:

> 'I was very fortunate to have a YOT management board and particularly a Chair who equally didn't believe it ["new youth justice"] to be the right thing to do. Instead, we had to engage much more broadly and preventatively to steer young people away from becoming involved in the formal YJS, because once youngsters were stigmatised as offenders, there was very little way back for them. It was abundantly clear that we had to follow the YJS requirements for working with young people, but the overall local strategy kicked off in a very different way [diversion, promoting positive outcomes]. Lots of work with colleagues and education, community safety. The police were fantastic in picking-up this agenda. They could see the potential benefits right from the kick off.'

The key contexts–mechanisms relationships identified when examining the role of professional lived experience, expertise and evidence generation in youth justice policy making are outlined in Appendix 11.

Conclusion: identities, expertise and evidence

This chapter has explored stakeholder perspectives and experiences of youth justice policy making in relation to three key contextual influences: political–policy discourses, the policy-making role and influence of the YJB and the influence of experts, expertise, evidence and experience. It can be concluded that macro-level political–policy discourses exert influence (for example on political and policy identities) in contexts that are historically dynamic and imbued with conflict and ambivalence. For example, experts interviewed highlighted the simultaneous, bifurcated pursuit of populist punitiveness alongside prevention–support–diversion agendas and the promotion of discourses that are disconnected from the evidence base for effective youth justice. In these complex contexts of political–policy discourse, key mechanisms for policy change were identified: governmental open-mindedness to external expert influence facilitated by a lack of political agenda and fluctuating power dynamics of government steering/being steered, mediated at all times by political and practical realities.

A secondary political–policy discourse was identified, the Welsh context of 'dragonised' youth justice. This was characterised by social justice and children's rights priorities and located within a nuanced national context that was poorly understood and marginalised by the UK government. In this national Welsh context, policy-making mechanisms such as universal children's rights policies were seen to cohere multi-agency and disparate agendas and to promote consensus, common ground, shared agendas and constructive collaboration between stakeholders, often under the radar of UK government and facilitated by small geographic size and a 'passive lack of scrutiny'.

When contextualising the policy-making role and influence of the YJB, stakeholders cited the organisation's relatively independent, ambiguous and fluid role and identity as a policy maker. Identified mechanisms that facilitated or obstructed policy making in YJB contexts were fulfilling a 'bridging' function between government and practice, engaging with practice (or neglecting to), albeit possibly in a strategic, instrumental and self-serving manner. The organisation's role as a policy influencer was facilitated by constructive relationships with civil servants and the managerialist prescription of policy into practice transfer, which was variously viewed as both a necessity immediately post-CDA 1998 and as a mechanism by which the YJB has dealt with persistent insecurity and threat relating to its role and identity. Several stakeholders preferred to categorise the YJB's policy-making role and identity as a strategic influencer, employing mechanisms of environmental scanning for emerging problems, using data and expert evidence, engaging stakeholders across multiple contexts, advising ministers and supporting practice improvement. Stakeholders concluded that the trajectory and nature of the YJB's policy influence was either waning or simply changing, perceiving this influence as dynamic, cyclical and related to the similarly dynamic identity of the YJB. Mechanisms seen to facilitate or debilitate YJB policy influence included a lack of legislation/policy vacuum (within which the MoJ and HMIP have become muscular) and the prioritisation of policy in practice contexts which has enabled the YJB to become more muscular and prescriptive again. In this way, the YJB identity as strategic influencer of policy displays elements of *stability* of expertise and independence, alongside change due to insecurity, instability, precarity and constant threat to its role and identity.

Feedback consistently focused on the significant influence of professionals identifying as experts, using their experience and generating evidence to shape policy. Interviewees recounted their experiences of policy making in dynamic and often fragile, insecure and precarious contexts that utilised the expertise of key professionals (such as MoJ civil servants, YJB strategists, HMIP officials, academics, practitioners, OCC representatives, third sector organisations) and employed an 'evidence mindset' (as an enabler) to engage with expert-generated evidence (practitioner data, academic/empirical evidence, for example). Attendant mechanisms operating within these contexts were identified as developing relationships (see next chapter) between like-minded, credible experts (particularly academics and practitioners), harnessing in-house expertise and realising an 'evidence mindset' through open-mindedness and boldness to challenge existing evidence and creating new evidence. Conversely, mechanisms that served as barriers to the use of experts in evidence included political and financial short-termism and sudden policy shifts. The recognition of practitioner expertise and the credibility of professional lived experience was central to the effective use of expert evidence, which typically occurred in contexts of YJB–practitioner engagement (with practitioners viewed as experts) and locally by practitioners who mediated and moderated centralised policy. The central mechanisms supporting these contexts of engagement were the development of local penal cultures, equitable collaboration between like-minded individuals (for example YJB and practitioners), support of influential advocates, and negotiation, discretion and innovation at the local level to support bottom-up policy making by practitioners operating as 'street-level bureaucrats'.

7

The centrality of relationships in youth justice policy making

The previous chapter examined the constructive influence of identity as constructed and animated in relational contexts through mechanisms operating at multiple levels of the social system:

- macro – for example, governmental identities and political policy discourses and agendas, the fluctuating organisational identity of the Youth Justice Board (YJB) as a policy maker and strategic policy influencer, the Welsh 'dragonised' youth justice identity;
- meso – for example, relationships within and between organisations as influencing self-identity and how the organisational and professional identities of others are perceived and responded to, adopting an open-minded, evidence mindset to the generation and use of expertise and evidence;
- micro – for example, ministerial agendas, professionals self-identifying as experts capable of offering guidance and challenging and creating evidence, local mediation and moderation of centralised policy prescriptions.

Chapter 7, the last of the thematic chapters analysing the semi-structured interview data from experts, extrapolates the conclusion of Chapter 6 that relationships exert a significant constructive influence on policy making. It explores relationships as shaping and shaped by dynamic policy-making identities occurring within and between policy-making contexts, organisations and professionals/individuals. The chapter begins with discussion of the *power dynamics* (see Chapter 1) shaping/shaped by organisational and individual identity and agenda as influencing the nature of relational policy making. There follows a focus on the *relational contexts occupied by the YJB* in their policy-making relationships with governmental actors (for example UK and Welsh Governments, ministers, senior policy advisers [SPADs], civil servants) and non-governmental actors (such as His Majesty's Inspectorate of Probation [HMIP], Welsh professionals, practitioners). What follows is a detailed exploration of the relational (relationship-based) contexts shaping key mechanisms of *collaborative policy-making*, focusing on:

- power dynamics within and between governmental and non-governmental policy-making organisations in the Youth Justice System (YJS);

- seeking common ground within collaborative policy-making relationships;
- using communication to build collaborative relationships;
- relational reciprocity as a vehicle for promoting equitable, supportive policy-making relationships.

Power dynamics influencing relational policy making

Expert feedback consistently identified *power dynamics* as a constructive influence on the relational contexts within which youth justice policy is made. Stakeholders perceived that power in these contexts is animated through the status, agenda, personalities and preconceptions of key policy makers. For example, power dynamics were seen to determine the extent to which certain governmental actors (such as government ministers, SPADs) exercised steer and placed pressure on the policy-making and policy-influencing activities of other groups (such as civil servants, YJB, practitioners) and to determine the extent to which more powerful groups are receptive to the advice, expertise and 'soft power' of others.

Political pressure as agenda-based steer

> 'Policy was set by the government [circa 1998], and once it was established, the YJB should have been given its head tocrack on with the work in the way that some other organisations are. But they [government] never left it alone. There were always ministerial and indeed prime ministerial fingers in the pie.' (YJB Chief Executive)

> 'You've got the ministerial pressure. All of those officers that sit within YJB or MoJ [Ministry of Justice] will then be then almost forced to apply that pressure to practice.' (AYM Chair)

Several experts recounted their experiences of the power of political agenda and policy discourse (see Chapter 6) being animated by the *identities*, *personalities* and *partialities* (biases, prejudices) of individual ministers, themselves often inextricably linked to macro-level political/government agenda. These micro- and macro-level agendas created power dynamics that shaped power-based policy-making contexts wherein mechanisms of political pressure, framed as 'steer', were exerted. In these contexts, pressure was experienced by representatives from the YJB and Youth Offending Team (YOT) managers associations as assertive, aggressive, unequivocal and non-negotiable, contrasting with their experiences of political steer couched as part of constructive dialogue with ministers and civil servants. Stakeholders recounted *ministerial agenda* as placing political pressure on civil servants, the YJB and practitioners around exactly how to frame their policy-influencing advice and guidance:

> 'It was very clear that the Justice Secretary had a particular agenda from his extensive career as a barrister and that a number of different issues had bothered him for many years. It was a personal approach, and policy colleagues had been made very aware [by his SPADs] that there were pieces of advice he would accept and red lines he would never cross. He wanted to be legislative, no matter what the evidence told us.' (YJB senior official)

> 'In the YCS [Youth Custody Service] it's really stark, the control that the minister has over policy. I hadn't really appreciated how much the views of ministers or our government really do impact on the ability to take forward policy. If the minister doesn't agree with something personally, whether it's the right thing to do or not, they won't agree to sign off that policy.' (YCS senior official, Association of YOT ManagersChair)

> 'You've got a government that has a particular position, and ministers are pushing their departments to take those positions and drive policy formation. That becomes difficult when it's at odds with what practitioners know is the right way to behave. Quite often, when they [ministers] take a really hard-line approach, you can't get past it. Departments in central government have an eye to not upsetting their ministers. That's the reality. That means not pushing things too far, taking a particular stance and being the good civil servants. They're looking to keep ministers happy.' (AYM Chair)

Having established a context of power dynamics influencing policy making through ministerial agenda and pressure/control, experts identified several mechanisms through which this power and pressure/control is exerted, typically linked to components of *ministerial personality*, including their *partialities* (for example agendas, areas of interest), *prejudices*, *animosities* and *stubbornness*:

> 'There is a certain extent to which it [policy] depends on the personalities of ministers and their personal areas of interest. So there will be periods when the department is very fertile soil for you and periods when it isn't. The trick is to recognise and be ready for periods when it is fertile, to be ready to exploit that as much as you can. Recognise that there's no linear march of progress in policy development.' (YJB Chief Executive)

When discussing his experiences of governmental, agenda-based policy making being animated by *prejudice and partiality*, an early YJB board member and senior academic reflected:

'What has most influence is how open-minded a policy maker is. The prejudices of Norman Warner's [first YJB Chair] always drove him, not policies. He couldn't stand social services or the civil service. So the YJB was set up as its own policy-making implementation machine, very counter-culture, locally based, but against social work and mainstream civil servants. There was no policy at all. It was a land grab. A lot of it was based on personality. Blunkett [Home Secretary] and Norman hated each other's guts. There was no love lost at all, so policy initiatives would take place depending on who put them forward. Charles Pollard [subsequent YJB Chair, interviewed for this book] had a lot of influence on how policy was made. He was a [restorative justice] zealot, but the government wanted a high-flying copper on the YJB, and so he got what he wanted.'

Numerous experts working in custodial contexts noted how political power and agenda was enacted in policy-making contexts through ministerial stubbornness and resistance to challenge by experts to their agendas and views. This stubbornness/intransigence influenced the nature of the policy-making relationships ministers could have with their civil servants and other professionals across the sector, along with their receptiveness to using expertise and evidence (see Chapter 6).

'The stubbornness of government, that even though it hadn't been involved, they still imagined they've got a better view of it [youth justice policy]. They went through the messages we [YCS] should communicate and were so wide of the mark. I was telling them what the goals were and they disagreed. I said you should read your own website, your text, your vision. Ask the Deputy Prime Minister to read it too.' (YCS manager)

'There's influence within the system that are impacting and delaying Secure Schools. Like Dominic Raab [Justice Secretary], who does not get this. He wants children locked up and throw away the key. It's a worry because I know if Robert Buckland [former Justice Secretary] was there, he'd get it. The YCS should be like an advisory board to government to tell them, this is what we need to do. I see government influencing policy, rather than the SPADs advising government on decision making, but it feels more the other way around.' (YCS manager)

Shifting power dynamics: civil servants steering government

When challenging academic and empirical understandings of governmental dominance of policy-making relationships, Souhami (2015a) argued that civil servants can be capable of steering political policy agendas rather than simply being steered by them (see Chapters 1 and 6), indicating the importance of the *institutional context of government administration* (Souhami, 2015a). Souhami asserts that civil servants often have to elaborate on ministerial decisions in order to put them into action and are routinely involved in formulating policy, having discretion in relation to small questions of implementation that define and change the shape of policy (see also Page and Jenkins 2005). Therefore, civil service bureaucracy can be a site at which policy ideas emerge and are promoted or resisted through the provision of formal advice and engaging in informal processes of influence and negotiation, which was reflected during interviews:

> 'There's been a shifting dynamic of power relationships between politicians and civil servants, which changes over time and changes in unexpected ways, partly as a consequence of contradictions, which emerge as policy makers try to shift the terrain in their own favour. So you get contradictions as a consequence of actions which were designed initially to increase their [politicians'] power. The unanticipated consequence of making it harder for them to implement what they would like to do.' (Senior academic)

> 'As Justice Secretary, I was a great believer in giving them [civil servants] a preliminary view about where my mind was in a meeting on policy. So, we should be doing this, tell me if I'm wrong. Give me some options here. It was very much two-way, but I was always anxious to make sure that they had a very clear steer from me and that the decision was clear. If it wasn't, they'd come back to me and say so. I felt very much part of a team, rather than some distant authority. The relationship I had with civil service was a very healthy and open one. It wasn't excessively hierarchical. I believe in much flatter structures.' (Government minister)

Exercising soft power: non-governmental actors steering government

Expert interviewees perceived that civil servants and certain non-governmental stakeholders (for example from the YJB and the Office of the Children's Commissioner [OCC]) were able to challenge and steer policy making, suggesting more balanced and equitable power dynamics within their relationships with government. Indeed, non-governmental stakeholders identified their own use of *soft power* (for example, through leverage) as a constructive influence on local and national policy making and policy influencing (see also Chapter 6), both within and outside of their relationships with governmental actors:

'We [YJB] are trying soft power from a variety of directions and trying to influence the practice of people who've got the levers. If you think about the Child First principle, it's not a formal MoJ policy, but it's something which we promote and incorporate in all of our documentation. We use it whenever we're interacting with other people. We incorporate it into our expectations around Youth Justice Plans. So it's not really a formal policy mechanism, it's more a campaign where we're trying to influence the whole system. Policy making without levers. We don't own any of these policies, but we try to influence their content.' (YJB Chief Executive)

'YJB doesn't have policy-making power per se, but it does have soft power. We think very hard about who we're meeting with and why. It's about the conversations that we have with people of influence at all sorts of levels, including people who have the experience of what the policy has done to them.' (YJB Chair)

'A challenge for the OCC is that sense of formal versus informal, soft power. How do you translate those big picture systems that people know are failing into another big picture system that works better for children? We're looking to effect change in the lives of children. Sometimes that requires systems to change. It's a delicate dance and the job of the Commissioner is to balance that situation. We don't have formal recommendation powers. We have powers of entry and data collection, the ability to require any public sector body to respond to our letters, the ability to raise issues with Parliament. We have the ability to make a noise. That's the art of the job rather than the science. How you can use that leverage or bring attention to an issue to actually effect change. Getting those wheels of government turning along a slightly different track.' (OCC senior official)

The central contexts–mechanisms relationships identified when examining power dynamics and their influence on relational policy making are outlined in Appendix 12.

YJB relationships in policy-making contexts

The predominance of YJB officials in the sampling frame for the semi-structured interview component (see reflections in Chapters 2 and 8), as well as their emerging significance as policy influencers, necessitates a more detailed analysis of the trajectory of the organisation's relationships with governmental and non-governmental actors in policy-making contexts.

YJB relationships with governmental actors: government and ministers

A board member (also a senior academic) expressed the view that government occupied a more directive, prescriptive and agenda-based role in their relationships with the YJB (that is, an inequitable power dynamic), which was reiterated by a board member and senior academic:

> 'What can be a barrier for the YJB at senior level is if you have a minister coming in with their senior officials [SPADs] and they don't agree with what the YJB wants to do or its direction of travel, because they have the power and authority to say no, you're not gonna do that and it doesn't happen. YJB has wanted to go in a certain direction and basically been told no, you can't do that for various reasons or that's not how we want to operate at this moment in time. Whereas in the past, perhaps a different ministerial team with whom we had a different set of relationships, might have been open to it and some ground might have been gained.'

Another senior academic noted the evolving and dynamic trajectory and nature of the YJB–government relationship and how this has caused tensions with civil servants in the MoJ due to the YJB becoming a more proactive policy maker and influencer in recent years:

> 'The history of the YJB relationship with central government and ministerial departments with responsibility for youth justice is interesting in how policy has developed. You can see how that relationship changed and how the role of the YJB became something quite different from what it had originally been. There are periods when that created tensions with the MoJ. YJB shifted from being an organisation starting to develop policy in advance of changes at the national political level and telling practitioners what to do, to trying to influence what politicians did as a reaction to failures in the existing policy regime. That's an interesting [power] dynamic change in what they thought was appropriate for them to do and their role within the policy-making process. More recently, their role was seriously truncated and a whole raft of their staff were moved out to the MoJ policy team and YCS. I see that in part as a consequence of their changing role and the MoJ becoming increasingly concerned to be seen as an asset. You saw this power battle between the board and the MoJ. It's gone into balance, but I suspect it still simmers and could easily come to the surface again if they are any particular points of serious disagreement.'

Perceptions of an evolving YJB relationship with government enabling an increasing YJB policy influence were reinforced by a Chief Executive. He linked the changing contexts of being steered by/steering government to the *agendas* and *personalities* (such as their open-mindedness) of individual ministers (see earlier in this chapter) exerting both positive and negative influence:

> 'My experience is that some justice secretaries are really focused on their agenda, and they'll drive it incredibly hard. They'll get their objective, but they might have damaged some other relationships along the way. There are others who are much more consultative and engaging with others, such as Robert Buckland. He was very clear that as an arm's-length body, we [YJB] were probably better placed to have conversations with some of the partners than the core department [MoJ], because this [youth justice] is our agenda. So there was bridge building. … light years away from the position we were in when I first went to the YJB where we were somewhat ostracised.'

A YJB Chief Executive reflected on the *churnover* (see Chapter 5) of justice ministers as actually facilitating contexts of constructive policy-influencing relationships with government through mechanisms of credibility, consistent messaging, empathy and open-mindedness:

> 'Gove was open to seeing how the YJB might be helpful to government. Truss took over and spent about six months deciding what her response to the Taylor Review (2016) would be, taking a lot of advice from policy officials. Using my previous capital, I managed gradually to get myself involved in discussions with ministers around what we might do, what the priorities might be and what their response might be. It was more personal than organisational, but the organisation gradually moved in behind me. Lee as minister joined us and he was a bit unsure as to what does this job mean? That gave me an opportunity to say, well I'm new too. Let's learn together and actually we did, we kicked stuff around in quite an open way [see 'opportunism' discussion in Chapter 6]. Agar followed on, and by then, I'd established credibility with the Minister's office [see also 'credibility' discussion in Chapter 6]. He used to routinely invite me to meetings that had policy officials, and he actually listened to their advice. He'd say, what does YJB think? They used us as a sounding board.'

YJB relationships with governmental actors: civil servants

YJB stakeholders reflected in depth on the evolving nature of their power dynamics and relationships with civil servants, from the Home Office in the expansionist area of youth justice policy making (see Chapter 3) and from the MoJ in the austerity era (see Chapter 4). YJB experts built upon academic discussions presented in earlier chapters (for example, Souhami, 2011, 2015a) that the creation of the YJB outside of departmental structures recognised the limitations of the civil service in producing youth justice policy and liberated it from notoriously conservative, compliant and risk-averse civil service culture (Kemp, 1990; Driscoll and Morris, 2001).

Reflecting on experience of the directive, prescriptive and steering approach to the YJB adopted by Home Office civil servants immediately after the Crime and Disorder Act 1998, two senior YJB officials commented that this was often experienced as intrusive and sudden/unpredicted:

> 'The research people in the Home Office came and said we've been looking at the way we've been calculating these figures and actually we don't think this is right, and so suddenly the figures turned on their heads. So from the policy looking like it had really delivered results on the ground, suddenly the figures weren't right. We weren't talking about anything that had changed in practice, but they [Home Office] changed, as researchers often do.' (YJB Chief Executive)

> 'There was an interesting relationship with our guardians in the civil service, who had privileged access to ministers. In 2010, after the Home Office had been reorganised as not fit for purpose, effectively we had two sponsoring authorities, an MoJ team shadowing me and a Home Office team shadowing the MoJ team, which was an interesting insight into central government. We were playing the field, and I had two sets of people watching what we did. So I have some experience of policy development.' (YJB board member, YOT manager)

The austerity era (post-2010) saw the replacement of the Home Office by the MoJ as sponsor of the YJB. Thereafter, the YJB–civil service relationship became more balanced, reciprocal and collaborative (in its power dynamics) and thus *influential in policy-making contexts*, according to senior YJB officials, although this influence was always *mediated by political realities*:

> 'We [YJB–MoJ] have a good relationship. We're always talking about what we're seeing and finding. They [MoJ] help to triangulate some of the stuff that we [YJB] see ourselves.' (YJB Chair)

> 'MoJ look at how policy is developed through evidence and horizon scanning. But you've also got the political with a small or big "P", so our policy colleagues are constantly having to navigate that political environment. YJB have to consider that less. Relationships are absolutely crucial. One of my major roles is managing the relationship with MoJ and being able to demonstrate our value and providing them with good evidence-based advice to support their policy development

> … to help them find the levers to use to push an evidence-based agenda.' (YJB senior official)

However, the nature of the YJB relationship with the civil service has not always been necessarily constructive or framed by equitable power dynamics. A series of YJB representatives addressed the inevitable tensions and *threats to the identity, status, role and influence* of each organisation (YJB and MoJ) caused by the evolution of youth justice policy-making contexts immediately once austerity measures kicked in, particularly as the YJB appeared to increase its policy influence:

> 'The MoJ was really starting to feel the squeeze on its resources [circa 2015], and children were in danger of being squeezed out at the expense of adults. Understandable, but that was just the reality. They were under real pressure. The YJB didn't have very much influence. Government and MoJ had just taken receipt of the Taylor Review, with a lot of stuff in there that said this [YJS] isn't working very well and could be done in a different way. I wasn't sure what role the YJB played. We were definitely on our own as an organisation supposedly looking at policy influencing, so that's where I started.' (YJB Chief Executive)

> 'Imagine you're a civil servant on the way up and get an offer of joining the MoJ Youth Justice Policy Unit, then you arrive to find the location of power and authority doesn't sit with you, but with a non-departmental public body [NDPB] [YJB]. There's not much of a job for you, other than man marking or giving advice or shaping policy. You're not at the forefront of proposing legislative agendas or change. Because for civil servants, a big badge for them is taking a bill through Parliament. That's how civil servants earn their spurs.' (YJB board member, YOT manager)

Shifting MoJ–YJB power dynamics: civil servants reclaiming the policy initiative

Interviewees suggested that the more recent trajectory and nature of the YJB–civil service (MoJ) relationship reflects a shifting power dynamic, with the MoJ adopting a more active policy-making role and assuming more power, authority and influence in youth justice policy-making contexts and the YJB's policy influence (allegedly) diminishing proportionately:

> 'MoJ has taken a more active role in recent years and is back designing policy and using the YJB as a sounding board, rather than how I experienced it, whereby YJB dreamt-up policy and cleared it through

the [MoJ] Policy Unit before it got to ministers. Really, since 2012, there's been very little legislative change. Yet YJB has the knowledge and experience and skills and it's engaged with policy delivery, but actually they aren't well controlled by ministers, because they're supposed to be independent, so they can say what they like. I think there's been a reigning in of the authority and power of the YJB, and civil servants have become more dominant.' (YJB board member, YOT manager)

'In terms of developing policy, what we should be doing is contributing to their [MoJ] understanding of the [youth justice] picture, identifying what we think needs to be improved and describing what we think good policy and practice should look like. Prior to the creation of the MoJ Youth Justice Policy Unit, I think the YJB did more policy making directly, but we don't anymore.' (YJB Chief Executive)

Some experts perceived the MoJ as becoming more 'muscular' in policy-making contexts in recent years, indicative of civil service ambition to seize policy-making power by recalibrating relational power dynamics in their favour. The MoJ was also seen as retaining a commitment to collaboration with the YJB, an organisation increasingly viewed (by some stakeholders) as relatively *directionless* in recent years (see also Chapter 6):

'MoJ has always been a Policy Unit that has dealt with some youth justice matters, although it's largely been benign and very much in the background. Certainly from the beginning of 2023, it seems to be flexing its muscles and being more questioning of the roles and responsibilities between the two [MoJ and YJB] and asking, why should the YJB be developing policy? No, that's the role of the Policy Unit. Should MoJ be involved in operational matters? No, that's the responsibility of the YJB. The relationship is never static, it's dynamic.' (YJB board member, senior academic)

'It's really interesting what's happening with the MoJ Youth Justice Policy Unit. There's almost a land grab going on, taking away from the YJB. It all started with the YCS, cause the whole custody element used to sit under YJB. But I don't get a sense that they're [MoJ] trying to dominate them [YJB] or push them out. I think they are trying to work alongside them and utilise their skills.' (AYM Chair)

YJB relationships with non-governmental actors: HMIP

Experts discussed the influence on policy making of the dynamic, evolving trajectory and context of the YJB–HMIP relationship; two governance organisations overseeing and guiding youth justice practice in the YJS. Particular attention was drawn to the perceived context of *incongruent practice agendas* across the youth justice sector in recent years (see also Chapter 4) due to growing YJB advocacy for their 'Child First' guiding principle and HMIP's resilient commitment to a risk management agenda (see Day, 2022; Case et al, 2023; Hampson in Case and Hazel, 2023). However, officials from both governance organisations had experienced and continue to advocate for the pursuit of constructive, effective working relationships between the two organisations, notably when collaborating in *seeking common ground* (see also later in this chapter) upon which to *reconcile differing professional agendas*:

> 'Trying to understand where there's common ground and build on it, there's no expectation that you should always have 100 per cent alignment with every stakeholder. You will have some different drivers, different objectives, different priorities. But equally, it's very unlikely that there'll be 100 per cent antagonism. You don't have to be in agreement about a subject to understand that both parties are coming to it with good intentions and honourable motives. You don't have to be set up into an oppositional relationship. You start by trying to recognise where you might have common ground. We have very few stakeholders that don't want to see better outcomes for children.' (YJB Chief Executive)

> 'I meet regularly with YJB leadership. We have regular catch-ups. We download recent inspections and talk about thematic findings. They have a particular role in terms of the guidance that they issue, their control, their ownership of assetPlus, their ability to support local YOTs on the ground. It's helpful to have them come in behind that when we've found problems. So when we do a thematic review, we can make recommendations to the YJB, as well as to government and to local YOTs.' (HMIP senior official)

> 'A good example of building common ground with HMIP is around the question of "risk". The sense of trying to manage what felt like almost irreconcilable positions gets in the way of the relationship we have with HMIP, an absolutely, critical stakeholder for us. So we try to work out what it is we can agree on, rather than focusing what it is that you can't agree on. If you can establish a position that doesn't say risky kids are bad kids but says children with a certain set of experiences may develop complex needs that need to be resolved, then you are able to reconcile what HMIP are looking for. The two are not irreconcilable, but you have to work to find the common ground.' (YJB Chief Executive)

A YJB board member (who was also a YOT manager) viewed HMIP becoming more muscular, aggressive and assertive in policy-making contexts in recent years, which he explained as due to a contemporary policy vacuum, the individual agenda of the HMIP Chief Inspector and a less influential YJB. He also perceived that the YJB had recognised this change of relational power dynamics and had embarked on a similar trajectory of becoming more directive, assertive and interventionist itself:

> 'HMIP has taken on this more muscular form, but there's clearly something in the water, because the YJB are now aping that. YJB seems to be a more expansionist, more muscular again, I find it really interesting that HMIP had gone through the same cycles just a bit earlier. They've had a few years of being muscular and they've been empowered to behave in ways which are counter-productive to do youth justice governance. I wonder whether there's been a vacuum left by the YJB. The [HMIP] Chief Inspector himself is pretty significant in that. Whereas you had a previous inspector who wasn't particularly interested in youth justice, the current leader seems very bothered to make his mark. So it's an individual thing, but it is clearly a space that he's been able to inhabit.'

YJB relationships with non-governmental actors: Wales

The policy-making context of youth justice in Wales merits further exploration in terms of the YJB's relationships with Welsh-centric stakeholder organisations, such as the Welsh government (notably its Crime and Justice Unit), YJB Cymru and YOT Managers Cymru (YMC). These relationships reflect the confluence of two unique and nuanced policy-making contexts and constructs in youth justice: the YJB as an NDPB situated between government and practice, and the partially devolved policy-making context in Wales (see Chapters 3 to 5). A range of experts with experience of the Welsh youth justice context reflected on the political, policy-based strategic and practical marginalisation of Welsh youth justice by the (English) centrism of UK government and YJB, who were, at times, seen as variously trying to control, neglect, ignore and disrespect their Welsh counterparts. However, stakeholders in Wales reported that the historical lack of attention paid to Wales, considered alongside its relatively small size geographically, were contexts enabling *collaborative policy-making* relationships nationally (in Wales) based on the development of *common ground* (some even argued *consensus*) and *shared agendas and identities* (see also Chapter 5). Furthermore, for some experts, the unique Welsh policy-making context has enabled *challenge and innovation* when faced with realising prescribed UK government youth justice policy in practice.

Stakeholders reflected upon the relational context of *English-centrism* within the UK government and how this was animated by anti-Welsh mechanisms of neglect, prejudice and lack of understanding:

> 'One of the issues for Wales is whether UK government policy in relation to the YJS considers Wales at all. The answer is generally not. At best, you'll get a statement in policy documents that says something like "and arrangements or consideration of what this means for Wales will follow in due course". It will be a very short statement because if the policy is coming from the UK government, it's formed from that direction. It's not always clear what the level of consultation has been in Wales, if any.' (YJB board member, senior academic)

> 'The YJB were so centrist and so determined that they had the answer that they didn't want to listen to somebody [such as the Welsh government] who thought that they might have an answer that wasn't the same as theirs. Warner [first YJB Chair] didn't like the drive down to Wales and always felt that the YJB were missing out on too much by coming away from London. It was by no means the case that the YJB could just look at YOT managers as being their property in Wales to do their bidding. They had to work through the political structure of Welsh government.' (YMC Chair, YOT manager)

Experiences of Anglo-centrism, combined with an emerging national identity for youth justice in Wales grounded in universalism, social justice and children's rights (see Chapters 3, 4 and 6), was seen as encouraging policy innovation and challenge among Welsh professionals. This included increased practice engagement with Welsh Government, who were considered more aligned with and empathetic to the Welsh youth justice identity and with practitioners than the UK government:

> 'Engagement with YJB Cymru was not particularly easy when [its former Chair] was there as she was very London-focused, which made life quite difficult. But in a sense, that encouraged a collective group within Wales. We actually had to work harder to get common consensus about things, and we lent a bit more towards Welsh Assembly government. (YMC Chair, YOT manager)

> 'I've heard anti-Welsh racism from ministers. What are they [the Welsh] bleating about now? I was seen as the grumpy Welsh ***** who was always saying "that doesn't apply to us". It was a bit of an invidious position, but for a while it worked really well in terms of the effective practice side. And we formalised it, we brought academics in, we

brought people from policy and practitioners and YJB getting together once a month for a chat and to share good stuff and to sometimes find a bit of money to do stuff. The argument was that almost like spread the love. We need to get some of this Welsh expertise into England.' (YJB Cymru Chair)

However, from the perspective of one YJB senior official, practitioner resistance and challenge to perceived Anglo-centric policy prescriptions could be experienced by Welsh strategists as unnecessary hostility, suspicion and intransigence, which served as relational barriers to establishing common ground and pursuing collaborative policy-making relationships in Wales:

'The YJB Cymru–YMC relationship was disappointingly difficult because I always felt like I was trying to do the best for them. I was trying to get more money and trying to put youth justice in the best position in a difficult environment, because Welsh government had no real political, economic, constitutional, imperative to do anything for youth justice. But I would often be treated with lots of suspicion and told, you have nothing to teach me, so you're not coming into my YOT. So I've been treated very rudely. That was disappointing. It got better as the years went by. I was able to be more inclusive and be more open and share things.' (YJB Cymru Chair)

Wales as a small policy-making context

'It feels a little like we've got away with something and they're gonna wake up to this in a minute.'

(YJB board member – Wales representative)

The relatively small size of Wales in political, geographical, demographic, financial and resource terms was clearly a double-edged sword to experts. On the negative side, as noted, Welsh stakeholders had experienced centrism, neglect, prejudice and repeated attempts to exert Anglo-centric control in policy-making contexts. On the positive side, stakeholders felt that its relative lack of size, profile and status had rendered Wales 'out of sight, out of mind' to the UK government, such that professionals could mediate/moderate UK government policy and develop Welsh-centric youth justice policy unilaterally:

'A passive lack of scrutiny can give us [Welsh government] a lot of freedom. It's been at the heart of how we want to work and ultimately, good youth justice practice and policy formation. It allows us to just get on and do good stuff without always needing to worry about where UK ministers might be on it.' (Welsh government senior civil servant)

> 'In Wales, we [YJB Cymru] kept our heads below the parapet and basically continued as we were. Wales is smaller and so scaling it is a key issue because all the key players we have probably follow each other around to each other's meetings all week. The relationships in Wales tend to be well known, and in terms of people's knowledge and understanding of each other, the regions in England cannot operate in the same way. But the YJB are in danger of seeing Wales as just another region, rather than the country in its own right with its own unique set of issues.' (YJB board member)

The posited Welsh national policy identity was progressed by the smaller national context, which allowed easier, more practical mechanisms through which to develop collaborative relationships and shared agendas:

> 'That ability to have those conversations with the YJB, but also Welsh government. Our opportunity to be able to have that in Wales far outstripped what they were ever gonna be able to do in England, really just cause of its size. You could have those conversations in Wales, where other people couldn't.' (YMC Chair)

> 'I could never understand this, but a lot of London-based board members couldn't stand talking to Wales. Whereas I [YJB Chief Executive] thought that the Welsh context was really interesting because it's a small country. When the Welsh talked about our children, they had a completely different way of thinking than when the English talked about the 11 million children in England at that time. There was a sense of responsibility, ownership, commitment, which was different and that played in very neatly and maybe was a consequence of the "Extending entitlement" [youth inclusion] agenda. So it was just a pleasure. And there were some great people there.' (YJB Chief Executive)

Several Welsh stakeholders believed that Wales' shared youth justice policy identity and small size could actually enhance its relationship with English stakeholders. These beneficial characteristics operated in contexts that enabled *challenge of English centrism*, requiring and facilitating the *education of English colleagues* (through new constructs such as the YJB Wales representative, for example) and fostering the development of innovative and constructive relationships of *mutual learning and respect*:

> 'The YJB now see Wales as this great test bed because it's small enough that if you have any innovation, you try it in Wales and then increase the scope, so it does offer real opportunity. What it does take is for both parties [England and Wales] to actually be open to learning

from each other. But sometimes there's quite a hostile approach in Westminster, quite dismissive of the devolved nations. So we [YJB] are trying to navigate that difficult position. Day-to-day, that means contact is more with Westminster and advocating on behalf of Wales, because invariably they [UK government] will forget that Wales has got these services and actually they need to be speaking with Wales, having those conversations and ensuring that Wales feel respected as a partner.' (YJB senior official)

'In Wales, youth justice is not wholly devolved, which makes it [policy development] much more difficult. You didn't really have any influence over anything really and you were just told what you needed to do. But to meet the English perspective in the policy-making context, there's a large amount of "Welshifying" you have to do with documents.' (YMC Chair)

'In one way, Welsh government was more important for the majority of our prevention policies and services for children, as opposed to the YJB being more associated with England. Generally, the relationship with the YJB was a good relationship, but they could see us [YMC] as a bunch of troublemakers making their lives difficult, so therefore, it was easier to try to get on with us. I felt that it was a useful relationship. We were a small number of organisations working with and for children and so being able to do things together made much more sense than trying to fight against each other.' (YMC Chair)

YJB relationships with non-governmental actors: YOTs

'We didn't seek to try and influence [YOTs] too much or directly. I thought that we should have been engaging with them at a higher, more strategic level, a more political level, rather than saying, you're not filling out your forms properly, which is probably what we used to do in the past.'

(YJB Chair)

Chapter 6 analysed the evolving relationship between the YJB and local YOTs in terms of its trajectory away from centralised managerialist prescription and towards more YJB (regional, localised) engagement with and empowerment of YOTs. The suggestion from stakeholders was that relational *power dynamics* had become more equitable due to an emerging *collaborative mindset* and more willingness to acknowledge and use *expertise* situated locally with practitioners. Furthermore, as Souhami (2015a) has noted, the development of the YJB's regional monitoring role appears to have facilitated a mutually beneficial relationship with YOTs, allowing the YJB to widen and deepen their influence in localities, thereby helping embed youth justice services into the local landscape, while enabling YOTs to become more firmly established among their local partners. In this relational context, it is instructive to compare and contrast the perspectives of expert stakeholders from the YJB and those from practice and practitioner organisations, typically representatives from YOT managers' organisations.

YJB experts advocated the importance of developing open, empathetic, supportive and challenging relationships with YOT managers' groups (AYM, YMC), YOTs and their individual practitioners:

> 'You will never be influential if you don't have seats at the table and if you don't have goodwill with stakeholders and partners. You have to actively build those relationships, trying to understand your stakeholders' drivers and objectives and finding ways of supporting them to navigate their issues. That creates goodwill that you will eventually benefit from … trying to make sure that we are seen as helpful and friendly and constructive to a lot of different groups, not just to the MoJ.' (YJB Chief Executive)

> 'There were times when they [YOTs] felt we [YJB] should have been arguing more strongly and banging the drum louder, normally for more money. We had a fairly open working relationship, so I would explain to them how far I thought I could go and without overstepping the mark. They [AYM] said to me toward the end of my tenure [as YJB Chief Executive] that they'd been really well served by us, certainly in terms of money. They got what they needed to continue. There were times when it was quite tricky because I was asking for evidence that would help me argue that this was a good investment. They were struggling with some of that. But they were supportive of the changes we made and supportive of us as an organisation, so were able to input to policy ideas.' (YJB Chief Executive)

> 'The relationship with the AYM is probably more open than it has been in the past. The YJB have worked hard to engage with the AYM, which I think has been a good thing in terms of each side being able to be honest with each other and challenging of each other. Because challenge is a good thing in all relationships.' (YJB board member)

From the perspective of YOT managers, their relationships (and associated power dynamics) with the YJB in policy-making contexts have evolved in recent years (since the 2016 Taylor Review, for example). The YJB–YOT managers' relationship is now perceived as more equitable, constructive and collaborative, wherein practitioner experience and expertise to challenge and innovate is increasingly recognised and used:

> 'We see each other as ollaborators, rather than adversaries, so that's shifted things. We've got longstanding relationships with YJB. A number of those colleagues were previously in YOTs and are now in YJB or vice versa, so the relationships are there and are strong. I also see that AYM clearly has the ability to say things and challenge things that YJB wouldn't be able to be seen to be doing or saying or challenging. It's a constructive relationship.' (AYM senior official, YOT manager)

> 'Initially, the AYM's role was very much challenging current policy and the expected practice that falls out of that policy. As the AYM has become more mature and able to engage with MoJ, YJB and latterly, YCS, we are in a better position to help [policy development] through active consultations and stakeholder engagement. That's why we've been able to do more influencing, meeting with the YJB Chair and Chief Executive on a regular basis. When we meet with the YJB, we'd be saying this is a consistent problem and it has been raised individually, but we are now bringing this as a collective voice.' (AYM Chair)

However, issues remain from a practitioner perspective regarding increasing *YJB prescriptiveness and control* (see MoJ–YJB relationship discussion):

> 'The YJB try to placate the AYM and don't want us to make a noise. They get confused thinking that they can tell us what to do, so it can be quite a difficult relationship to manage. They absolutely think we're a pain in their ****. But if it's making a difference to children, then I'm gonna be a pain. YJB don't like that because a lot of the people there haven't worked in practice. But there has definitely been a shift change [towards more prescriptiveness] with the new Chief Executive and because the YJB feel quite vulnerable at the moment [2023].' (AYM Chair)

> I have a lot of meetings with the YJB, and the relationship is good. But what's been really interesting this year [2023] is that they've started to become more prescriptive, and we're starting to see ringfence funding coming through again. This year for the Youth Justice Plan, we all got letters in April with prescriptive templates. The Chief Executive has obviously come with the new thinking and approach.' (AYM Chair)

The most significant contexts–mechanisms relationships identified when exploring the power dynamics of YJB relationships with non-governmental organisations are outlined in Appendix 13.

Mechanisms of relational and collaborative policy making: common ground, communication and reciprocity

> 'It's always about relationships. Everything comes down to relationships … the dialogue is so important. I'm building links. Let's bring people along with us and to breakdown some of the misconceptions as well.'
> (HMIP senior official)

This chapter has established from the experiences and perspectives of experts that youth justice policy making occurs in relational contexts shaped by power dynamics, including political identity and agenda, personalities, agendas, stubbornness, prejudice, soft power and centrism in different national and local contexts. The chapter now moves to more detailed identification and exploration of the mechanisms through which relationships operate and policy making occurs in contexts characterised by consensus and collaboration. Interviewee experiences align with a central conclusion from literature regarding effective social policy making, namely that priority should be given to establishing *common ground* to enable compromise and to constructively reconcile and/or manage differences (while avoiding organisational siloes), rather than necessarily pursuing a consensus between stakeholder groups or privileging a particular organisational agenda (Ansell et al, 2017; Hudson et al, 2019).

A consistently identified contextual barrier to policy making is ineffective collaborative relationships, most notably the development of policy in distinct administrative silos (Hill and Hupe, 2015). It is clear, both from empirical research and from the expert experience solicited in the current project, that policy implementation in particular is highly dependent on local context (see Brathwaite et al, 2018) and that centralised youth justice policy and strategy is 'made' real at the local level (see Goldson and Briggs, 2021). Consequently, effective policy making in youth justice contexts requires continuous collaboration with a range of stakeholders at multiple political, policy-making, managerial and administrative levels (Case and Browning, 2021a; Day, 2022). As stated previously (see, for example, Chapter 6), effective policy making often demonstrates 'local universality' (Sausman et al, 2016), whereby centralised policy/strategy is shaped/tailored by practitioners to fit local contexts and practices, which necessitates the engagement of local 'downstream' implementation actors ('street-level bureaucrats') such as end users, frontline staff and a range of local service agencies (see Ansell et al, 2017). In this section, therefore, the expert interview data is analysed to identify the mechanisms that may drive relational and collaborative policy making in youth justice contexts, mechanisms presenting as:

- seeking common ground through challenging barriers to collaborative, relational policy making such as agenda change/shift and staff churnover (by rebuilding relationships and re-educating colleagues, for example) and through developing shared agendas, networking/building alliances with the right people, advocacy and brokering relationships;

- using communication to build collaborative relationships, including the effective use of dialogue, language, diplomacy and consistent, cogent messaging, narrative storytelling;
- relational reciprocity promoting equitable and supportive relationships and equitable power dynamics through mechanisms of empathy, immersion, trust, respect and valuing professional lived experience and expertise by being inclusive and developing evidence-led and collaborative mindsets.

Seeking common ground: networking, building alliances, advocating and brokering

> 'Trying to see others' priorities is crucial. How they see what we're doing helps us [YJB] to support them, because people will have different ideas about how to deal with the same issue. You have to work with all those different actors to try and get a view that is relatively consistent.'
>
> (YJB Chair)

A common weakness of collaborative policy making is the failure to establish *common ground* for public problem solving through the constructive management of difference (Hill and Hupe, 2015). Indeed, scholars argue that effective collaborative policy making should not be a long and cumbersome search for unanimous consent or consensus but rather a search for sufficient common ground to proceed and to avoid ongoing conflicts over policy legitimacy and organisational mission (Ansell et al, 2017; Braithwaite et al, 2018; Case and Browning, 2021a). Expert experiences coalesced around the notion of *pursuing common ground* through establishing a *collaborative mindset*, often by using *multi-agency partnership working*, to build constructive, empathetic relationships between national and local stakeholders:

> 'Showing yourself [Alliance for Youth Justice (AYJ)] to be an asset to the work of others means that they want you around the table and want to have another catch-up with you, because it's a mutually beneficial relationship, not just an influencing relationship. Make it really clear, even in your first interactions, that this is how you want that relationship to be, that you're not just there to have a go at them or to push your agenda. You understand that they're working in a particular context and that you want to work together to try and achieve things that have mutual benefit.' (AYJ Chair)

'I've got close links with the MoJ Deputy Director and we [HMIP] have started having more frequent liaison. I do feedback sessions with Heads of Service, Directors of Children's Services as well. We have an expert advisory group of academics and other people within the YJS. We also have a working group that consists of youth justice service [YOT] managers and certainly the AYM has a place around that table. So you're gonna get some commonality in terms of the understanding and expectations, and I'm keen that our language is reflective of that. It feels like a much more collaborative set of relationships, understanding how the sector experience us so that we're on the same page.' (HMIP senior official)

According to a Children's Commissioner, *developing shared agendas* is a key mechanism for establishing common ground for policy progress, reconciling tensions/conflicting agendas and being open-minded and empathetic to alternative perspectives and expertise:

'Connecting with local practitioners is really important because it helps to support their [local] agenda and it supports our [OCC] agenda. It's always keeping your mind open about how can you knit people together. Meet both your outcomes. There's no right answer about it, but what you do need to be really clear about whatever is the policy around youth justice is, it has to hang and sit in the right places, so that the statutory bodies own it collectively and that no single body has the greater priority.' (Children's Commissioner, local government official)

Having established *collaborative mindset* as a key mechanism shaping the pursuit of common ground and shared agenda in youth justice policy-making contexts, experts elaborated by identifying a number of barriers to initiating and particularly maintaining this mindset in relational contexts. A notable influence on *political agenda change/shift* was staff 'churnover' (see Chapter 5), which necessitated the *rebuilding of relationships* and the *re-education of colleagues*:

'Obviously, there will be individuals who are obstacles, who say, I'm doing this because this is my agenda. That causes tension because you don't get an alignment. When priorities change, people then stop listening because they're now focused on the next priority. That doesn't help to keep things flowing or get people to keep being interested and investing. When people leave, relationships stop, or you have to rebuild and start again. That's often a big barrier because then you either get the new person not interested, so you can't get them into your camp, or actually you get fatigued by the fact you're saying the same old thing and you're trying to get people involved again.' (Children's Commissioner)

'One of the biggest challenges is that personnel changes quite frequently occur with policy colleagues. You're always trying to resell your story and it'sifficult to build those relationships with the right people, because the right people often change, and then you end up spending time getting the right people up to speed again. Then the opportunity is gone. It's all a bit of a perfect storm.' (HMIP senior official)

Networking to build collaborative policy-making relationships

'Knowing where your friends are and making the case was key. You've got all the big beasts that you've got to engage with. You cut your cloth. It's that mixture of hard power and soft power.'

(YJB Chair)

Networking was identified by experts as an effective mechanism for *building relationships/alliances* with key colleagues (political connections, advocates), often underpinned by perceived *professional legitimacy/credibility*. Networking was also seen as useful for garnering and utilising the political and policy-making *leverage* required to effect policy change using empathy and challenge. Reflecting on the use of networking to create and enable policy-making leverage, stakeholders commented that

'[s]ometimes it does feel like a game, and you feel that you constantly have to second guess and try to frame things in ways that you're gonna get the most leverage and interaction. Understanding and trying to see things from other people's perspectives.' (YJB senior official)

'Having the YJB has changed the dynamic around policy agenda setting. For all its strengths or weaknesses, it has been a game changer in terms of bringing together partners to have a constructive conversation around youth justice.' (YJB board member, YOT manager)

'We [HMIP] are shining a light on practice that colleagues [YJB, YOTs] really need to think about and need to change. Increasingly, I have youth justice services saying, you shone a light on stuff, some of it we knew, some of it we didn't know. We've given people [YOTs] leverage in terms of things that they needed to do, particularly from a [local] partnership perspective, and that they've helped move things along. People have found it really valuable and helpful.' (HMIP senior official)

Building alliances with the right people was highlighted as a pivotal networking mechanism for creating policy influence in relational contexts of collaboration:

'The board [YJB] members were so important to me. The Chair would tell me, with ACPO [Association of Chief Police Officers], you need to meet with XYZ and he would set-up the meeting. I would meet with them and Bob's your uncle. Then we had a board member who could give us access into their network, another into their network and so on.' (YJB Chief Executive)

'Building alliances is probably the most unique role YJB has, but there aren't too many other parties who really grasp its importance. Civil servants don't understand that influence comes from building alliances. Their whole drive is to satisfy ministers. At the YJB, I took our primary function as being to build up the whole alliance for the YJS. That meant that we had to have a trusting relationship with sentencers, with the judiciary, inputs that improved practice in the courts, which we did in publications and training programs. We needed to have a great relationship with the police chiefs. So the ACPO lead on youth justice was immensely important to me. They had the child-centred policing concept, and I encouraged it and so it wasn't difficult to find a common cause.' (YJB Chief Executive)

'As YJB Chief Executive, I recognised the unique places I could go to talk about youth justice, so that gave me a particular responsibility. I could do media stuff, and the voice would be heard in a way that other people's voices wouldn't. I'd always do local media as much as possible. My role was to big up the local leaders … this what they're doing. These are their policies. You're given the privilege of having a platform and building alliances.' (YJB Chief Executive)

Powerful advocates advocating powerfully

A key element of networking and building alliances with the right people (like-minded colleagues, for example) to support collaborative, relational policy making in youth justice contexts was identifying and utilising *powerful, like-minded advocates* and *advocating* for less powerful partners:

'As Children's Commissioner, I found advocates everywhere. Here's a great person who works in National Health Service etc and you go off and chat with them and they're doing something wonderful. Then you advocate for what they're doing. They advocate for what you're doing. It's relationship building.' (Children's Commissioner)

'You gain policy momentum with like-minded individuals. When you've got really good YOT managers who are saying I wanna make a difference. I'm gonna pull in these individual people and they might not necessarily have the policy or the reasons or the mandate, but because they wanna make a difference, because they're passionate about it, they will go and do it anyway. That's what we need. We need to support and champion people who do that.' (AYM Chair)

'They [government] were very happy with my recommendation of YJB Chair. That was not the source of any debate, even though sometimes these issues can be quite tense and difficult. I'm somebody who always tries to find a way through and seek consensus and seeks solutions. I generally felt that in the YJS, I wasn't having to push water uphill in order to get to get the desired objective, because a lot of the groundwork that had been laid was proving to be successful, so I supported it.' (Government minister)

Brokering collaborative relationships

A key element of advocacy was identified by experts as the *brokering* of collaborative relationships and shared agendas and ideas between like-minded individuals and organisations (for example building alliances with the right people) across local and national contexts:

'We [Welsh government Crime and Justice Unit] are very much the convener and the conduit. We recognise that the Welsh government's approach to youth justice cuts across a range of policy areas. So the delivery of education in youth justice contexts sits with the Education Minister, the delivery of healthcare sits with the Health Minister etc. Our conversation is, who needs to be in the room? Sometimes that's just us being a passive conduit, making sure the right people are in touch with each other. Sometimes that's more an active facilitation role in terms of, how are we gonna get these crazy kids to work together? Fundamentally, we make sure that the right partners come together and are able to structure the right conversations. We don't have all the answers. We take a step back and look at the system, ask the right questions and facilitate the right discussions.' (Welsh government senior civil servant)

'You work out who you need to talk to by asking around or by looking on the MoJ directory. You work out who you need to warm-up. I will cold call people, not literally on the phone, but just drop an e-mail and say, we've just got this piece of work and think you'd be interested in it. Let's get together and talk about it.' (HMIP senior official)

Using communication: diplomacy, dialogue, common language and effective messaging

According to experts, collaborative, empathetic policy-making contexts were shaped by mechanisms of communication: "It's all about communication and understanding where colleagues are coming from" (AYM Chair). Effective communicative mechanisms identified by experts included the use of *diplomacy*, *dialogue*, *common language*, *consistent*, *cogent messaging* (for example persistent, well pitched, attention grabbing) and effective *narrative storytelling*. These were seen as facilitating the pursuit of common ground and shared agendas, networking (including building alliances with the right people) and brokerage of relationships while encouraging the building of empathy, trust and respect.

Diplomacy as a communicative mechanism of policy making

Diplomacy was highlighted as a powerful communicative tool and barrier (when absent) in policy-making contexts, particularly when used to criticise and challenge in *tactful and tactical* ways:

> 'You've got to be diplomatic. You've got to recognise that colleagues have political constraints and political drivers. And so for me, I would try to work out where's the process we can do on this? How can we handle this?' (YJB Chief Executive)

> 'Knowing when to have conversations in private and when to come out and talk about things openly, particularly if you're being critical, is something the AYJ has always done really well. We've had a really good balance in terms of having the ear of people involved in policy, and we've always had a sense that there are some things that you can discuss privately and that not everything that we disagree with, we're going to come out and trying to be getting the headlines in the *Guardian* [newspaper]. That does come down to relationships.' (AYJ Chair)

> 'I don't think I was a very good Chair of the YJB. I wasn't sufficiently subtle in getting my arguments across within Whitehall. Too often talked from public platforms in front of ministers offering a critique. I was naive. I should never have appeared as I did on television news talking about the numbers [of children in custody]. I should have been much more subtle by using quieter backstream channels.' (YJB Chair)

Dialogue as a communicative mechanism

Establishing a constructive, diplomatic (tactful and tactical) *dialogue* was considered an important mechanism for engendering collaborative contexts underpinned by empathy to the agendas and challenges of others:

> 'You need to establish a dialogue with the people who are actually delivering the policy, I firmly believe that the YJB and the creation of the YOT was a fundamentally good model. But in order to see it through, it needed to be nurtured and understood. As it evolved, it couldn't be directed straightforwardly from the centre.' (YJB Chair)

> 'There are times when policy officials will take exception to people in an arm's-length body [YJB] having a view. That "keep your tanks off my lawn" stuff. There are times when YJB probably got stuff wrong or went too far, overstepping the mark. It's steering your way through, and it's all about relationships. Working out what you can bring to the party that others will support you on. Most of the time, it was trying to do stuff collaboratively. We were pretty good at coming up with ideas that policy people could then run with and at grabbing an opportunity and helping other people run with stuff.' (YJB Chief Executive)

Common language as a communicative mechanism

> 'It's about reframing, because you can say the same thing in two very different ways. One will get over the line with policy change, the other won't. So it's about finding the right words in order to be able to sell what it is you're you wanting to deliver.'
>
> (YJB senior official)

Diplomacy and dialogue as constructive influences on collaborative policy-making contexts were facilitated by the promotion of *common language* supporting *cogent narratives/messaging* for the development of shared agendas and common ground:

> 'We all agree with Child First principles, but colleagues may label it differently as child practice or child-centred policing. But even if it's different language used, you've just got to get to a common understanding, because it's the right thing to do for children.' (YMC Chair)

> 'I put a lot of effort into ensuring the management board level within the MoJ talked about "children" and recognised that they had a responsibility directly for children and that children weren't the

same as adults. They needed to be dealt with as individuals, and the thinking within that was important. When Charlie Taylor became YJB Chair, he was really worried about that because he thought it would land really badly politically. Gradually, we [YJB] got it to the point where now it's been accepted. Quite a significant change actually, that language change. Dropping that in constantly with ministers.' (YJB Chief Executive)

'Robert Buckland [Justice Minister] thought it would be great to hear the sector use that language [of Child First] because it reinforces the importance of thinking about children as children. It worked for him because he was in the space of trying to get other government departments to think about what they could do for the children that, ultimately, he was responsible for, and he worked that in and used that language well.' (YJB senior official)

Consistent messaging as a communicative mechanism

'That's the thing with influencing policy from the bottom. You just gotta keep at it until something gives.' (AYM senior representative, YOT manager)

'We go on about it. That's what we do. We go on about it in every arena we can, and we keep raising it.' (YMC Chair)

Consistent, cogent messaging was a key vehicle for and identified component of employing and encouraging common language use as a mechanism of collaborative policy making in relational contexts:

'We [AYJ] monitor the YJB's work and try to constantly be that irritant, that grit in the oyster. But that means that you're always there and you're being consistent in what you're saying. Policy influencing is not necessarily always about positive change but limiting potential damage. It's about nipping things in the bud so that they don't create a groundswell where, all of a sudden, we're back in the '90s again. For example, we made a massive song and dance about Knife Crime Prevention Orders and went to town on doing so behind the scenes [diplomatically], writing letters in the *Times* [newspaper] and calling it the knife crime ASBO [Antisocial Behaviour Order] to make the association with the failed ASBO. We did lots of parliamentary work, but also did loads of stuff in the media and on social media to really try and stop that from becoming the next big problem.' (AYJ Chair)

> 'It's rare to get anybody that understands the devolved world [Wales]. You say, what you're talking about relates to England, but it doesn't relate here in Wales. What you do is continually keep talking about the issues that they need to understand, continually telling them that perhaps it won't work in the same way here. Continually trying to chip away in terms of helping understanding, explaining the context.' (YJB Cymru Chair)

Narrative storytelling as a communicative mechanism

> 'A drip, drip, drip approach and enabling people to have conversations and constructively challenging ourselves. Not making people feel that they're saying the wrong thing, but really trying to work with them to explore why they might think a certain way.'
>
> (YJB senior official)

> 'There are certain tricks of the trade. I learned that no-one reads Chief Inspector of Probation reports, and they are completely ignored by the media. But if you want to grab any attention, you've got to use unusual words or sharp phrases.'
>
> (YJB Chair)

Presenting a compelling narrative that is drip-fed, appropriately pitched and attention grabbing was cited as an enabler of consistent, cogent messaging that supported collaborative policy making. These common stakeholder perspectives align with policy-making research indicating that rather than being neutral arbiters of technical information, officials create particular constructions of problems and solutions, in other words, 'good stories' which can be presented to ministers (Stevens, 2011).

> 'What helps is being able to narrate a little about why this [evidence] makes sense and why it's important. We used a lot of data visualisation, a lot of videos, trying to get politicians to really connect with what on earth this evidence was all about because it does feel a bit out there. It can be a bit woolly, so what are the tangibles with the evidence that suggest it's gonna work?' (Children's Commissioner)

Relational reciprocity: promoting equitable and supportive relationships

> 'I really did want the realities on the ground of youth justice practice to reach up into the highest levels of policy making.'
>
> (YJB board member – Wales representative)

Stakeholders identified a series of important mechanisms that they associated with the pursuit of collaborative, supportive relationships in contexts of *relational reciprocity*. These mechanisms, operating in contexts characterised by equitable and empathetic power dynamics, included building empathy, developing trust and respect, valuing professional/personal lived experience and expertise.

Building empathy

Experts considered *building empathy* to be a critical contextual mechanism for pursuing collaborative relationships (based on common ground, shared agendas) that acknowledge political and practical realities, differing organisational agendas/priorities and differing/conflicting professional perspectives in policy-making contexts:

> 'I'd always take the time with the partners to understand what their win looks like, I knew what my win was, but I always tried to understand what theirs was too. If possible, we both could get a win. If I'm gonna win at their expense, then I've got a lot of convincing to do, or they had nothing to get out of the process. Relationship is partnership. Being relaxed enough to be actively seeking to support your partners' outcomes as well as your own. Build a "we're in it together" scenario.' (Children's Commissioner)

> 'Understanding other people's perspectives is key. It's getting people around the table and sitting there and saying "what's this like for you?" "What do you think are the pros and the cons, and where do we cross over?" That's the only way you can move forward. We listen to our partners, but actually we have to have a shared vision. That doesn't mean that we're all wanting the same thing, but there must be things that you need to achieve as a result of improving outcomes for children. Find that middle ground. Find those shared interests. The mutual benefits for both of us.' (AYM Chair)

Immersion as empathy building

> 'I think that some [MoJ] staff would benefit from spending a week or so with us [AYM] in different YOTs. It would give them a bit of credibility and also a bit of insight.'
>
> (AYM Chair)

Stakeholders working across a range of contexts espoused the utility of *immersion* (self-imposed and requested of others) within and exposure to the practical contexts (realities) of colleagues as a key mechanism to support the development of empathetic policy-making contexts:

> 'Spend time with people, immersing them in situations, take them along to the sorts of things you're talking about, getting them involved in hearing directly from children. That was an important part of us [OCC] bringing together decision makers from across the borough [see also 'Networking' and 'Brokering' discussions] … to get closer to understanding why this [child-friendly policy] is so important from a young person's perspective.' (Children's Commissioner, local government official)

> 'I keep one day a month free for myself [senior MoJ official] to visit and experience the YJS, to do some frontline visit of sorts. Visiting a custodial establishment, spending a day with a charity or a YOT, that type of thing just sat quietly in the background or speaking to the frontline practitioners to give me and us [MoJ] a better sense of what is and isn't working.' (MoJ senior official)

> 'One of the things I did was that the YJB, instead of always meeting in our offices in London, I would go on the road. I was never going to learn what was actually happening by sitting in a big office in Whitehall. I should get out there, meet the troops on the ground, talk to them and understand their day-to-day operational issues. Likewise, the YJB would frequently meet in different local authorities, where we'd spend the morning having a big meeting with senior staff, chief executives, other senior local authority councillors etc about how the YOT and its policy is fitted in with other parts of the local authority framework.' (YJB Chair)

Developing trust and respect

Contexts of relational reciprocity were seen as shaping/shaped by mutual *trust and respect* for colleagues' credibility, expertise and professional lived experience and expertise. Mechanisms of developing trust and respect were frequently highlighted as enablers of and barriers to collaborative, empathetic policy making:

> 'There has to be trust and mutual respect. Those are two of the cornerstones of relationships. Also, honesty and compromise. Know when to push and see those opportunities, but also know when to wind it back in order to navigate and develop trusted relationships with policy colleagues, so that they will be open as well as guiding them through some of the barriers that they will inevitably face. It's gotta be a partnership. Work out how we are going to be able to achieve our respective goals.' (YJB senior official)

> 'David Blunkett [Home Secretary] was suspicious of the police. There was no trust really. So he would have said a police officer should never be chairman of the YJB because he had closed his mind to the police. I didn't feel I could ever communicate satisfactorily with him. He kept me at arm's length.' (YJB Chair)

> 'Trying to help people find the answer around what they need to be doing, that's where that degree of trust comes in. We [YJB] try to walk a sensitive line in relation to the conversations we'll have privately and those that we'll have publicly with other stakeholders and within government. People have got to be able to trust us that we think very carefully before we make something public. You use that soft power with a good degree of thought behind it.' (YJB Chair)

Valuing professional experience was identified as a valuable policy-making mechanism linked to the development of empathy, trust and respect within collaborative contexts. It was a mechanism of policy making exemplified by components such as *using expertise*, *power sharing*, *inclusion/listening* and *open, evidence-led mindsets*:

> 'Understanding what's in the centre with those voices of experience. Making sure that they feed into our policies in a much more direct and systematic way. We do a lot of listening to organisations in that space.' (Welsh government senior civil servant)

> 'As a YOT manager, I was motivating staff. I valued them. I listened to them in regards to what they were telling me and was always willing to be involved at the operational level, so they didn't ever think that I was divorced from the reality of their work.' (AYM senior official, YOT manager)

> 'My own passion, my own understanding of the situation and my own experience, drove me. Unusually perhaps for modern justice secretaries, because I've been a criminal practitioner for so long, I had lived knowledge and experience when it came to youth justice. I knew that locking loads of boys up together in large detention centres was a guaranteed way of creating criminals in the future and seeing them return to the adult estate. But I didn't come into the role with a preconceived set of ideas that this is my vision and I have a better knowledge. I listened to the professionals in the field. I thought, it's not my job to start interfering and disrupting where I can see evidence of things working.' (Government minister)

Certain stakeholders discussed their preference for a form of *proactive empathy* through offering *support* and prioritising *inclusion* when shaping policy influence processes:

> 'The more it's about structure and process, the less connection with the individual child. Different bits of the jigsaw are missing for different children in different contexts in different parts of the country, and so you need to have a YJS able to respond at that micro-level. That's critical for youth justice policy. If you start at the top and try creating policy, you're gonna create a system. You're looking through the wrong end of the telescope. What works is good responsible adults forming strong relationships with children, giving them the support they need. If structures are getting in the way of that happening, then the structures need to be changed.' (YJB Chair)

> 'Liking people, having really good relationships with them and including them. I would include people within different departments and loads of people from the [practice] field. I'd rather have you involved now to tell me it's [policy] a bit ropey so we can get it better before it hits the real world. Gives a bit of leeway if we make mistakes. When you include people across departments, you get better results too. Talking to people, sharing and being inclusive seems to implement policies more smoothly than keeping things under wraps. Explaining why you're doing things seems to work better than just doing them and then saying that's the policy.' (YJB Cymru Chair)

Valuing the personal lived experience and expertise of children in imparting their own life stories and contributing to policy-making decisions was a significant, albeit under-developed, strategic context identified by adult experts:

> 'I feel very strongly about the role of children in terms of helping us [HMIP] develop our future programme and develop the influence of children.' (HMIP senior official)

> 'Wales was the first UK country to appoint a Children's Commissioner. They would refer to a national shame around not listening to the voices of children. Wales made the Commissioner remit very broad. The role needed to focus on children, protecting and upholding children's rights and holding duty bearers to account. That means understanding what children think and feel, their lived experiences.' (Children's Commissioner)

> 'Under our [AYJ] new strategy, we did a huge piece of work with our young advocates where we got their views about what they thought was important [in youth justice]. Then we got our members together to focus on where is it we can be the glue between the more detailed policy work our members are doing and the big picture stuff around supporting a Child First approach, for example.' (AYJ Chair)

The key contexts–mechanisms relationships identified when investigating relational, collaborative policy making are outlined in Appendix 14.

Conclusion: contexts and mechanisms of relational policy making

This final thematic analysis of the interview data has examined the constructive influence of relationships on youth justice policy making, specifically in contexts shaped by differing power dynamics between stakeholder organisations. When investigating how power dynamics influence relational policy making, analyses indicated the constructive influence of mechanisms of agenda, steer, pressure and control operating in political/governmental contexts. For example, ministerial identity and personality were experienced as exerting pressure through mechanisms of partiality, prejudice, animosity and stubbornness. Contexts in which non-governmental actor influence was identified were typified by the strategic exercise of soft power (for example by YJB, OCC, AYJ) and the use of communicative and relational mechanisms of diplomacy, expert challenge and seeding constructive conversations.

Analyses developed a detailed focus upon power dynamics within relational contexts occupied and shaped by the YJB. The general conclusion was that power dynamics in policy-making contexts between the YJB and both governmental and non-governmental organisations have become more equitable in recent years. For example, YJB relationships with government actors (government ministers, civil servants) have moved slowly away from early governmental/civil service prescriptiveness and steering of the YJB and towards more equitable power dynamics with government more amenable to being steered, challenged and being receptive to YJB expertise. However, these power dynamics are perennially mediated by political and financial realities as barriers and challenges to policy making.

More recent relational trajectories have been accompanied by a parallel increase in the assertiveness and muscularity of the civil service/MoJ, as well as HMIP, for example, due to threatened organisational identities and the need to fill a perceived policy vacuum in youth justice. This, in turn, has apparently led the YJB to tentatively return to its former managerialist prescription agenda to protect its role, status and identity, contrary to the recent trajectory of developing more equitable power dynamics with practitioners and encouraging practice challenge, innovation and expertise. Analyses also explored the YJB's policy-making relationship with Welsh professionals in contexts of UK government centrism (perceived as a barrier) and a passive lack of scrutiny (perceived as an enabler), characterised by Welsh stakeholders as signifying prejudice, hostility, suspicion, neglect and lack of understanding by English stakeholder organisations. However, these barriers were able to be addressed effectively by using mechanisms of relationship building, mutual learning and educating English colleagues.

The final analytical section focused on mechanisms of relational and collaborative policy making in commonly identified contexts of seeking common ground, using communication and pursuing relational reciprocity. Stakeholders consistently reported that seeking common ground (as a priority over the more ambitious seeking of consensus) was facilitated by mechanisms of developing shared agendas, rebuilding relationships and re-educating colleagues when faced with policy-making barriers and through networking, building alliances and brokering relationships. Communicative influences on effective policy making in youth justice contexts (viewed as policy-making enablers) included the tactful and tactical use of diplomacy and dialogue, employing common language, consistent/cogent messaging and narrative storytelling. Finally, stakeholders emphasised the constructive influence of contexts of relational reciprocity, facilitated by mechanisms of empathy building (through immersion, for example), developing trust and respect and valuing professional and personal (for example, children's) lived experiences as expertise.

8

Discussion: towards a contextualised understanding of youth justice policy making

The ambition of this analytical project was to enhance understandings of youth justice policy making in England and Wales the period sincethe ground-breaking Crime and Disorder Act 1998. The book took up the challenge of Souhami (2015a: 152, 164), who asserted that 'a wider view is required of what constitutes [youth justice] policy and where and by whom it is made' in order that youth justice policy making can be better understood as 'a complex arena of social practice, incorporating a diverse range of actors, practices, relationships and networks'. Accordingly, analyses of policy documents and expert stakeholder perspectives focused on five central research questions (RQs):

1. What is youth justice 'policy'?
2. Who are the 'makers' of youth justice policy?
3. How is youth justice policy making understood, re/constructed, experienced and made meaningful by policy makers working in different contexts?
4. What are the barriers, challenges, enablers and opportunities for policy making?
5. How can youth justice policy making be improved?

Analyses brought into sharp focus the pressing need for 'improved' understandings of policy making that move beyond the reductionist, linear (Policy Cycle Model) explanations of governmental actors producing static 'products' and 'measures' to animate their decisions/agendas and then prescribing the nature of policy implementation in practice. Instead, operationalising youth justice 'policy' (RQ1) and examining the extent and nature of the 'makers' (RQ2) and 'making' of youth justice policy (RQ3/4) demands a lens of *necessary complexity* that conceptualises policy making as a series of dynamic processes, trajectories, relationships and interactions that are constantly re/constructed by a range of governmental *and* non-governmental policy actors. The qualitative methodology employed highlighted that the complexity of youth justice policy making is made meaningful by expert stakeholders in *relational contexts*. Therefore, context is constructed and experienced by experts as the relational and dynamic features[1] shaping the mechanisms through which policies work, seeing context as operating in a dynamic, emergent way over time at multiple different levels of the social system (Greenhalgh and Manzano, 2021). These relational contexts can be both stable (for example, consensual, cyclical) and subject to change (for example, unstable, precarious), but are always complex (for example multi-layered, fragmented, contested/contingent). However, while these complex contexts present as ostensibly chaotic, random and unpredictable, it is possible to discern a degree of coherence and predictability or 'patterns in the noise', indicative of the conflict, ambivalence and contemporary hybridity (for example, polyfurcation, 'messy complexities') characterising the socio-historical construction of youth justice (Case, 2018/21).

In the spirit of reflexivity that characterises the analyses throughout the book, the project findings, interpretations, conclusions and recommendations are presented with a significant caveat, itself reflective of the oft-dichotomised and bifurcated nature of the socio-historical construction of youth justice (see Chapter 1). The arguments, interpretations and conclusions throughout the book are deliberately generalised and somewhat caricatured (for example, the expansionist and austerity period characterisations in Chapters 3 and 4), intended to offer broad-brush, hard-hitting headline messages and lessons from the analyses as a foundation/touchstone for further dialogue around, exploration of and recommendations for youth justice policy making. Simultaneously, those same arguments, interpretations and conclusions are avowedly *partial* in origins, scope and perspective, the product of researcher positionality (for example, expertise, experience, evidence, subjectivity, prejudice[2]) imposed upon a deliberately limited analytical timeframe (1996–present) and, similarly, a sampling frame of policy documents and interviewees inherently limited by their availability and access through existing researcher networks and relationships (see Chapter 2). It remains important for the reflexive reader to be aware of this caveat of *generalisation–partiality* when engaging with the conclusions and recommendations of this project in order to evaluate their validity and to encourage reader reflexivity moving forwards.

Policy question: reader positionality

At this point in our analytical journey, what is your personal and professional position regarding how youth justice policy is, could and should be made? What constructive influences underpin your positionality, for example, in relation to your professional and academic/disciplinary backgrounds, your personal and professional experiences and values and your interpretations of available evidence, including the arguments presented in this book?

So, let's reflect on what the analyses tell us in response to the research questions that guide this project:

RQ1: what is youth justice 'policy'?

Analyses of the policy literature and expert stakeholder perspectives and experiences indicated that basic professional understandings in the youth justice sector align with the operationalisation of 'policy' as (variously) a stated intention, current/past action, formal/claimed status and organisational practice (after Levin, 1997; see also Chapter 1). Policy was typically represented and understood by experts as the position statement (of intent), direction of travel and dominant agenda of government (for example, manifestoes, Green/White Papers, legislation), all of which require subsequent implementation in practice. Consequent stakeholder interpretations of what constitutes policy cohered around the static 'products' and 'measures' (see Souhami, 2015a) decided upon and formulated by governmental actors. These dominant governmental actors were typically understood to prescribe the 'effective' and 'evidence-based' practice that allegedly maximises the potential for faithful policy transfer into practice and minimises policy implementation failures or gaps. However, critique of the 'Policy Cycle Model' and detailed analyses of project data highlighted the reductionism (for example, over-simplification, invalidity, linearity, partiality) of this explanatory framework, due, for example, to an increasingly complex and nuanced youth justice context in England and Wales since 1996. This contextualised complexity has been reflected in a number of new constructions, including: the introduction of the Youth Justice Board (YJB) (a non-departmental public body expert strategic adviser and practice guide), the growing prescriptive influence of His Majesty's Inspectorate of Probation (practice inspector), the 'dragonised' policy/strategy identity of the Welsh government and Welsh youth justice sector (in a partially devolved youth justice policy context) and the growing local mediation/moderation of policy prescriptions led by practitioner organisations and Youth Offending Teams. Taken together, post-1996 youth justice trajectories and policy developments indicate the need for youth justice 'policy' to be explored through the aforementioned lens of necessary complexity as a dynamic, contested, contingent and contextualised *social construction* subject to constant re/creation and re/making through *processes, relationships and interactions* between governmental and non-governmental policy actors and their organisations. Consequently, if policy can be understood as static at any point in time, it certainly does not remain static for very long.

RQ2: who are the 'makers' of youth justice policy?

It has been established that 'policy' in the youth justice arena is something more than simply a static product, output or outcome (that is, policy context as observable features): it is a constantly evolving process of re/construction shaped by relationships between contexts and mechanisms (for example, constructive influences) that are inherently dynamic, contested and contingent (after Greenhalgh and Manzano, 2021). The trajectory and nature of policy 'making' is one of fluctuating and even simultaneous stability and change characterised by complex developments, interactions and relationships within and between different 'stages' of policy making (for example agenda setting, formulating, implementing) and between the range of different professionals and organisations (with their attendant dynamic 'identities') who can be understood as policy 'makers'. Indeed, the nature of policy making was rendered more dynamic and complex by the variety of contextualised mechanisms employed by professional policy makers[3] (such as civil servants, YJB, practitioners) above and beyond traditionally understood 'stages' of policy 'making', including policy influencing (explicitly and in a 'dead hand' manner), steering, advising, networking, brokering, advocating, challenging and mediating/moderating.

The making of policy in the youth justice sector can be discerned as variously complex, chaotic and coherent, indicative of the conflict, ambivalence and ambiguity that has characterised the socio-historical construction of youth justice. The complexity of policy making is made redolent at the macro level by its 'melting pot of multiple discourses' and policy 'modes' (Fergusson, 2007) and by the contested and increasingly hybrid and *polyfurcated* nature of policy 'models' (Goldson, 2020; Case and Smith, 2023). Complexity is further illustrated by the multi-layered and nuanced contexts emerging both nationally (for example in Wales) and locally as a result of policy-making identities (for example 'dragonised' youth justice in Wales, local penal cultures) and local mediation/moderation of centralised policy prescriptions (Case et al, 2019; see also Chapters 6 and 7). Analyses clearly indicated the chaotic nature of youth justice policy making through macro- and meso-level processes, identities and relationships that can be, to some extent, chaotic and unstable in the sense of fragmented, precarious, unpredictable, sudden, random, opaque and opportunistic. These identity-based and relational contexts can also be shaped by capricious, volatile, mercurial, subjective, personality- and agenda-driven organisational and professional constructive influences. However, it was also possible to discern a degree of *coherence* to youth justice policy making, a stable, cyclical consistency characterised by the pursuit of consensus, common ground/shared agendas, along with strategic, instrumental, measured (for example gradual development) and ostensibly predictable (but not necessarily linear) trajectories and pathways. These commonly occurring contexts and mechanisms of coherence, not to mention the recurring characteristics of chaos, 'stable instability' and 'predictable unpredictability', present as 'patterns in the noise' for those seeking to better understand, shape and enhance youth justice policy making.

RQ3: how is youth justice policy making understood, re/constructed, experienced and made meaningful by policy makers working in different contexts?

The constructive and contextualised trajectories and influences identified through the qualitative documentary analysis and the semi-structured interviews strongly suggest that sector understandings of youth justice policy making are more complex and nuanced than implied by traditional representations of policy making as government-dominated, linear, bifurcated and dichotomous. Expert analyses of policy documentation and youth justice trajectories (see Chapters 3 and 4) and expert perceptions/experiences (see Chapters 5, 6 and 7) indicate that youth justice policy making is subject to dynamic, contemporaneous, overlapping and fluctuating re/constructions along a 'continuum of complexity', if not multiple, interrelated 'continua', which can be understood as *contexts* for policy making. The contextualised, constructive influences of policy discourses, modes, agendas, identities, roles, personalities, mindsets (for example evidence based, collaborative), relationships and other related mechanisms (such as communication) of youth justice policy making are situated along these continua, which themselves reflect the complex, hybrid, polyfurcated nature of contemporary youth justice. For example, analyses identified political policy-generation periods of expansion–austerity and broad policy development continua of stability–change (including gradual–sudden), predictability–unpredictability, clarity–ambiguity and consensus–conflict, all shaped/characterised by contextualised policy-making mechanisms (continua) such as power/governance–collaboration, prescription–empowerment, centralisation–local mediation and steering–being steered. Of course, the nature of these continua and the position of an organisation or professional along them is dynamic, contested and contingent on who is recounting their experiences/perceptions, with whom and focused on which point in time, not to mention the ever-present influence of researcher positionality.

RQ4: what are the barriers, challenges, enablers and opportunities for policy making?

A series of constructive influences/mechanisms were identified by expert stakeholders as enablers/facilitators and barriers/challenges for youth justice policy making in contexts that can be characterised as power based, identity-led and relational. The contexts–mechanisms relationships emerging as constructive influences on policy making can be discerned along broad, generalised, interrelated and mutually reinforcing continua of power–collaboration, opacity–transparency and chaos–consistency (see Chapters 5, 6 and 7).

Certain policy-making contexts were characterised by a hierarchy of *power and governance* manifested by *inequitable power dynamics*, wherein governmental actors (especially government ministers and their senior policy advisers [SPADs]) dominated decision making/agenda setting, policy formulation and, ultimately, policy implementation through the steering and pressurising of civil servants (for example Ministry of Justice [MoJ] officials). These power/governance-based contexts often generated *opaque and chaotic* policy-making mechanisms/constructive influences (as barriers/challenges) such as the 'dead hand' influence of Number 10 and right-wing newspaper media, and unclear, confused/contradictory and polyfurcated policy discourses, agendas and partialities, sudden agenda and personnel changes (for example churnover), policy–knowledge/evidence ruptures and ambiguous, unstable and precarious organisational roles and identities. This latter context–mechanism relationship was also experienced as a policy-making enabler/opportunity by the YJB, whose representatives reported that the organisation could exploit its slippery and fluid identity and status to introduce policy-based strategic developments (such as Child First) and to empower local practitioners to mediate/moderate centralised policy prescriptions. YJB experts reported that the organisation was able to exploit chaotic and unpredictable socio-political contexts through utilising *opportunism* to build policy-making networks and alliances with powerful advocates at governmental level and by filling a contemporary policy vacuum with an expertise in evidence in the context of socio-political and economic uncertainty and flux.

Power/governance-based contexts were also experienced as engendering transparent and consistent policy-making mechanisms (as barriers/challenges to policy making). In particular, inequitable power dynamics were experienced as leading to explicit governmental steer, pressure and prescription of the policy into practice activities of non-governmental organisations. In addition, these contexts fostered *governmental resistance* to challenge and to engaging/collaborating with inconvenient evidence or with the expertise of other stakeholders, including *deprofessionalising the civil service/MoJ* and *threatening the identity of the YJB*, which has arguably encouraged both organisations to pursue increased power/governance in relation to their own policy-making roles and identities, while neglecting the nuanced context and expertise on Welsh youth justice. To this latter point, Welsh stakeholders reported their relative neglect by the UK government and the YJB as a potential policy-making enabler/opportunity for developing 'dragonised' strategies and a principled national identity youth justice 'under the radar' and by exploiting a context characterised by a 'passive lack of scrutiny'.

At the other end of the power–collaboration continuum, contexts of power/governance were superseded by contexts of *collaboration*, often engendering constructive influences/mechanisms experienced by stakeholders as enablers of/opportunities for effective youth justice policy-making. These *relational contexts* were the sites at which policy actors began to address barriers/challenges to policy making and the inherent complexity, chaos, fragmentation, instability and unpredictability of their professional lived experiences by utilising collaborative, *transparent* and *consistent mechanisms* of policy development. For example, barriers presented by inequitable power dynamics, conflicting agendas and opaque, ostensibly chaotic policy-making discourses and processes were tackled in relational contexts wherein powerful policy actors (such as ministers, YJB) were *open-minded and receptive* to collaborative policy making. This open-mindedness and receptiveness often manifested in the form of steer, challenge, discretion/innovation, diplomatic dialogue, engaging with external expertise/evidence and empowering (rather than prescribing) YJB strategy and local penal cultures and mediation/ moderation. The barriers and challenges of incoherent, fragmented and conflicting policy contexts and agendas could be reconciled in relational contexts through transparent and consistent mechanisms cohering around the use of *soft power* (by YJB, Office of the Children's Commissioner [OCC], Welsh government) and collaborative relationship building between 'like-minded' professionals operating at different levels of the social system. These collaborative mechanisms were identified as: *seeking common ground/ shared agendas* through networking, building alliances, brokering and advocating; *communicating effectively* through diplomatic and constructive dialogue, common language, cogent messaging and narrative storytelling; and developing *relational reciprocity* by using empathy (for example for the challenges and realities of others), immersion, trust, respect, inclusion and valuing lived experience.

RQ5: how can youth justice policy making be improved?

> 'There's two things you should never see being made. One is sausages, the other is policy. Because it doesn't happen like people think ... able Oxbridge civil servants carefully crafting based on evidence, theory and the wishes of their political masters. It's much messier.'
>
> (YJB board member, senior academic)

Despite the improvements made to policy development through the contributions of expanding knowledge and evidence bases, politicians, civil servants, practitioners and academics continue to express concerns about the way policy is made (Hoornbeek and Peters, 2017; see also Croci et al, 2022). Accordingly, the final research question focuses on the ways in which youth justice policy making could be improved and rendered more 'effective', for example in terms of its sustainability, coherence, validity, evidence base and faithfulness of transfer into practice. Inevitably, this speculative exercise, related as it is to 'mapping the future', is 'complex and challenging' in the inherently unstable and uncertain context of youth justice (Goldson, 2020). However, critical reflection on the barriers, challenges, enablers and opportunities identified by stakeholders throughout this project can identify 'patterns in the noise' and thus offer coherence, consistency and confidence that more effective policy making is possible in these contexts of chaos, all the while being attendant/empathetic to the political and practical realities[4] faced by stakeholders. So, how can youth justice policy-making progress be enhanced by using the lessons learned from this project?

Reject reductionism, embrace complexity

> 'There's no linear march of progress in policy development.'
>
> (YJB Chief Executive)

A central lesson from this project is that the understanding, execution and experience of policy making can be enhanced by rejecting blind acceptance of reductionist (for example linear, government-dominated) explanatory frameworks and embracing the complexity (for example, construction, contextualisation, chaos) inherent to the making of youth justice policy. Findings reinforce the assertion that the Policy Cycle Model of policy process is unrealistic (Institute for Government, 2011; see also Chapter 1) because policy making does not take place in distinct, linear stages (agenda setting–formulation–implementation, evidence dictating policy, for example), but rather through 'stages' that are often inseparable, overlapping and interrelating as real-world policy problems and solutions emerge contemporaneously (Institute for Government, 2011) at the macro, meso and micro levels of the social system. Indeed, the relational and contextualised nature of youth justice policy making demands that we reject reductionism and embrace complexity. Human social relations are rarely, if ever, mechanistic in nature and can be more accurately described as open, dynamic, complex systems (see Case and Haines, 2014). Therefore, the human behaviour underpinning policy making cannot be understood through linear, consistent and predictable analyses, as this necessitates a level of abstraction and generalisation that renders any conclusions so distant from the original social reality as to make them worthless artefacts (Case and Haines, 2014). Relatedly, the ostensibly chaotic nature of policy making in youth justice contexts is not necessarily definitive or inevitable. Developments, processes, constructions (such as identities) and relationships that present as chaotic, random and unpredictable may actually hold a degree of meaning/sense, strategy/instrumentalism, consistency and coherence in the constructed realities of different policy makers in specific contexts at specific times. Therefore, the coherence in chaos or 'patterns in the noise' elucidated by this project can become transparent and accessible by talking to policy actors and should hopefully become accessible to policy makers themselves as they seek to enhance their policy-making practices.

Reject fear, embrace challenges

> 'Policy formation needs to take place knowing what has worked before. How does that feed into a political policy process now that's relevant for the next ten years, rather than us being condemned to revisit what has happened before? How do we get people building on the shoulders of what's gone before, yet recognising that the context may have changed?'
>
> (YJB Chief Executive)

The 'coherence in chaos' and 'patterns in the noise' identified provide lessons for effective policy making that may go some way to explaining contemporary 'successes' across the Youth Justice System (YJS) (see Taylor, 2016), such as the long-term trajectory of annual reductions in first-time entrants, reoffending rates and custody levels (see Case, 2018/21). We would certainly be remiss as critical professionals if we did not at least reflect on the constructive influences and contexts–mechanisms relationships identified across this project and their potential contribution to recent and future policy successes.

> 'Perhaps we just need to be realistic and understand that youth justice is a quiet success. I'm happier when youth justice isn't in the headlines or being talked about, because then it allows everybody to just get on and deliver it. We know what works, we know what doesn't work. We know what's cost effective, we know what will be a waste of money.' (Government minister)

The headline findings and lessons learned from this project can and should be used to embrace the challenges and opportunities facing effective policy making in the future. Much like attempts to bridge the policy–practice and rhetoric–reality divides, these exercises in critical reflection and the transfer of research findings into policy-making processes seek to avoid knowledge/evidence–policy ruptures, gaps and failures. The most valid and potentially effective approach presents as one which enhances the enablers of youth justice policy making in relational contexts wherein a range of expert stakeholders engage collaboratively with expertise/expert identities, experience and evidence, seek common ground, pursue effective communication and promote relational reciprocity. The corollary of fostering these particular contexts–mechanisms relationships is that identified barriers to policy making are reconciled or minimised, notably the power-based, opaque, chaotic, unpredictable and precarious contexts within which policy is often made.

Reject power, embrace expertise, experience and evidence

Analyses of semi-structured interviews indicate that power-based policy making in hierarchical contexts, founded in inequitable power dynamics and dominated by governmental actors, is experienced negatively by stakeholders. In contrast, collaborative policy making in relational contexts that engages with a broader range of policy-making and policy-maker expertise, experience and evidence is experienced more positively and linked by stakeholders to contemporary successes and progress in principle in the YJS. Project findings align with the conclusion that enhancing relational contexts is essential to enable professionals working at the intersection of different expert practices to jointly expand interpretations of a problem and, by bringing their specialist expertise to bear, enrich responses to it (Rickinson and Edwards, 2021). Findings reinforce the necessity for better understandings of the connection between evidence, expertise and (youth justice) policy making and the role that ideas and values (for example positionality, political agenda) have in shaping policy (Oliver and Boaz, 2019; Belfiore, 2021).

Central to the pursuit of a better understanding of youth justice policy-making roles and influences is the acknowledgement of a broader range of policy makers in explanatory frameworks and policy-making processes, in other words, the 'messy engagement of multiple players with diverse sources of knowledge' (Davies et al, 2008: 188). For example, project findings reject the enduring assumption in academic and policy debates that policy formation is the sole domain of ministers and SPADs and that the role of supporting bureaucracy (for example, MoJ civil servants, YJB) is largely confined to policy implementation (Page and Jenkins, 2005). In reality, the division of policy-making responsibility is less clear, and government officials (MoJ) and related officials (YJB) are often intrinsically involved in policy-making processes (see Souhami, 2015a). Civil servants and the YJB often elaborate on ministerial decisions in order to put them into action (see also Souhami, 2011; Case, 2014). Therefore, rather than civil servants and YJB officials being neutral arbiters of technical information, they can be engaged in informal processes of influence and negotiation at all policy-making stages, for example by constructing policy problems and solutions in the form of 'good stories' to present to ministers (see also Stevens, 2011). Indeed, the YJB has reflected upon the nature of its policy influence in the updated 'YJB Business Plan 2023 to 2024' (YJB, 2023), which outlines a series of 'strategic pillars' designed to drive system improvement and to effectively deliver system oversight by improving policy and practice and ensuring that 'experience from practice informs policy development' (YJB, 2023: 16). These pillars include commitments to developing a memorandum of understanding with the MoJ to enhance policy development relationships and to providing systematic, evidence-based advice to a range of governmental and non-governmental stakeholder partners in relational contexts of policy making (YJB, 2023).

Project findings highlighted an exponential trajectory of practitioner expertise influencing policy making, which was identified by representatives from practitioner bodies (Association of Youth Offending Team [YOT] Managers [AYM], YOT Managers Cymru [YMC]) and by organisations working in relational contexts with these practitioners (for example, MoJ, YJB, OCC, Alliance for Youth Justice [AYJ]). Interview feedback confirmed the widespread local mediation and moderation of centralised policy prescriptions by frontline practitioners as 'street-level bureaucrats' (Lipsky, 1980) who are typically closer to, and have a better understanding of, the realities of implementing policy in the real world than centralised governance and policy-making organisations (Hudson et al, 2019). This reinforced conclusions regarding the 'local universality' of policy implementation (Sausman et al, 2016), whereby centralised policy is shaped/tailored to fit local contexts and practices (see also Braithwaite et al, 2018) and reinforced empirical findings that the conversion of national youth justice policy into local practice is largely contingent on the discretionary and relational actions, adaptations, discernments and decisions of local actors (Goldson and Briggs, 2021; see also Evans et al, 2022). However, the experiences and perceptions of expert stakeholders also challenged the reductionist focus on practitioners functioning as policy implementers, making sense of and mediating/moderating policy prescriptions in local contexts through local penal cultures. A key finding across the interviews was the growing policy influence of expert practitioners at different policy-making stages (for example agenda setting, policy formulation) not confined to policy implementation, with their expertise, professional lived experience and professional data and evidence increasingly valued, empowered and solicited in collaborative contexts by a range of non/governmental partners. Therefore, the necessity for an increasing focus on the policy-making contexts of the local and of practice in order to enhance understandings and processes of youth justice policy making aligns with the conclusion that lessons can be learned in national policy-making contexts from the way justice is done in 'small places' (Scott and Staines, 2021), an assertion reinforced by a YJB Chief Executive:

> 'The YJB and the MoJ Youth Justice Policy Unit have to understand how policy is made, where it's made and what are the preconditions for that because that needs then to shape what they're doing. They need to understand the systems that actually operate at an operational

> level and how they can harvest the learning, insight and understanding from that.'

A final, absolutely crucial point to make regarding the neglected expertise relates to the absence of *children's voices* in youth justice policy development processes (see also Case et al, 2020) and in this book. It almost feels like an afterthought to introduce this necessity so late in proceedings and with such little consideration relative to the influence of other expert stakeholder groups, especially when, in reality, engagement with children's voices in policy-making processes is worthy of an entire book in itself. The lack of discussion in this book of children as policy makers is in large part due to the relative neglect of the issue in youth justice policy making (processes and research) historically and in the policy documentation and stakeholder interviews/experiences that provide the data analysed in this book, with children's input only briefly touched upon by individual experts from the AYM, AYJ and (inevitably and appropriately) the OCC. That said, it is important to acknowledge that other, nascent structures exist to support eliciting children's participation and collaboration in policy making, both within governance organisations (for example, the YJB 'Youth Advisory Network') and the third sector (AYJ Young Advocates for Youth Justice, Peer Power, User Voice, for example), in conjunction with a burgeoning academic literature championing the importance of integrating children's voices and children's rights considerations into policy-making processes (see Case and Hazel, 2023). However, more work is needed to move this advocacy of the importance of children's voices as 'experts by experience' (Creaney, 2020) beyond policy and strategy rhetoric and into its practical realisation within collaborative contexts of youth justice policy making.

Conclusion: youth justice policy making as complex, constructed and contextualised

Analyses strongly indicated that youth justice policy making since 1996 in England and Wales has been mediated, moderated and shaped by constructive influences/mechanisms operating in dynamic and relational contexts at multiple levels of the social system. These macro-, meso- and micro-level contexts are characterised by continua that can be operationalised and categorised as power–collaboration, opacity–transparency and chaos–consistency. These identified contexts and the mechanisms shaped by them constitute analytical frameworks that can help make sense of and bring coherence to the ostensibly complex, chaotic, unstable and precarious contexts of youth justice policy making. The overarching conclusions from this inevitably complex exercise of identifying coherence from chaos emphasise the necessary complexity required to generate holistic, valid understandings of youth justice policy making that are grounded in the real-world experiences, perceptions and constructions of policy actors. The project findings consolidate Souhami's assertions that if we want to understand youth justice policy making, we need to look at what youth justice policy makers do and understand the culture and institutions (contexts, for example) in which they work in order to understand the way that they do it (in Case, 2018/21). In this regard, it is crucial to acknowledge that 'policy' represents much more than static policy 'products' and 'measures' such as legislation, Green/ White Papers and ministerial rhetoric. Moreover, policy emerges in the spaces between defined parameters of legislation and guidance (Souhami in Case, 2018/21) presents as a series of dynamic, relational processes that are 'made' within and between a range of policy actors (see also Case et al, 2019).

Coherence from chaos

The central aim of this project was to explore possibilities for discerning coherence, consistency and predictability from policy contexts that often present as chaotic, unstable and unpredictable, in order to identify potential improvements to how youth justice policy and policy making is understood and actualised. This necessarily complex and long-term process has now been initiated through the identification of influential contexts–mechanisms relationships. What this project has clearly established, reflective of Souhami's inspirational YJB ethnography, is that such cohesion is only accessible and feasible if we look, listen and learn from the realities of those at the heart of policy making rather than uncritically accepting reductionist, superficial and political, power-based assumptions about how youth justice policy is 'made'. Clearly, there are multiple ways of viewing and constructing reality and knowledge in the youth justice sector. In order to execute such a challenging and complex project successfully, it is essential to critically reflect upon the positionality, assumptions and biases that shape the perceptions, experiences, instructions, decisions and practices of policy actors and of the researchers seeking to understand their world. It has become evident that holistic and ecologically valid understandings of youth justice policy making (by both stakeholders and researchers) necessitate the management of power dynamics, empathy with the needs, challenges, constraints and realities of others, sensitivity to context and representation and legitimisation of diverse voices (see Reed and Rudman, 2023). This project has concluded that there are multiple ways of viewing and constructing reality and knowledge in the youth justice sector. It seems appropriate, therefore, to conclude with a minor adaptation of the highly perceptive and suitably optimistic assertion of Reed and Rudman (2023: 967) that '[b]y considering how [youth justice policy] generation processes are mediated by context, power and voice, it may be possible to envision just transformations of knowledge systems that foreground the knowledge and needs of diverse groups … without systematically recognising or privileging one group over another'.

APPENDIX 1

List of stakeholder interviewees

Stakeholder	Policy position
Colin Allars	Chief Executive Youth Justice Board (YJB)
Dr Tim Bateman	Senior academic, National Association for Youth Justice (NAYJ) representative
Jacqui Belfield-Smith	Chair of Association of Youth Offending Team (YOT) Managers (AYM)
Jamie Bennett	Head of Strategy YJB
Andrea Brazier	His Majesty's Inspectorate of Probation (HMIP) Head of Youth Inspection Programme
Robert Buckland	Justice Secretary
Ben Byrne	YJB board member, YOT manager, NAYJ representative
Prof. John Drew	Chief Executive YJB
James Searle, Ali Lott, Sarah Evans (focus group interview)	Welsh Government Crime and Justice Unit
Brendan Finegan	YJB Head of Strategy, AYM
Elizabeth Flowers	Office of the Children's Commissioner (OCC) Wales Policy Adviser
Keith Fraser	Chair of YJB
Dr Pippa Goodfellow	Alliance for Youth Justice Chair
Samuel Howells	OCC England Policy Adviser
Eddie Isles	Swansea YOT manager, Chair of YOT Managers Cymru (YMC)
Dusty Kennedy	Chair YJB Cymru
Lord Tom McNally	Chair of YJB
Helen Mercer	Head of Strategy and Planning HMIP, YJB official
Prof. Rod Morgan	Chair of YJB, senior academic
Mary O'Grady	Chair of YMC
Sir Charles Pollard	Chair of YJB
Graham Robb	Chair of YJB
Michaela Rogers	Chair of YMC
Ellie Roy	Chief Executive YJB
Justin Russell	Chief Inspector HMIP, senior policy adviser
Charlie Spencer	Deputy Chair AYM

Stakeholder	Policy position
Prof. Martin Stephenson	Unitas, YJB board member, senior academic
Claudia Sturt	Chief Executive YJB
Geeta Subramaniam-Mooney	OCC Newham
Charlie Taylor	Chair YJB
Sue Thomas	YJB board member, senior academic
Keith Towler	OCC Wales, YJB board member
Lesley Tregear	Chair of AYM
Alan Webster	Ministry of Justice: Head of Youth Justice Division
Steve Chalke, Andrew Willetts (focus group interview)	Oasis Medway Secure School
Paula Williams	Head of Policy YJB
Hazel Williamson	Chair AYM
Prof. Howard Williamson	YJB board member, senior academic

APPENDIX 2

Critical commentary: researcher reflection on the introduction of the Scaled Approach

I'd like to share my professional experiences of the development of the Scaled Approach, which will indicate (my view of) the degree to which the framework was a political project, as opposed to the evidence-based practice enhancement it was claimed to be. In 2009, I published the book *Understanding Youth Offending: Risk Factor Research, Policy and Practice* (Case and Haines, 2009), a detailed critical evaluation of risk factor theories, associated research and their application in the Youth Justice System (YJS). As part of the research, we examined the theoretical and evidential bases of the Risk Factor Prevention Paradigm (RFPP) and made an alarming discovery. Despite claims that the Scaled Approach was 'evidence based' (YJB, 2009) and grounded in a longstanding, reliable and validated body of empirical research (see also Loeber et al, 2003), there was a worrying paucity of evidence that risk-focused intervention actually worked in practice (Haines and Case, 2008). In reality, much of the developmental and life-course research that influenced the RFPP (for example, West and Farrington, 1973; Sampson and Laub, 1993) did not even attempt interventions to reduce/prevent risk factors. Indeed, the original application of risk factor theories to the prevention of offending in the Cambridge-Somerville Youth Study (Cabot, 1940) had discovered that risk-focused intervention was often ineffective and could be actively harmful (McCord and McCord, 1959; McCord, 1978). Other studies that evaluated the impact of long-term, risk-focused interventions with children demonstrated very limited and inconsistent evidence of success (for example Bottoms and McClintock, 1973; Thornberry and Krohn, 2003); moreover evidence of the deleterious (harmful) consequences of risk-focused preventative intervention when delivered through contact with the YJS (for example McAra and McVie, 2007). Consequently, the evidence base for the expansion of the Scaled Approach was seriously questionable, as was the claim that risk-focused early intervention is effective. However, this contradictory evidence base did not deter the government from supporting the Scaled Approach, indicating a preformed political project being rolled out regardless of inconvenient academic evidence.

My academic perspective and experience of the Scaled Approach roll-out was that of a project of political expediency rather than being evidence based (see Goddard and Myers, 2017), which was compounded by professional experience of the framework's development (2008–9) prior to its inception. I worked with an Open University consultancy team developing Youth Justice Board (YJB)-funded training materials for Youth Offending Team (YOT) managers preparing to implement the Scaled Approach. These materials consisted of a series of modules unpacking the RFPP, its origins and evidence base, how it should be implemented and how practitioners should critically reflect on risk-based practice. My role was to encourage critical reflection by practitioners through evaluating the methodology, analysis, evidence, conclusions and ethics of the framework, how it could be adapted and whether it was appropriate based on its (lack of) validity and reliability, a critical point that was rather off message for the YJB. The reaction to my course materials was one of outrage from the YJB and from the external training provider contracted to produce the materials. I had 'caricatured' youth justice practice and the key elements of the RFPP, to the point that practitioners may find the approach impractical and inappropriate. I disagreed, as did the Open University consultancy team manager and the external reviewer (a respected critical youth justice academic researcher), who argued that I was 'encouraging practitioners to reflect critically on their practice in a challenging way, very much in the spirit of reflective practice and quality academic scholarship'. Ironically, such reflection aligned with YJB requirements for YOT practice but apparently were less encouraged if targeted at the evidential basis of youth justice policy and practice. My overwhelming impression was that the government/YJB commitment to the RFPP/Scaled Approach was fixed and indicative of a 'sunk cost fallacy', so any reflection must be focused on how to implement it effectively, not whether to implement it at all. That way, any failure of the Scaled Approach 'policy' would lie in its practice implementation, not in its policy formulation by governmental actors and the YJB. The emphasis seemed more on generating policy-based evidence than evidence-based policy.

My view was soon reinforced when attending a conference presentation to youth justice practitioners – a critique of the Scaled Approach by two critical academics. A senior policy adviser from the YJB gate crashed the session and proceeded to interrupt the post-presentation critical question-and-answer panel by informing practitioners in the audience that "you will be doing this", regardless of their expressed concerns. Once again, the Scaled Approach was being presented (in this case by senior policy makers) as a done deal, and practitioners were being browbeaten into its implementation. They had, after all, been through a consultation exercise regarding the new framework. However, this consultation had taken the form of a prescriptive and pre-judged reflection exercise along the lines of 'this is what you will be doing, so how can you make sure that it works?' In my experience, this was an all-too-common approach to 'consultation' with practitioners in the YJS at that time – key stakeholders from the centre (government, civil servants, YJB) presenting a preformed and politically agreed policy/practice proposal and expecting YOT staff to accept it and make it work (with YJB support of course). The implementation of the Scaled Approach appeared to me to exemplify such an unreflective and self-fulfilling process, which I have characterised elsewhere as 'a prescription without a consultation' (Case, 2007: 174).

APPENDIX 3

The Child First 'Strategy Implementation Project'

While the Child First guiding principle is well established in youth justice policy, strategy and practice guidance, consolidated by a significant research evidence base (Case and Browning, 2021a), the principle remains relatively underdeveloped in practice. Academic experts have begun to address the policy into practice (that is, policy transfer) issue being faced by the Youth Justice System (YJS) of England and Wales through their empirical research in collaboration with key policy-maker stakeholders such as strategists and practitioners (see Day, 2022). The enhanced focus on youth justice policy implementation was evidenced by the 'Child First Strategy Implementation Project' (hereafter the 'SIP'), which was designed to examine implementation of the guiding principle in practice, focusing on stakeholder perspectives of how it is understood, issues affecting implementation (for example enablers, barriers, challenges, opportunities) and the support needs crucial to making Child First a practical reality (Case and Browning, 2021b). The SIP was underpinned by a series of workshops with 73 expert stakeholders working in different contexts and organisations across the youth justice sector: community (practitioners, managers, heads of service); custody (practitioners, management); strategy (policy leads, strategic advisers, analysts, senior managers); inspectorate (secondees, inspectors, senior management); and research (academic, organisational researchers).

Feedback elicited three key themes as central to the implementation of Child First across stakeholder groups – child-centrism, cognisance and professional relationships:

- Child-centrism: developing child-friendly and child-focused strategies for working with children, which are focused on:
  - engagement – communicating and collaborating with children, understanding children, valuing their voices, building trusting relationships;
  - realising children's rights and entitlements – realising rights to childhood, universal access to support services;
  - prioritising needs – recognising, responding to and addressing children's needs;
  - positive intervention focus – avoiding stigmatisation, promoting minimal intervention and positive, desistance-focused approaches;

  - developmental sensitivity – responding to children according to their maturity and developmental stage.
- Cognisance: knowledge, understanding and information regarding Child First, underpinned by:
  - knowledge – development and sharing of new knowledge;
  - development of understanding – promoting system-wide awareness of Child First, promoting relevant terminology;
  - guidance/information/support – making available practice guidance and support for staff, ensuring understanding of Child First tenets;
  - incongruence – addressing incompatibility, disagreement, contradiction and conflict between policies and practices, ensuring appropriate structures, systems, mechanisms and processes for implementation.
- Professional relationships: developing strategies and practices to address elements of inter- and multi-agency working relationships that influence implementation, particularly:
  - philosophical and cultural differences – differing beliefs, values, cultures and terminology, competing philosophies;
  - inter-agency partnership working – working together to support positive outcomes for children;
  - educating others – educating colleagues about Child First, defending professional decisions;
  - organisational identity – maintaining clarity of purpose and organisational integrity, respecting practitioner knowledge, enabling discretion. (See Case and Browning, 2021b for detailed analysis and discussion of findings)

The SIP offered a detailed, contextualised investigation of a wide range of stakeholder understandings, perceptions and experiences of Child First, notably the conceptual, relational and practical issues and challenges shaping its implementation. Findings clearly demonstrated that the implementation of youth justice policy principles (mobilised through strategy) in real-world practice is a complex, multi-faceted process subject to adaptation at the discretion of key stakeholders working in different local and organisational contexts (Braithwaite et al, 2018). The SIP recommended that implementation complexity should not be underestimated in the Child First context, particularly as such underestimation contributes to policy failure (Hudson et al, 2019). Instead, complexity should be addressed through bespoke support and guidance mechanisms, designed and administered in collaboration with stakeholder groups in order to meet organisational needs, while remaining true to Child First principles (Case and Browning, 2021b).

Findings corroborated conclusions that policy implementation is highly dependent on local context (Brathwaite et al, 2018) and that centralised youth justice policy and strategy is 'made' real at the local level (Goldson and Briggs, 2021). Crucially, analyses illuminated the centrality of holistic collaboration to prevent policy failure. The debilitating influence of 'inadequate collaborative policy-making' (Hudson et al, 2019) on the policy implementation gap supports the SIP's prioritisation of stakeholder collaboration at multiple levels, including enhanced engagement of frontline practitioners. The SIP concluded that Child First policy implementation processes should be designed in a way that 'connects actors vertically and horizontally in the process of collaboration and joint deliberation' (Ansell et al, 2017). This collaborative emphasis was intended to facilitate the constructive management of differences within and between organisations and to encourage the search for sufficient common ground to proceed with the implementation of Child First policy/strategy, rather than seeking (unrealistic) unanimous consent and privileging policy legitimacy and organisational missions/agendas (Ansell et al, 2017).

The SIP project concluded with a recommendation that the Youth Justice Board (YJB) act as 'implementation broker' for Child First, offering expert, evidence-led support tailored to local contexts and being sensitive to 'bottom-up' discretion and dilemmas. Implementation support, it was recommended, should be focused on problem solving through collaboration – providing technical support, troubleshooting problems, brokering areas of dispute and encouraging the use of research and evidence (Hudson et al. 2019). It was also recommended that the YJB extend their mechanisms of collaboration with stakeholders (including children) to inform their practice guidance and to expand its purview to incorporate emerging areas of practice significance such as trauma-informed practice, adverse childhood experiences and communication issues (see Case and Browning, 2021b). For example, it was recommended that the YJB re-evaluate and appropriately revise their 'National standards' guidance to practitioners regarding out-of-court processes. It was suggested that current guidance does not fully address stakeholder concerns regarding child-centrism, largely because 'there is no explicit indication that rights, best interests or minimising levels of intervention should contribute to the decision-making process, as might be expected in guidance intended to direct child first practice' (Bateman, 2020: 5). Finally, His Majesty's Inspectorate of Probation were encouraged to critically reflect upon the incongruence between project evidence and their preferred, risk-led evidence base (Case and Browning, 2021a), to fulfil their stated intention 'to follow the evidence as it evolves ... [to] determine where the academic research leads us to refine and amend our approach to inspection' (HMIP, 2021: 6).

The SIP concluded by making 15 recommendations for more effective implementation of Child First in practice, mainly targeted at youth justice governance organisations and practitioners. Of these, 11 were fully accepted the YJB in a detailed response to the authors (YJB, 2021, private correspondence), with the remaining four being partially accepted because of resource limitations (YJB should address perceptual, practice and training gaps in understandings of Child First) or because they were owned by other organisations: revisit out-of-court guidance/'National standards' (owned by the Justice Minister), develop KPI-related concrete positive outcome measures (owned by the government), promote Youth Offending Team leadership of the Child First agenda (dependent on local governance arrangements). Notwithstanding the general requirement for constant reflective improvement in terms of policy into practice transfer activity, however, it was tentatively concluded that the Child First principle was being increasingly mobilised and realised in the YJS, moving practice away from being prescriptive and process driven and towards becoming more discretionary and outcomes focused. Indeed, the support offered to the SIP research by expert stakeholder groups strongly indicated both the desire and capacity for cultural change and continued critical reflection, offering encouragement that this could be conducted in collaborative, child-focused ways (Case and Browning, 2021b).

APPENDIX 4

What is youth justice policy making?

Contexts	Mechanisms
Complex, contested, multi-layered, multi-systemic	Identity, role and status ambiguity and conflict
Fragmented	Cohering fragmentation and reconciling agendas Collaboration and consensus Universal policy, shared objectives, seeking alignment

APPENDIX 5

Who makes youth justice policy? Governmental actors

Contexts	Mechanisms
Government, ministers, politicians	Dead hand influence of Number 10 Dead hand influence of right-wing newspaper media Steering civil servants
Senior policy advisers	Advising ministers, manifesto commitments Steering civil servants and other officials
Civil servants	Being steered Challenging and steering government policy Advising government as policy architects Retraction and deprofessionalisation

APPENDIX 6

Who makes youth justice policy? Non-governmental actors

Contexts	Mechanisms
Youth Justice Board	Contested, ambiguous identity and role Advisory and supportive Soft power
Office of the Children's Commissioner	Identifying problems, brokering solutions Soft power
Welsh youth justice (national)	Development of national policy identity Soft power Seeking consensus, common ground
Managers/practitioners, third sector	Localised mediation and moderation Challenge, innovation

APPENDIX 7

How does youth justice policy making happen?

Contexts	Mechanisms
Stability, change, instability	Cyclical, gradual development
Conflict and ambivalence	Seeking consensus and common ground
	Clarity and consistency of approach and messaging
Chaotic, random	Political short-termism and precarity
Sudden agenda change	Financial short-termism and precarity
Change of government	Opacity and incoherence
Staff 'churnover'	Re-education
External events	Opportunism and instrumentalism

APPENDIX 8

Policy discourses as governmental identity

Contexts	Mechanisms
Political policy discourses Conflict and ambivalence Hybridity, confusion Populist punitiveness Prevention–support–diversion Discourse–evidence rupture	Governmental open-mindedness to external expert influence Lack of political agenda Steering versus being steered Political and media agenda Political and practical realities
Welsh 'dragonised' Social justice Children's rights Partially devolved Poorly understood, marginalised	Universal children's rights policy Seeking consensus and common ground Developing and cohering shared agendas Collaboration Under the radar

APPENDIX 9

Youth Justice Board policy-making role and influence

Contexts	Mechanisms
Policy-making role Independence	Lack of practitioner engagement Bridging function Strategic, instrumental
Policy influencer Ambiguous, fluid role	Relationships with civil servants Managerialist prescription as necessity, visited by government, tool of insecurity and threat
Strategic influencer Expert, independent Unstable, fluctuating, threatened	Environmental scanning for emerging problems Utilising data and expert evidence Engaging stakeholders across multiple contexts Advising ministers Supporting practice improvement
Waning/changing influence Dynamic, cyclical Changing identity and role	Lack of legislation and policy vacuum Ministry of Justice and His Majesty's Inspectorate of Probation becoming more muscular Policy into practice (Youth Justice Board more muscular)

APPENDIX 10

Experts, experience and evidence

Contexts	Mechanisms
Expertise and experience	Relationships between experts Identifying like-minded, credible experts Harnessing in-house expertise
'Evidence mindset' Dynamic, fluctuating, fragile	Open-mindedness to evidence Boldness to challenge and create new evidence Partiality and inconvenient evidence Short-termism, sudden policy shifts Utilising professional lived experience
Using expert evidence Twin-track approach	Generating and challenging evidence Relationships with academic experts Relationships with practitioner experts

APPENDIX 11

Professional lived experience, expertise and evidence generation

Contexts	Mechanisms
Youth Justice Board (YJB) – practitioner relationships	Recognising/using practitioner expertise and credibility Prioritising localised, micro-level engagement Instrumental, self-serving YJB engagement
Practitioners as experts	Challenge/resistance to centralised prescription Development of local penal cultures Collaboration between like-minded individuals Support of influential advocates Negotiation, discretion, innovation
Local mediation and moderation of centralised policy	Bottom-up policy making by 'street-level bureaucrats' Engagement with stakeholders/advocates

APPENDIX 12

Power dynamics as relational policy making

Contexts	Mechanisms
Political, governmental	Ministerial pressure, agenda, steer, control
Minister identity, personality	Partialities, prejudices, animosity, stubbornness
Non-governmental influence	Soft power Strategic use of steer and leverage Diplomatic, expert challenge Constructive conversations

APPENDIX 13

Power dynamics and YJB relationships with non-governmental organisations

Contexts	Mechanisms
Government Steering/being steered	Centralised prescription and steering of Youth Justice Board (YJB) Constructive challenge Governmental receptiveness to being steered
Civil servants Tensions Increasing YJB influence Threatened identity	Directive, prescriptive, steering of YJB by Home Office More balanced, collaborative, influential relationship with Ministry of Justice (MoJ) MoJ more muscular, assertive (mirrored by YJB) Relationship mediated by political realities
His Majesty's Inspectorate of Probation (HMIP) Governance organisations	Reconciling incongruent practice agendas Seeking common ground HMIP more muscular, assertive (mirrored by YJB)
Wales UK government centrism Lack of scrutiny	UK government and YJB prejudice, hostility, suspicion Neglect, lack of understanding Smaller context facilitating relationship building Mutual learning and educating the English
Youth Offending Teams (YOTs) Collaborative mindset Practitioner expertise	Openness to expertise, inclusivity, equity (YJB view) Practice expertise, challenge, innovation (YOT view) Increasing influence of the Association of YOT Managers (YOT view)

APPENDIX 14

Mechanisms of relational, collaborative policy making

Contexts	Mechanisms
Seeking common ground Dynamic, contested, contingent Agenda shift, churnover	Rebuilding relationships, re-educating colleagues Collaborative mindset, shared agendas Networking Building alliances with the right people Brokering collaborative relationships
Using communication	Dialogue, diplomacy Common language Consistent, cogent messaging Narrative storytelling, drip fed, attention grabbing
Relational reciprocity	Empathy, immersion Developing trust, respect Being inclusive Valuing professional and personal lived experience

Notes

Introduction

1 Underpinned by the *expertise*, *evidence* and *experience* developed over my career; essential components of policy making that are discussed throughout this book.

Chapter 1

1 From this point, individuals coming to the attention of youth justice systems and services will be referred to as 'children' rather than young people, in accordance with the operational definition of the United Nations Convention on the Rights of the Child (UNCRC, 1989), which categorises a child as anyone below the age of 18.

2 For example, national (central) and local governments and criminal justice agencies such as the police, courts, community-based organisations (e.g. youth justice/offending teams, third sector groups) and custodial institutions.

3 Following the CDA 1998, youth justice policy-making responsibilities became the remit of the newly created, partially devolved governments of Scotland and Northern Ireland, with the UK government remaining in place to exercise overall power and retaining specific 'reserved' (non-devolved) policy responsibilities. While a new partially devolved government was also created for Wales, youth and criminal justice (also policing) were non-devolved policy areas controlled by the UK government in Westminster, England.

4 The microsystem is closely associated with a further identified level, the 'exosystem', containing environments that can impact upon microsystems, for example, the mass media. Additionally, Bronfenbrenner identified the 'chronosystem' as a fifth level of social system consisting of environmental changes that occur over a lifetime and influence development, such as major life events (for example, economic austerity).

5 As opposed to context solely as the static, observable feature (space, place, people, things) operating at one moment in time and setting in motion a deterministic chain reaction of events.

6 The Home Secretary leads the Home Office (the lead government department for immigration and passports, drugs policy, crime, fire, counter-terrorism and police) and is responsible for making sure that communities in all force areas of the UK are kept safe and secure and for protecting the UK's national borders and security. The Minister of Justice (also known as the Secretary of State for Justice) oversees Her Majesty's Prison Service in England and Wales, probation matters and the judiciary and heads the Ministry of Justice, a major government department at the heart of the justice system working to protect and advance the principles of justice.

7 Note that children are rarely considered as key stakeholders in the making of youth justice policy (Creaney, 2020) or social policy (Mitra, 2009).

8 The relative neglect of practitioners' expertise in youth justice policy-making contexts indicates, by extension, the even greater neglect of *children* as policy-maker experts, an issue that will discussed further as we progress. For example, the crucial perspective of children as receivers of policy and holders of expert views regarding the implementation of policy into practice has been glaringly absent from policy-making debates, processes and mechanisms in the youth justice field (Case et al, 2020).

9 For example, the production of evidence by 'expert' sources such as government data analysts, academics, opinion polls, think tank reports, policy papers by civil service, independent inquiries, inspectorate reports, press reports, television programmes, personal experience/opinion (Stevens, 2011).

Chapter 2

1 A philosophical approach to classifying and understanding the nature of reality and 'real-world' operations, processes and knowledge construction.

2 With expert guidance from Dr Anna Souhami, Professor John Drew, Dr Kathy Hampson, Professor Kevin Haines, Dr Tim Bateman and Dusty Kennedy.

3 Double-checked and augmented to increase the 'trustworthiness' (a common reliability measure in qualitative research) and internal validity (for example, accuracy, completeness, honesty) of the study findings and conclusions in order to develop deeper understandings of the topic (see Dalgliesh et al, 2020).

4 This inclusion criterion resulted in the exclusion of children from the sample, rendering the research sampling and analysis more focused and manageable, but at the same time compounding the neglect of children as 'experts by experience' from adult-centric policy-making studies. The implications of this exclusion on the study findings, conclusions and recommendations are discussed throughout.

5 In addition, data have been included from a series of interviews conducted in 2018 with key stakeholders. These interviews accessed Alun Michael (former Minister of State for Home affairs and Welsh Secretary), Professor Kevin Haines, Dr Anna Souhami and Professor John Drew and Dusty Kennedy (both interviewed for this project).

6 Subtitled 'The Mechanisms of Government and Politics, and How to Investigate Them', which illustrates the author's privileging of governmental actors and contexts as driving policy making.

7 Some stakeholders have occupied multiple organisational contexts over their careers.

Chapter 3

1 When he became Labour leader in 1994, Blair pronounced that "we should never excuse the commission of criminal acts on the grounds of social conditions" (Blair, 1994, in Scraton and Haydon, 2002), having previously characterised youth offending as a descent into "moral chaos" (Scraton and Haydon, 2002).

2 Northern Ireland ceded from direct English rule in 1998 following the ratification of the 'Good Friday Agreement' and the establishment of the Northern Ireland Assembly, which took control of youth and criminal justice policy making. Scotland partially devolved in 1999 following the Scotland Act 1998, taking independent control over a number of policy areas including criminal justice but with others remaining under Westminster rule. Wales achieved partial devolution in 1999 following the Government of Wales Act 1998 and its subsequent 2006 iteration, which introduced a range of primary law-making powers and created an executive body, the Welsh Assembly Government ('Welsh Government' since 2011), holding devolved responsibility for certain policy issues (such as education, health, housing) but with other areas non-devolved, notably criminal and youth justice.

3 In its early years, New Labour published a series of documents articulating a clear commitment to modernisation and evidence-based policy formation, notably the 'Modernising government' White Paper (Cabinet Office, 1999: 31), which proclaimed that 'policy decisions should be based on sound evidence'.

4 Indeed, specialisation is deliberately avoided in the civil service as staff are expected to move to new posts frequently and because short-term posts reduce the possibility of officials developing intellectual or ideological attachment (or specific expertise, of course) to a particular approach to policy problems (Page and Jenkins, 2005).

5 The AYM was created in 2001 'to promote the role and status of YOT managers and to agree policy initiatives that put young people at the heart of the Youth Justice System' (AYM website). An equivalent organisation followed in Wales, entitled YOT Managers Cymru (YMC).

6 In addition to the three main KPIs for England and Wales, there were four Wales-specific KPIs[24] known as Youth Justice Indicators: education, training and employment (ETE), accommodation, substance use, mental health, emotional health and well-being.

7 Education, Training and Employment, Mental Health, Substance Use, Young People Who Sexually Abuse, Offending Behaviour Programmes, Parenting, Restorative Justice, Mentoring, Targeted Neighbourhood Prevention, Final Warning Interventions, Swift Administration of Justice, Supervision and Surveillance Programmes, Custody and Resettlement, and Assessment, Planning Interventions and Supervision (YJB, 2003).

8 Wacquant (2009: 1) observed that this 'new punitive common sense' was born in the United States and exported internationally, evidenced through 'vertical expansion' (for example, burgeoning prison populations) and 'horizontal expansion' (such as the proliferation and diversification of technologies of regulation, control and surveillance).

9 The authors of the 'Engaging Young People Who Offend' KEEP.

10 Asset required YOT staff to rate a child's likelihood of reoffending (more accurately, their risk of reconviction) based on their (current or recent) exposure to psychosocial 'risk factors' in 12 domains of life: living arrangements, family and personal relationships, education, training and employment, neighbourhood, lifestyle, substance use, physical health, emotional and mental health, perception of self and others, thinking and behaviour, attitudes to offending and motivation to change (YJB, 2000). The risk domains were supplemented by sections measuring the influence of positive (protective) factors, indicators of vulnerability, indicators of risk of serious harm to others and a self-assessment 'What do you think?' section.

11 A 'scientific', experimental, framework privileged by the UK government (Cabinet Office, 2021) and YJB as the central rationale for KEEPs (see Stephenson et al, 2011) and for evaluating the robustness and 'effectiveness' of crime prevention interventions based on comparisons of intervention effects between control and recipient groups (see Sherman et al, 1998; Sutton et al, 2021).

12 At the time of writing, the First Minister for Wales.

13 See Appendix 2 for my 'Critical commentary' on my experience of the Scaled Approach's introduction as a new youth justice process/strategy.

14 The Department for Children, Schools and Families became the Department for Education in May 2010, at which point, government sponsorship of and responsibility for youth justice and the YJB became the sole domain of the Ministry of Justice.

Chapter 4

1 A government department populated by civil servants working with and for the Department of Justice (led by the government's Minister for Justice) and other government departments to monitor and manage the Criminal Justice System, in order to protect the public, reduce reoffending and deliver swift access to justice. The MoJ assumed sole sponsorship of the YJB from the Home Office and Department for Children, Schools and Families in 2010.

2 Relatedly, following 'Breaking the cycle', the YJB (understandably keen to reinforce its policy currency and identity) collaborated with the 'Children and young people now' newsletter to produce a short report entitled 'Prevention matters: how sustained investment in prevention programmes has reduced youth offending' (YJB and CYP Now, 2010). 'Prevention matters' detailed the youth justice work conducted over the past ten years aimed at 'preventing children and young people from becoming involved in crime' (YJB and CYP Now, 2010: 2). Using local case study examples and testimony from children who have desisted from offending, the publication championed 'a robust raft of targeted interventions' (YJB and CYP Now, 2010: 2), notably YIPs, YISPs, Safer

Schools Partnerships and parenting programmes, which had purportedly demonstrated success and cost-effectiveness in reducing offending.

3 I reviewed this text for *Youth Justice Journal* (Case, 2011: 106–8). My review was extremely critical, to the point of being scathing and overly subjective, but it is still of value to the reader to illustrate my positionality regarding youth justice policy making at that time.

4 In May 2022, the Conservative government announced a £300 million funding package for youth justice over the next three years 'to support every single council across England and Wales in catching and preventing youth offending earlier than ever, helping to stop these children and teenagers from moving on to further, more serious offending'. The announcement included the 'Turnaround' scheme, 'a new early intervention scheme backed by £60 million, through which YOTs will be given extra funding to connect children and teenagers to targeted, wraparound support to stop them going down a path of criminality'. The package also included an uplift in core funding for YOTs, such that together with Turnaround funding, central government funding for YOTs will be around £100m a year, compared to around £75m currently.

5 Recommendations being revisited and updated by Professor Jonathan Evans and colleagues (Evans et al, 2023) at the time of writing.

6 At the time of writing (early 2023), however, only one Secure School has been planned, in Medway (its senior staff have been interviewed for this book), and its opening has been consistently delayed (now due in mid-2024).

7 There have been strategic developments in related youth justice policy areas over this period. For example, the National Police Chiefs' Council 'Child centred policing' national strategy document states that '[i]t is crucial that in all encounters with the police those below the age of 18 should be treated as children first' (NPCC, 2015: 9). Subsequently, the Sentencing Council produced their 'Sentencing children and young people' guidelines and principles, which stated that 'the approach to sentencing should be individualistic and focused on the child or young person, as opposed to offence focused' (Sentencing Council, 2017: 4), thus Child First, not offence or offender first.

8 In order to bolster the evidence base for the effective implementation of Child First in practice, since 2021 the YJB has funded a series of evaluations of Child First 'Pathfinder' projects in different YOTs, which are now beginning to disseminate their early findings. The YJB also now requires all YOTs to detail their Child First practice and intentions in their annual 'Youth justice plan' document. Since 2022, the AYM have convened regular 'Child First in practice' webinars to discuss and explore evidence of effective implementation of the guiding principle.

9 The potential incompatibilities between these practice agendas is explored further in Appendix 3, which discusses the 'Strategy Implementation Project' stakeholder consultation project (Case and Browning, 2021b).

10 In the absence of comprehensive training/guidance on implementing the AssetPlus framework/instrument, there has been inevitable regression to risk-informed practice (Hampson, 2018; Creaney, 2020).

11 This YJB quote is particularly notable for its emphasis on the policy-making role of *evidence* developed by a range of *experts* in the contemporary YJS, but also for the identification of 'policy makers' as a category somehow distinct from practitioners, academics and, indeed, the YJB itself. My inclination (positionality alert) is that such a perspective could foster a reductionist view of policy making and policy makers – one that will be explored and challenged in forthcoming analyses.

Chapter 5

1 These senior civil servants work closely with ministers and government officials to develop and implement policy.

2 The main statutory duties of the YJB under the Crime and Disorder Act 1998 are: monitoring the operation of the youth justice system; advising the Secretary of State (Home Secretary) on the operation of the youth justice system, national standards and on how the aim of preventing offending by children and young people can most effectively be pursued; identifying and disseminating effective practice across youth justice services; making grants to YOTs and other organisations to support development and delivery of effective practice.

3 The custodial institutions of the YJS of England and Wales: Young Offender Institutions, Secure Training Centres and Secure Children's Homes, currently overseen by the Youth Custody Service.

4 Note that Lipsky defined the 'street-level bureaucrat' in entirely adult-centric terms, without consideration of the potential for children subject to and experiencing practice to fulfil this expert role in some way.

5 Cycles of reforms advocating either lenient treatment or harsh punishments for juvenile delinquents (see Chapter 1), with this cycle driven by several unchanging ideas that force us to repeat, rather than learn from, our history (Bernard and Kurlychek, 2010).

6 A broader example of governmental/organisational churn is the change of YJB sponsorship from the Home Office (1998–2007) to joint sponsorship between the DCSF and the MoJ (2007–10) to sponsorship by the MoJ (2010 onwards).

7 What is youth justice 'policy'?; Who are the 'makers' of youth justice policy?; How is youth justice policy making understood, re/constructed, experienced and made meaningful by policy makers working in different contexts?; What are the barriers, challenges, enablers and opportunities for policy making?; How can youth justice policy-making be improved?

Chapter 6

1 Enabling closer analyses of RQs 3 and 4: how is youth justice policy making understood, re/constructed, experienced, and made meaningful by policy makers working in different contexts? What are the barriers, challenges, enablers and opportunities for youth justice policy making?

2 It must be acknowledged again that children were missing from this range of 'expert stakeholders', in part to keep the scope of the research manageable but also because they are not currently viewed by adult stakeholders as experts by experience in relation to youth justice policy making. However, as will be emphasised in the discussion recommendation, children absolutely must be included as an expert policy-maker group in future policy-making processes and analyses.

3 The YJB has long classified Wales as a 'region' for performance management purposes.

4 By 2006, a series of organisational, structural and political shifts had eroded YJB influence. For example, organisational changes within the YJB had begun to alter its relationship with Whitehall, notably its dramatic expansion (growing from six to 212 staff in less than a decade), which now necessitated physical separation from the Home Office in a dedicated building. This organisational change both removed officials from the scrutiny and influence of ministerial staff and allowed for the development of new ways of working, routines and processes (for example, more space for the routine, expert criticism of government youth justice policy). Furthermore, a broader political 'crisis of confidence' occurred, wherein government departments were continually being split and reorganised, leading to sudden transformations in initiatives, priorities and careers. For example, the Cabinet Office increased its control of new policy initiatives through the establishment of the Prime Minister's Delivery Unit, a policy-making change that was particularly strongly felt in relation to youth justice, which straddled multiple policy areas, such that youth justice lost its political status (Souhami, 2015a). Taken together, therefore, consistent and

unpredictable organisational changes and political crises were conspiring to render the YJB's function, role and identity ever more precarious, ambiguous and insecure in the policy-making context.

Chapter 8

1 In contrast to constructing contexts in reductionist, linear ways as the observable features (space, place, people, things) that trigger or block policy development, assuming the context operates one moment in time and sets in motion a chain reaction of events (see Greenhalgh and Manzano, 2021).

2 In particular, my longstanding opposition to risk-based youth justice and my strong advocacy for principled Child First alternatives.

3 Once again, it must be stressed that children as experts were excluded from the analyses across this book. While this exclusion is representative of the absence of the child's voice in policy-making processes and relationships since 1998, it also means that the findings and conclusions are *not* representative of the full complexity and breadth of policy making and policy mak*ers* in the youth justice sector.

4 For example, the scientific aspirations of advocates of 'evidence-based' policy and practice (see Chapter 3) will always be limited by other constructive influences such as democratic political debates, stakeholder lobbying and popular opinion (Head, 2015).

References

Allcock, C., Dorman, F., Taunt, R. and Dixon, J. (2015) 'Constructive comfort: accelerating change in the NHS', London: Health Foundation.

Allen, R. (1991) 'Out of jail: the reduction in the use of penal custody for male juveniles 1981–1988', *Howard Journal*, 30(1): 30–52.

Allen, R. (2011) 'Written evidence to the Justice Committee on the proposed abolition of the Youth Justice Board', Available from: https://publications.parliament.uk/pa/cm201012/cmselect/cmjust/1547/1547vw07.htm

Andrews, D.A. and Bonta, J. (2010) *The Psychology of Criminal Conduct*, London: Routledge.

Ansell, C., Sørensen, E. and Torfing, J. (2017) 'Improving policy implementation through collaborative policymaking', *Policy and Politics*, 45(3): 467–86.

Audit Commission (1996) 'Misspent youth: young people and crime', London: Audit Commission.

Audit Commission (2004) 'Youth justice 2004', London: Audit Commission.

Bandalli, S. (2000) 'Children, responsibility and the new youth justice', in B. Goldson (ed) *The New Youth Justice*, Lyme Regis: Russell House, pp 81–95.

Bardach, E. and Patashnik, E. (2015) *A Practical Guide for Policy Analysis: The Eightfold Path to More Effective Problem Solving*, Thousand Oaks: CQ Press.

Bateman, T. (2011) 'Punishing poverty: the "Scaled Approach" and youth justice practice', *Howard Journal of Penal Reform*, 50(2): 171–83.

Bateman, T. (2012) 'Children in conflict with the law: an overview of trends and developments – 2010/2011', London: NAYJ.

Bateman, T. (2016) 'The state of youth custody', London: NAYJ.

Bateman, T. (2017) 'The state of youth justice 2017: an overview of trends and developments', London: NAYJ.

Bateman, T. (2020) 'Unjust pains: the impact of COVID-19 on children in prison', *Journal of Children's Services*, Available from: www.emerald.com/insight/content/doi/10.1108/JCS-07-2020-0045/full/html

Belfiore, E. (2021) 'Is it *really* about the evidence? Argument, persuasion, and the power of ideas in cultural policy', *Cultural Trends*, 31(4): 293–310, Available from: https://doi.org/10.1080/09548963.2021.1991230

Bernard, B. and Kurlychek, M. (2010) *The Cycle of Juvenile Justice*, Oxford: Oxford University Press.

Bottoms, A.E. and McClintock, F.H. (1973) *Criminals Coming of Age: A Study of Institutional Adaptation in the Treatment of Adolescent Offenders*, London: Heinemann.

Braithwaite, J. and Mugford, S. (1994) 'Conditions of successful reintegration ceremonies', *British Journal of Criminology*, 34(2): 139–71.

Braithwaite, J., Churruca, K., Long, J.C., Ellis, L.A. and Herkes, J. (2018) 'When complexity science meets implementation science: a theoretical and empirical analysis of systems change', *BMC Medicine*, 16(63).

Braun, V. and Clarke, V. (2006) 'Using thematic analysis in psychology', *Qualitative Research in Psychology*, 3(2): 77–101.

Braun, V. and Clarke, V. (2022) *Thematic Analysis*, London: Sage.

Brett, J. (2018) 'Learning from history by seeing it differently: frameworks for understanding the socio-historical development of youth justice', *Howard League ECAN Bulletin*, 1(37): 34–9.

Brewster, D. and Jones, R. (2019) 'Distinctly divergent or hanging onto English coat-tails? Drug policy in post-devolution Wales', *Criminology and Criminal Justice*, 19(3): 364–81.

Briggs, D. (2013) 'Conceptualising risk and need: the rise of actuarialism and the death of welfare? Practitioner assessment and intervention in the Youth Offending Service', *Youth Justice*, 13(1): 17–30.

Bronfenbrenner, U. (1995) 'Developmental ecology through space and time: a future perspective', in P. Moen, G.H. Elder Jr and K. Lüscher (eds) *Examining Lives in Context: Perspectives on the Ecology of Human Development*, Washington, DC: American Psychological Association, pp 619–47, Available from: https://doi.org/10.1037/10176-018

Brown, R. (2013) 'Evidence-based policy or policy-based evidence? Higher education policies and policymaking 1987–2012', *Perspectives: Policy and Practice in Higher Education*, 17(4): 118–23.

Cabinet Office (1999) 'Modernising government', London: Cabinet Office.

Cabinet Office (2010) 'Building the Big Society', London: Cabinet Office.

Cabot, R. (1940) 'A long-term study of children: the Cambridge-Somerville Youth Study', *Child Development*, 11(2): 143–51.

Cairney, P. and Oliver, K. (2020) 'How should academics engage in policymaking to achieve impact?', *Political Studies Review*, 18(2): 228–44.

Cameron, D. (2009) 'The Big Society', Hugo Young Memorial Lecture, Available from: www.conservatives.com/News/Speeches/2009/11/David_Cameron_The_Big_Society

Cameron, D. (2011) 'Building a bigger, stronger society', speech, 23 May, Available from: www.conservatives.com/News/Speeches/2011/05/David_Cameron_Building_a_bigger_stronger_society

Capano, G. and Pritoni, A. (2020) 'Policy cycle', in P. Harris, A. Bitonti, C. Fleisher and A. Skorkjær (eds) *The Palgrave Encyclopaedia of Interest Groups, Lobbying and Public Affairs*, Cham: Palgrave Macmillan.

Case, S.P. (2006) 'Young people "at risk" of what? Challenging risk-focused early intervention as crime prevention', *Youth Justice*, 6(3): 171–9.

Case, S.P. (2007) 'Questioning the "evidence" of risk that underpins evidence-led youth justice interventions', *Youth Justice*, 7(2): 91–106.

Case, S.P. (2011) 'A new response to youth crime (D.J. Smith)', *Youth Justice*, 11(1): 106–8.

Case, S.P. (2014) 'Strategic complexities and opportunities in Welsh youth justice: exploring YJB Cymru', *Safer Communities*, 13(3): 109–19.

Case, S.P. (2018/21) *Youth Justice: A Critical Introduction*, London: Routledge.

Case, S.P. (2022) 'Challenging the reductionism of "evidence-based" youth justice', *Sustainability*, 13(4): 1735.

Case, S.P. and Browning, A. (2021a) 'Child First: the research evidence-base', Loughborough University, Available from: https://www.lboro.ac.uk/subjects/social-policy-studies/research/child-first-justice/

Case, S.P. and Browning, A. (2021b) 'The Child First Strategy Implementation Project', Loughborough University, Available from: https://www.lboro.ac.uk/subjects/social-policy-studies/research/child-first-justice/

Case, S.P. and Haines, K.R. (2009) *Understanding Youth Offending: Risk Factor Research Policy and Practice*, Cullompton: Willan.

Case, S.P. and Haines, K.R. (2012) 'Supporting an evolving and devolving Youth Justice Board', *Criminal Justice Matters*, 88(1): 38–40.

Case, S.P. and Haines, K.R. (2014) 'Youth justice: from linear risk paradigm to complexity', in A. Pycroft and C. Bartollas (eds) *Applying Complexity Theory: Whole Systems Approaches in Criminal Justice and Social Work*, Bristol: Policy Press, pp 119–39.

Case, S.P. and Haines, K.R. (2015) 'Children first, offenders second positive promotion: reframing the prevention debate', *Youth Justice Journal*, 15(3): 226–39.

Case, S.P. and Haines, K.R. (2021) Abolishing youth justice systems: Children first, offenders nowhere. *Youth Justice Journal,* 21(1): 3–17.

Case, S.P. and Hampson, K. (2019) 'Youth justice pathways to change: drivers, challenges and opportunities', *Youth Justice*, 19(1): 25–41.

Case, S.P. and Hazel, N. (eds) (2023) *Child First: Developing a New Youth Justice System*, London: Palgrave.

Case, S.P., Browning, A. and Hampson, K. (2023) 'The Child First Strategy Implementation Project: translating strategy into practice', *Youth Justice*, Available from: https://doi.org/10.1177/14732254231191978

Case, S.P., Drew, J., Hampson, K., Jones, G. and Kennedy, D. (2020) 'Professional perspectives of youth justice policy implementation: contextual and coalface challenges', *Howard Journal of Criminal Justice*, 59(2): 214–32.

Case, S.P., Sutton, C., Monaghan, M., Greenhalgh, J. and Wright, J. (2022) 'Contextualising evaluations of interventions to prevent youth offending: "what works" and EMMIE', *Safer Communities*, 21(4): 272–89.

Chapman, T. and O'Mahony, D. (2007) 'Youth and criminal justice in Northern Ireland: developments in social work with offenders', in G. McIvor and P. Raynor (eds) *Developments in Social Work with Offenders*, London: Jessica Kingsley.

Coldwell, M. (2019) 'Reconsidering context: six underlying features of context to improve learning from evaluation', *Evaluation*, 25(1): 99–117.

Creaney, S. (2020) 'Children's voices: are we listening? Progressing peer mentoring in the youth justice system', *Child Care in Practice*, 26(1): 22–37, Available from: https://doi.org/10.1080/13575279.2018.152138

Croci, G., Laycock, G. and Chainey, S. (2022) 'A realistic approach to policy formulation: the adapted EMMIE framework', *Policy Studies*, 44(4): 433–53.

CYP Now (2011) 'Interview with Crispin Blunt', 8 February.

Dalglish, S., Khalid, H. and McMahon, S (2020) 'Document analysis in health policy research: the READ approach', *Health Policy and Planning*, 35(10): 1424–31.

Davies, H., Nutley, S. and Walter, I. (2008) 'Why "knowledge transfer" is misconceived for applied social research', *Journal of Health Services Research & Policy*, 18(3): 188–90.

Day, A. (2020) 'Time to stop and smell the roses: On 'rushing headlong' into service delivery without really knowing what it is we are doing', *Criminal and Mental Health Behavior*, 31(1): 5–8.

Day, A. (2022) '"It's a hard balance to find": the perspectives of youth justice practitioners in England on the place of "risk" in an emerging "Child First" world', *Youth Justice*, 23(1), Available from: https://doi.org/10.1177/14732254221075205

DCSF, MoJ, Home Office (2008) 'Youth crime action plan', London: DCSF, MoJ, Home Office.

Department for Education and Skills (2003) 'Every child matters', London: DfES.

Department for Education and Skills (2005) 'Youth matters', London: DfES.

Drakeford, M. (2009) 'Children first, offenders second: youth justice in a devolved Wales', *Criminal Justice Matters*, 78(1): 8–9.

Drakeford, M. (2010) 'Devolution and youth justice in Wales', *Criminology & Criminal Justice*, 10(2): 137–54.

Driscoll, A. and Morris, J. (2001) 'Stepping out: rhetorical devices and culture change management in the UK civil service', *Public Administration*, 79(4): 803–24.

Dunkel, F. (2014) 'Juvenile justice systems in Europe: reform developments between justice, welfare and "new punitiveness"', *Kriminologijos studijos*, 1: 31–76.

Etzioni, A. (1995) *The Spirit of Community*, London: Fontana.

Evans, J., Raynor, P. and Heath, B. (2022) 'Locality, legitimacy and the limits of diversion: reviewing youth justice in Jersey', *Howard Journal of Crime and Justice*, 61(3): 367–80.

Evans, K. (2011) '"Big Society" in the UK: a policy review', *Children & Society*, 25(2): 164–71.

Farrington, D.P. (2000) 'Developmental criminology and risk-focussed prevention', in M. Maguire, R. Morgan and R. Reiner (eds) *The Oxford Handbook of Criminology* (3rd edn), Oxford: Oxford University Press.

Farrington, D.P. (2007) 'Childhood risk factors and risk-focused prevention', in M. Maguire, R. Morgan and R. Reiner (eds) *The Oxford Handbook of Criminology* (4th edn), Oxford: Oxford University Press.

Fergusson, R. (2007) 'Making sense of the melting pot: multiple discourses in youth justice policy', *Youth Justice*, 7(3): 179–94.

Finlay, L. (2002) 'Outing the researcher: the provenance, process and practice of reflexivity', *Qualitative Health Research*, 12(4): 531–45.

Flanagan, R. (2008) 'The review of policing: final report', London: HMSO.

Gains, F. (1999) 'Implementing privatization policies in "Next Steps" agencies', *Public Administration*, 77(4): 713–30.

Gains, F. (2003) 'Executive agencies in government: the impact of bureaucratic networks on policy outcomes', *Journal of Public Policy*, 23(1): 55–79.

Garland, D. (2001) *Culture of Control*, Oxford: Oxford University Press.

Goddard, T. and Myers, R. (2017) 'Against evidence-based oppression: marginalized youth and the politics of risk-based assessment and intervention', *Theoretical Criminology*, 21(2): 151–67.

Goldson, B. (2000) *The New Youth Justice*, Lyme Regis: Russell House.

Goldson, B. (2003) 'Tough on children: tough on justice', paper presented at the Centre for Studies in Crime and Social Justice (Edge Hill) in collaboration with the European Group for the Study of Deviance and Social Control, Chester, UK.

Goldson, B. (2010) 'The sleep of (criminological) reason: knowledge–policy rupture and New Labour's youth justice legacy', *Criminology and Criminal Justice*, 10(2): 155–78.

Goldson, B. (2011) 'The Independent Commission on Youth Crime and Antisocial Behaviour: fresh start or false dawn?', *Journal of Children's Services*, 6(2): 77–85.

Goldson, B. (ed) (2017) *Juvenile Justice in Europe: Past, Present and Future?*, London: Routledge.

Goldson, B. (2020) 'Excavating youth justice reform: historical mapping and speculative prospects', *Howard Journal of Crime and Justice*, 59(3): 317–34.

Goldson, B. and Briggs, D. (2021) 'Making youth justice: local penal cultures and differential outcomes; lessons and prospects for policy and practice', London: Howard League.

Goldson, B. and Hughes, G. (2010) 'Sociological criminology and youth justice: comparative policy analysis and academic intervention', *Criminology and Criminal Justice*, 10(2): 211–30.

Goldson, B. and Muncie, J. (2006) 'Rethinking youth justice: comparative analysis, international human rights and research evidence', *Youth Justice*, 6(2): 91–106.

Goldson, B. and Muncie, J. (2009) 'Editors introduction', in B. Goldson and J. Muncie (eds) *Youth Crime and Juvenile Justice*, vol 2, *Juvenile Corrections*, London: Sage.

Goldson, B. and Muncie, J. (eds) (2015) *Youth Crime and Justice*, London: Sage.

Greenhalgh, J. and Manzano, A. (2021) 'Understanding "context" in realist evaluation synthesis', *International Journal of Social Research Methodology*, 5: 583–95.

Gunn, L.A. (1978) 'Why is implementation so difficult?', *Management Services in Government*, 33: 169–76.

Haines, K.R. (2010) 'The dragonisation of youth justice', in W. Taylor, R. Hester and R. Earle (eds) *Youth Justice Handbook*, Cullompton: Willan.

Haines, K.R. and Case, S.P. (2008) 'The rhetoric and reality of the Risk Factor Prevention Paradigm approach to preventing and reducing youth offending', *Youth Justice*, 8(1): 5–20.

Haines, K.R. and Case, S.P. (2011) 'Risks, rights or both? Evaluating the common aetiology of negative and positive outcomes for young people to inform youth justice practice', *Social Work Review*, 2: 109–22.

Haines, K.R. and Case, S.P. (2012) 'The failed approach?', *Youth Justice*, 12(3): 212–28.

Haines, K.R. and Case, S.P. (2015) *Positive Youth Justice: Children First, Offenders Second*, Bristol: Policy Press.

Haines, K.R. and Drakeford, M. (1998) *Young People and Youth Justice*, London: Macmillan.

Haines, A., Goldson, B., Haycox, A., Houten, R., Lane, S., McGuire, J., Nathan, T., Perkins, E., Richards, S. and Whittington, R. (2012) *Evaluation of the Youth Justice Liaison and Diversion (YJLD) Pilot Scheme. Final Report*, Liverpool, UK: University of Liverpool.

Haines, K.R., Case, S.P., Charles, A.D. and Davies, K. (2013) 'The Swansea Bureau: a model of diversion from the youth justice system', *International Journal of Law, Crime and Justice*, 41(2): 167–87.

Hampson, K.S. (2018) 'Desistance approaches in youth justice: the next passing fad or a sea-change for the positive?', *Youth Justice*, 18(1): 18–33.

Hampson, K.S. (2023) 'Cementing 'Child First' in practice', in S. Case and N. Hazel (eds) *Child First: Developing a New Youth Justice System*, London: Palgrave, pp 301–31.

Hart, D. (2014) 'What's in a name? The identification of children in trouble with the law', London: SCYJ.

Hawkins, J.D. and Catalano, R.F. (1992) *Communities that Care*, San Francisco: Jossey-Bass.

Hazel, N. (2008) 'Cross-national comparison of youth justice', London: Youth Justice Board.

Hazel, N. and Bateman, T. (2021) 'Supporting children's resettlement after custody: beyond the risk paradigm', *Youth Justice*, 21(1): 71–89.

Head, B.W. and Alford, J. (2015) 'Wicked problems: implications for public policy and management', *Administration & Society*, 47(6): 711–39.

Hendrick, H. (2015) 'Histories of youth crime and youth justice', in B. Goldson and J. Muncie (eds) *Youth Crime and Justice*, London: Sage, pp 3–17.

Higher Education Policy Institute and Loughborough University (2023) *How to Talk to Poly Makers about Research*. London: HEPI/LU.

Hill, M. and Hupe, P. (2015) *Implementing Public Policy* (3rd edn), London: Sage.

HM Government (2003) 'Respect and responsibility: taking a stand against antisocial behaviour', London: HM government.

HM Government (2008) 'Criminal Justice and Immigration Act', London: HMSO.

HM Government (2011) 'Public Bodies Act', London: HM government.

HMIP (2006) 'Joint inspection of youth offending teams of England and Wales', London: HMIP.

HMIP (2020) 'Inspecting desistance: a response from HMIP Asst Chief Inspector of Probation Head of the Youth Offending Inspection Programme', presentation to annual NAYJ conference.

HMIP (2021) 'Inspecting desistence', Manchester: HMIP.

HMIP (2022) 'Youth offending services inspection', Available from: https://www.justiceinspectorates.gov.uk/hmiprobation/about-hmi-probation/about-our-work/documentation-area/youth-offending-services-inspection

Home Office (1997) 'No more excuses: a new approach to tackling youth crime in England and Wales', London: HMSO.

Home Office (1998) 'Crime and Disorder Act 1998', London: Home Office.

Home Office (2012) 'Assessing young people in police custody: an examination of triage schemes', London: Home Office.

Hoornbeek, J. and Peters, B. (2017) 'Understanding policy problems: a refinement of past work', *Policy and Society*, 36(3): 365–84.

Hopkins-Burke, R. (2016) *Young People, Crime and Justice*, Abingdon: Routledge.

House of Commons (2012) 'The big society: further report with the government's response to the committee's seventh report of session 2010–2012', London: HMSO.

Howlett, M. (2018) 'The criteria for effective policy design: character and context in policy instrument choice', *Journal of Asian Public Policy*, 11(3): 245–66.

Huckel-Schneider, C. and Blyth, F. (2017) 'Challenges of integrating evidence into health policy and planning: linking multiple disciplinary approaches', *Public Health Research & Practice*, 27(2): e2721719.

Hudson, B., Hunter, D. and Peckham, S. (2019) 'Policy failure and the policy-implementation gap: can policy support programs help?', *Policy Design and Practice*, 2(1): 1–14.

Independent Commission on Youth Crime and Antisocial Behaviour (2010) 'Time for a fresh start', Available from: www.youthcrimecommission.org.uk

Institute for Government (2011) 'Making policy better', London: Institute for Government.

Jann, W. and Wegrich, K. (2007) 'Theories of the policy cycle', in F. Fischer, G. Miller and M. Sidney (eds) *Handbook of Public Policy Analysis: Theory, Politics and Methods*, Milton Park: Taylor & Francis, pp 43–62.

Jones, C. (1993) 'Auditing criminal justice', *British Journal of Criminology*, 33(3): 187–202.

Jones, D. (2001) '"Misjudged youth": a critique of the Audit Commission's reports on youth justice', *British Journal of Criminology*, 41(2): 362–80.

Jones, R. and Wyn Jones, R. (2019) *Justice at the Jagged Edge in Wales*, Cardiff: Cardiff University.

Joyce, P. (2017) *Criminal Justice: An Introduction*, London: Routledge.

Kehl, D., Guo, P. and Kessler, S. (2017) *Algorithms in the Criminal Justice System: Assessing the Use of Risk Assessments in Sentencing.* Responsive Communities Initiative, Berkman Klein Center for Internet and Society, Harvard Law School.

Kelly, L. and Armitage, V. (2015) 'Diverse diversions: youth justice reform, localized practices, and a "New Interventionist Diversion"?', *Youth Justice*, 15(2): 117–33.

Kemp, P. (1990) 'Next steps for the British civil service', *Governance: An International Journal of Policy and Administration*, 3(2): 186–96.

Kemshall, H. (2008) Risk, rights and justice: Understanding and responding to youth risk. *Youth Justice*, 8(1): 21–38.

Kingdon, J.W. (2011) *Agendas, Alternatives and Public Policies* (2nd edn), Boston, MA: Longman.

Kisby, B. (2010) 'The Big Society: power to the people', *The Political Quarterly*, 81(4): 484–91.

Klammer, U., Leiber, S. and Leitner, S. (2021) *Social Work and the Making of Social Policy*, in association with the European Social Work Research Association, Bristol: Policy Press.

Kuhn, T.S. (1996) *The Structure of Scientific Revolutions*, Chicago: University of Chicago Press.

Labour Party (1995) 'Safer communities, safer Britain: Labour's proposals for tough action on crime', London: Labour Party.

Lawrence, P. (2012) 'History, criminology and the "use" of the past', *Theoretical Criminology*, 16(3): 313–28.

Lawrence, P. (2019) 'Historical criminology and the explanatory power of the past', *Criminology and Criminal Justice*, 19(4): 493–511.

Lea, J. and Young, J. (1984) *What is to be Done About Law and Order?* Harmondsworth, UK: Penguin.

Levin, P. (1997) *Making Social Policy: The Mechanisms of Government and Politics, and How to Investigate Them*, Buckingham: Open University Press.

Lipsky, M. (1980) *Street-Level Bureaucracy*, New York: Russell Sage Foundation.

Loeber, R., Farrington, D.P., Stouthamer-Loeber, M., Moffitt, T.E., Caspi, A., White, H. et al (2003) 'The development of male offending: key findings from fourteen years of the Pittsburgh Youth Study', in T.P. Thornberry and M.D. Krohn (eds) *Taking Stock of Delinquency: An Overview of Findings from Contemporary Longitudinal Studies*, New York: Kluwer.

Luttrell, W. (2019) 'Reflexive qualitative research', in G. Noblit (ed) *Oxford Research Encyclopedia of Education*, New York: Oxford University Press.

Magarey, S. (1978) 'The invention of juvenile delinquency in early nineteenth century England', *Labour History*, 34: 1–27.

May, M. (1973) 'Innocence and experience: the evolution of the concept of juvenile delinquency in the mid-nineteenth century', *Victorian Studies*, 17(1): 7–29.

May, T. (2010) 'Moving beyond the ASBO', speech to the Coin Street Community Centre, 28 July.

McAra, L. (2010) 'Models of youth justice', in D.J. Smith (ed) *A New Response to Youth Crime*, Cullompton: Willan.

McAra, L. (2023) 'Youth justice in an age of uncertainty: principles, performance, and prospects', in A. Liebling, S. Maruna, L. McAra (eds) *Oxford Handbook of Criminology*, chapter 32, Oxford: Oxford University Press.

McAra, L. and McVie, S. (2007) 'Youth justice? The impact of system contact on patterns of desistance from offending', *European Journal of Criminology*, 4(3): 315–45.

McAra, L. and McVie, S. (2010) 'Youth crime and justice: key messages from the Edinburgh Study of Youth Transitions and Crime', *Criminology & Criminal Justice*, 10(2): 211–30.

McCord, J. (1978) 'A thirty-year follow-up of treatment effects', *American Psychologist*, 33(3): 284–9.

McCord, J. and McCord, W. (1959) 'A follow-up report on the Cambridge-Somerville Youth Study', *The ANNALS of the American Academy of Political and Social Science*, 322(1): 89–96.

McQuail, D. (1993) *Media Performance*, London: Sage.

McSweeney, B. (1988) 'Accounting for the Audit Commission', *The Political Quarterly*, 59(1): 28–43.

Merriam, S.B. and Tisdell, E.J. (2016) *Qualitative Research and Case Study Applications in Education*, San Francisco: John Wiley & Sons.

Ministry of Justice (MoJ) (2010) 'Breaking the cycle: effective punishment, rehabilitation and sentencing of offenders', London: MoJ.

Ministry of Justice (MoJ) (2012) 'Youth Justice Board for England and Wales (triennial review)', London: MOJ.

Ministry of Justice and Youth Justice Board (MoJ and YJB) (2013) 'Youth out-of-court disposals', London: MoJ/YJB.

Ministry of Justice and Youth Justice Board (MoJ and YJB) (2019) 'Standards for children in the Youth Justice System', London: MoJ/YJB.

Mitra, A. (2009) 'Moral, ethical, and social responsibilities', *Decision Sciences*, 7(2): 346–48.

Morgan Harris Burrows (2003) 'Evaluation of the Youth Inclusion Programme', London: Youth Justice Board.

Morgan, R. (2009) 'Report to the Welsh Assembly government on the question of devolution of youth justice responsibilities', Cardiff: Welsh government.

Muncie, J. (2008) 'The "punitive" turn in juvenile justice: cultures of control and rights compliance in Western Europe and the USA', *Youth Justice*, 8(2): 107–21.

Muncie, J. (2014) *Youth and Crime*, London: Sage.

Muncie, J., Hughes, G. and McLaughlin, E. (eds) (2002) *Youth Justice: Critical Readings*, London: Sage.

Murray, C. (1994) *Underclass: The Crisis Deepens*, London: Institute of Economic Affairs.

Myers, R., Goddard, T. and Davidtz, J. (2020) 'Reconnecting youth: beyond individualized programs and risks', *Youth Justice*, 21(1): 55–70.

National Assembly Policy Unit (2002) 'Extending entitlement: support for 11 to 25 year olds in Wales; direction and guidance', Cardiff: National Assembly for Wales.

National Police Chiefs' Council (2015) 'Child-centred policing: national strategy for the policing of children and young people', London: NPCC.

Oliver, K. and Boaz, K. (2019) 'Transforming evidence for policy and practice: creating space for new conversations', *Palgrave Communications*, 5(60), Available from: https://doi.org/10.1057/s41599-019-0266-1

Page, E. and Jenkins, B. (2005) *Policy Bureaucracy*, Oxford: Oxford University Press.

Perl, A. (2020) 'Studying policy dynamics: policy cycles and regimes', in G. Capano and M. Howlett (eds) *A Modern Guide to Public Policy*, Cheltenham: Edward Elgar Publishing, pp 22–40.

Phoenix, J. (2016) 'Against youth justice and governance, for youth penalty', *British Journal of Criminology*, 56(1): 123–40.

Pitts, J. (2001) 'Korrectional karaoke: New Labour and the zombification of youth justice', *Youth Justice*, 1(2): 3–16.

Pitts, J. (2003) *The New Politics of Youth Crime: Discipline or Solidarity?*, Lyme Regis: Russell House.

Pliatzky, L. (1992) 'Quangos and agencies', *Public Administration*, 70(4): 555–63.

Porteus, D. (2007) 'The prevention of youth crime: a risky business?', in B. Thom, R. Sales and J. Pearce (eds) *Growing Up with Risk*, Bristol: Policy Press.

Prior, D. and Mason, P. (2010) 'A different kind of evidence: looking for "what works" in engaging young offenders', *Youth Justice*, 10(3): 211–26.

Reed, M. and Rudman, D. (2023) 'Re-thinking research impact: voice, context and power at the interface of science, policy and practice', *Sustainability Science*, 18: 967–81.

Renshaw, J. and Perfect, M. (1997) 'Out of order', *Community Care*, 8 January: 20–1.

Richards, K. (2014) 'Blurred Lines: Reconsidering the Concept of "Diversion" in Youth Justice Systems in Australia', *Youth Justice*, 14(2): 122–39.

Rickinson, M. and Edwards, A. (2021) 'The relational features of evidence use', *Cambridge Journal of Education*, 51(4): 509–26.

Rose, N. (1996) 'The death of the social? Refiguring the territory of government', *Economy and Society*, 25(3): 327–56.

Sampson, R.J. and Laub, J.H. (1993) *Crime in the Making: Pathways and Turning Points through Life*, Cambridge, MA: Harvard University Press.

Sandberg, S. (2021) 'Narrative analysis in criminology', *Journal of Criminal Justice Education*, 33(2): 212–29.

Sanderson, E. (2011) 'Evidence-based policy or policy-based evidence? Reflections on Scottish experience', *Evidence and Policy*, 7(1): 59–76.

Sausman, C., Oborn, E. and Barrett, M. (2016) 'Policy translation through localisation: implementing national policy in the UK', *Policy & Politics*, 44(4): 563–89.

Savard, J., with the collaboration of R. Banville (2012) 'Policy cycles', in L. Côté and J-F. Savard (eds) *Encyclopedic Dictionary of Public Administration*, Quebec: L'Observatoire de l'administration publique, Available from: www.dictionnaire.enap.ca

Scott, J. and Staines, S. (2021) 'Charting the place of islands in criminology: on isolation, integration and insularity', *Theoretical Criminology*, 25(4): 578–600.

Scraton, P. and Haydon, D. (2002) 'Challenging the criminalisation of children and young people: securing a rights-based agenda', in J. Muncie, G. Hughes and E. McLaughlin (eds) *Youth Justice: Critical Readings*, London: Sage, pp 311–28.

Sentencing Council (2017) 'Sentencing children and young people', Available from: https://www.sentencingcouncil.org.uk/overarching-guides/magistrates-court/item/sentencing-children-and-young-people

Sherman, L., Gottfredson, D., MacKenzie, D., Eck, J., Reuter, P. and Bushway, S. (1998) *Preventing Crime: What Works, What Doesn't, What's Promising*, Washington, DC: U.S. Department of Justice, Office of Justice Programs.

Shore, H. (2011) 'Reforming the juvenile in nineteenth- and early twentieth-century England', *Prison Service Journal*, 197: 4–9.

Silk Commission (2014) 'Empowerment and responsibility: legislative powers to strengthen Wales', Cardiff, UK: Commission on Devolution in Wales.

Smith, D.J. (2006) 'Social inclusion and early desistance from crime', *Edinburgh Study of Youth Transitions and Crime Research Digest*, 12.

Smith, D.J. (ed) (2010) *A New Response to Youth Crime*, Cullompton: Willan.
Smith, R. (2014) 'Reinventing diversion', *Youth Justice*, 14(2): 109–21.
Smith, R. (2016) *Youth Justice: Ideas, Policy, Practice*, Abingdon: Routledge.
Smith, R. and Gray, P. (2019) 'The changing shape of youth justice: models of practice', *Criminology & Criminal Justice*, 19(5): 554–71.
Social Exclusion Unit (2000) 'Report of Policy Action Team 12: young people', London: SEU.
Social Exclusion Unit (2001) 'National strategy for neighbourhood renewal', London: SEU.
Solomon, E. and Garside, R. (2008) 'Ten years of Labour's youth justice reforms: an independent audit', London: Centre for Crime and Justice Studies, King's College London.
Souhami, A. (2007) *Transforming Youth Justice. Occupational Identity and Cultural Change*, Cullompton, UK: Willan.
Souhami, A. (2011) 'Inside the Youth Justice Board: ambiguity and influence in New Labour's youth justice', *Critical Social Policy*, 10(3): 7–16.
Souhami, A. (2015a) 'Creating the Youth Justice Board: policy and policy-making in English and Welsh youth justice', *Criminology and Criminal Justice*, 15: 152–68.
Souhami, A. (2015b) 'The central institutions of youth justice: government bureaucracy and the importance of the Youth Justice Board for England and Wales', *Youth Justice*, 14: 209–25.
Stephenson, M. and Allen, R. (2013) *Youth Justice: Challenges to Practice*, London: Unitas.
Stephenson, M., Giller, H. and Brown, S. (2007) *Effective Practice in Youth Justice*, Cullompton: Willan.
Straw, J. and Michael, A. (1996) 'Tackling the causes of crime: Labour's proposals to prevent crime and criminality', London: Labour Party.
Stevens, A. (2011) 'Telling policy stories: an ethnographic study of the use of evidence in policy-making in the UK', *Journal of Social Policy*, 40(2): 237–56.
Sutherland, A. (2009) 'The "Scaled Approach" to youth justice: fools rush in …', *Youth Justice Journal*, 9(1): 44–60.
Sutton, C., Monaghan, M., Case, S.P., Greenhalgh, J. and Wright, J. (2021) 'Contextualising youth justice interventions: making the case for realist synthesis', *Sustainability*, 14(2): 854.
Taylor, C. (2016) *Review of the Youth Justice System in England and Wales*. London: Ministry of Justice.
Taylor, S.P. (2018) 'Critical realism vs social constructionism & social constructivism: application to a social housing research study', *International Journal of Sciences: Basic and Applied Research*, 37(2): 216–22.
Thornberry, T.P. and Krohn, M.D. (2003) *Taking Stock of Delinquency: An Overview of Findings from Contemporary Longitudinal Studies*, New York: Kluwer.

Turnbull, G. and Spence, J. (2011) 'What's at risk? The proliferation of risk across child and youth policy in England', *Journal of Youth Studies*, 14(8): 939–59.

UNICEF (1999) 'United Nations Convention on the Rights of the Child', Geneva: UNICEF.

Vergari, S. (2015) 'Mechanisms for the development of educational policy', in J. Wright (ed) *International Encyclopedia of the Social and Behavioural Sciences*, np: Elsevier.

Wacquant, L. (2009) *Punishing the Poor: The Neoliberal Government of Social Insecurity*, Durham, NC: Duke University Press.

Ward, T. (2021) 'Why theoretical literacy is essential for forensic research and practice', *Criminal and Mental Health*, 31(1): 1–4.

Welsh Government (2011) *Devolution of Youth Justice: Cabinet Briefing*, Cardiff, UK: Welsh Government.

Welsh Government (2012) 'Proposals to improve services in Wales to better meet the needs of children and young people who are at risk of entering, or are already in, the Youth Justice System', Cardiff, UK: Welsh Government.

Welsh Government (2018) 'Commission on justice in Wales: written evidence submitted by the Welsh government', Cardiff: Welsh Government.

Welsh Government and YJB (2004) 'All Wales youth offending strategy', Cardiff: Welsh Government.

Welsh Government and YJB (2014) 'Children and young people first', Cardiff: Welsh Government/YJB, Available from: https://www.gov.uk/government/publications/youth-justice-strategy-for-wales-children-and-young-people-first

West, D.J. and Farrington, D.P. (1973) *Who Becomes Delinquent?*, London: Heinemann.

Whitehead, P. and Arthur, R. (2011) '"Let no one despise your youth": a sociological approach to youth justice under New Labour 1997–2010', *International Journal of Sociology and Social Policy*, 31(7/8): 469–85.

Whyte, B. (2009) *Youth Justice in Practice*, London: Policy Press.

Wilcox, A. (2003) 'Evidence-based youth justice? Some valuable lessons from an evaluation for the Youth Justice Board', *Youth Justice*, 3(1): 21–35.

Yates, J. (2012) 'What prospects youth justice? Children in trouble in the age of austerity', *Journal of Social Policy and Administration*, 46(4): 432–47.

YOT Managers Cymru (2013) Available from: www.yotmanagerscymru.org.uk/

Youth Justice Board (2000) 'ASSET', London: YJB.

Youth Justice Board (2003) 'Assessment, planning interventions and supervision', London: YJB.

Youth Justice Board (2006) 'YIP management guidance', London: YJB.

Youth Justice Board (2008) 'Assessment, planning interventions and supervision', London: YJB.

Youth Justice Board (2009) 'Youth justice: the Scaled Approach; a framework for assessment and interventions; post-consultation version two', London: YJB.

Youth Justice Board (2010) 'Process evaluation of the pilot of a risk-based approach to interventions', London: YJB.

Youth Justice Board (2013) 'Assessment and planning interventions framework: AssetPlus', London: YJB.

Youth Justice Board (2014) 'AssetPlus rationale', London: YJB.

Youth Justice Board (2018) 'Proposed definition of "children first, offenders second": board information paper', London: YJB.

Youth Justice Board (2020) 'Business plan 2019–2022', London: YJB.

Youth Justice Board (2021) 'Youth Justice Board for England and Wales: strategic plan 2021–2024', London: YJB, Available from: https://assets.publishing.service.gov.uk/government/uploads/system/uploads/attachment_data/file/802702/YJB_Strategic_Plan_2019_to_2022.pdf

Youth Justice Board (2022) 'Strategic Plan 2021–2024', Londoon: YJB.

Youth Justice Board (2023) 'YJB Business Plann 2023–24', London: YJB.

Youth Justice Board Cymru (2012) 'A Blueprint for Promoting Effective Practice and Improving Youth Justice Performance in Wales', London: YJB.

Youth Justice Board/Ministry of Justice (YJB/MoJ) (2012) *Youth Justice Statistics,* London: YJB/MoJ.

Index

References to endnotes show both the page number and the note number (231n3).

K

L

M

N